A. Dmitrenko,
E. Kuznetsova,
O. Petrova,
N. Fyodorova

FIFTY RUSSIAN ARTISTS

Raduga Publishers
Moscow

Translated from the Russian
by *Angus Roxburg*

Designed by *Viktor Chistyakov*

English translation

© Raduga Publishers 1985. Illustrated

ISBN 5-05-000066-1

CONTENTS

CONTENTS

Late Nineteenth-Early Twentieth Centuries

FIFTY RUSSIAN ARTISTS

FOURTEENTH–
SEVENTEENTH
CENTURIES

FIFTY
RUSSIAN
ARTISTS
9

Theophanes the GREEK

(1330s-c. 1415)

1

'A famous sage, a wise philosopher, a master who excelled in decoration of manuscripts and the best of icon-painters', such were the words of the educated monk Epiphany the Wise about his contemporary Theophanes the Greek.

Theophanes, one of the greatest medieval Russian painters, was born in Byzantium, and was therefore known in Russia as 'the Greek'. It is estimated that he was born in the thirties of the fourteenth century. When he came to Rus he was 35-40 and already decorated more than forty stone churches in Constantinople, Chalkidike and Galata. From Byzantium he travelled first to Kaffa (Feodosia), at that time a rich Genoese colony, and then to Novgorod.

In Rus, which was developing as a result of the inchoate struggle for the liberation and unification of the lands around Moscow, Theophanes found a fruitful outlet for his enormous talent. His extremely distinctive art, based on Byzantine traditions, both influenced and came under the influence of Russian culture.

The first paintings done by Theophanes in Russia were the frescos in one of the splendid cathedrals of Novgorod—the *Church of Our Saviour (Transfiguration)* in Ilyin Street, built in 1374. The frescos were commissioned by the boyar Vasily Danilovich and the citizens of Ilyin Street, and Theophanes worked on them during the summer of 1378.

These frescos have been partly preserved. In the cupola there is a depiction of the Pantocrator (Christ the Almighty) and four seraphim. On the walls between the windows are the figures of Adam, Abel, Noah, Seir, Melchizedek, Enoch, the prophet Elijah and John the Baptist, and in the chapel, specially commissioned by the boyar, are five stylites, *The Holy Trinity* and in medallions are depicted the Saints John Climacos, Agathon, Akaky and Makary.

All the saints painted by Theophanes the Greek are different, each with individual, complex features. But at the same time they all have something in common: the wrathful, mighty

1. St. Akaky, fresco in the Church of Our Saviour, Ilyin Street, Novgorod

FIFTY
RUSSIAN
ARTISTS
10

THEOPHANES THE GREEK

FOURTEENTH–
SEVENTEENTH
CENTURIES

Pantokrator, the wise, majestic Noah, the sombre Adam, the menacing prophet Elijah and the self-absorbed stylites are all strong in spirit and steadfast in character, people torn by contradictions, people whose outer calm conceals their inner struggle against raging passions.

Even the composition of *The Holy Trinity* shows no appeasement. No youthful mildness can be sensed in the figures of the angels, whose beautiful faces are severe and aloof. The central figure is particularly expressive, his immobility only serving to emphasize the tenseness of his inner self. His outstretched wings overshadow the other two angels, unifying the composition and lending it austere completeness and a monumental character.

Theophanes' figures have a powerful emotional effect and strike a moving, tragic chord. There was a sharp, dramatic quality in his very manner of painting, which was impetuous and spirited. He fashioned his figures with bold, vigorous strokes, applying vivid highlights to achieve emotionality and intensity of expression. His palette is as a rule laconic and restrained, but the colour is saturated and meaningful, and the overall expressiveness of the figures is further intensified by the abrupt, sharp lines and the complex rhythm of the compositional structure.

Theophanes the Greek's paintings testify to his profound knowledge of life. His powerful figures are full of intense dramatic emotions; they are deeply philosophical and reveal the penetrating mind and passionate philosophical temperament of their author.

The artist's contemporaries were impressed by his originality of thought and by the range of his creative imagination. 'When he painted, no one ever saw him following standard patterns —unlike some of our icon-painters, who spend more time perplexedly studying models than painting. He paints with his hands, but constantly is on the move, chatting with callers, cogitating things wise and elevated, and seeing goodness with eyes of reason.'

The frescos in the Church of Our Saviour are among the most precious examples of Novgorod monumental art and influenced the work of many other icon-painters. Closest to them are the murals in the Fyodor Stratilat Church and the Church of the Dormition in Volotovo Pole, which were probably done by Theophanes' pupils.

Theophanes appears to have lived in Novgorod for quite a long time, and then, after working for a while in Nizhny Novgorod, to have gone to Moscow. There is more information available about this period in his work. It is likely that Theophanes had his own studio and carried out commissions with the help of his pupils. The works mentioned in chronicles of the time cover the ten years from 1395 to 1405, during which the artist decorated three cathedrals in the Moscow Kremlin—the *Church of the Nativity of the Virgin Mary* (1395), the *Cathedral of the Archangel* (1399) and the *Cathedral of the Annunciation* (1405)—and also painted some secular works—frescos in the terem-palace of the Grand Prince Vasily Dmitrievich and in the palace of Prince Vladimir Andreyevich Khrabry (the cousin of Dmitry Donskoy).

Of all these works, the only one still extant is the iconostasis * in the Kremlin Cathedral of the Annunciation, which Theophanes painted together with Andrei Rublyov and the monk Prokhor from Gorodets. Rublyov worked on the icons depicting the festivals, while Theophanes painted most of those in the central row, the so-called 'Deesis range': *The Saviour, The Virgin, John the Baptist, The Archangel Gabriel, The Apostle Paul, John Chrysostomos* and *Basil the Great.*

The iconostasis has an overall unifying design, however, and a precise, harmonious composition. In the centre is the stern judge—the Saviour, seated on a throne; on either side are

---

* The iconostasis was a wall, decorated with icons, separating the altar from the central part of the cathedral. The icons were arranged in rows according to a strict religious hierarchical system: 'local' icons in the lowest row, then the 'Deesis range', above it rows dedicated to festivals and prophets, and at the very top—the Crucifixion.

FOURTEENTH–
SEVENTEENTH
CENTURIES

THEOPHANES THE GREEK

FIFTY
RUSSIAN
ARTISTS
11

2. Church of Our Saviour, Ilyin
   Street, Novgorod
3. Noah, fresco in the Church of Our
   Saviour, Ilyin Street, Novgorod
4. The Pantocrator (Christ the
   Almighty), fresco in the Church
   of Our Saviour, Ilyin Street, Novgorod
5. The Pantocrator. Detail
6. St. Makary of the Egypt, fresco in
   the Church of Our Saviour, Ilyin
   Street, Novgorod

FIFTY
RUSSIAN
ARTISTS
12

THEOPHANES THE GREEK

FOURTEENTH–
SEVENTEENTH
CENTURIES

saints, interceding with Christ for sinful mankind. As before, Theophanes' saints are powerful and individualised. But here there are also new qualities: they are more restrained and majestic. There is more warmth in the image of the Virgin, more gentleness in that of the Archangel Gabriel and more tranquility in the wise apostle Paul.

The icons are exceptionally monumental in character. The figures are clearly silhouetted against a brilliant gold background, and the colours of their garments are vibrant—Christ robed in snow white, the Virgin Mary in velvety blue, and John in green. And although in his icons Theophanes retains the general style of his murals, his lines are simpler and more distinct and restrained.

The task of decorating the Cathedral of the Annunciation brought together two great masters of ancient Rus, who each in his own way gave expression to an age full of dramatic conflicts: Theophanes in tragic, titanic images, Rublyov in harmonious, serene images, expressing a dream of peace and harmony among people. It was these two artists who created the classical form of the Russian iconostasis.

The work on the Cathedral was completed in one year. What happened to Theophanes thereafter, and what other works he painted, is unknown. Scholars believe that he worked as a miniaturist, and some consider that the miniatures for two ancient Russian manuscripts—the Koshka and the Khitrovo Gospels—were painted in Theophanes' studio and were possibly designed by him. Where he spent the last years of his life is also not known. He appears to have died between 1405 and 1415, since a letter written by Epiphany the Wise mentions that in 1415 the great artist was no longer alive.

A native of Byzantium, Theophanes found his second homeland in Rus. His impassioned, inspired art was in keeping with the general disposition of the Russian people and exercised a beneficial influence both on his contemporaries and on later generations of Russian artists.

6

FOURTEENTH–
SEVENTEENTH
CENTURIES

FIFTY
RUSSIAN
ARTISTS
13

Andrei RUBLYOV

(c. 1370-1430)

1. The Archangel Michael

In one of the halls of the Tretyakov Gallery in Moscow there is a work which ranks among the greatest achievements of world art—the icon entitled *The Holy Trinity*.

In his depiction of the traditional Biblical subject—the appearance of the three angels to Sarah and Abraham—the artist expresses a profoundly human, philosophical idea. Painted more than five hundred years ago, *The Holy Trinity* still appeals to modern man because of the noble emotions, delicate poetry and inspired beauty of the figures.

The laconic composition concentrates one's attention on the figures of the angels. Elegant and beautiful, they seem to be immersed in their inner worlds; the atmosphere is one of sadness, meekness and inner determination. The rounded lines of the figures lend the whole composition a certain equilibrium and solemnity. The light, pure, almost luminous colours—blues, silver-greens, golden-yellows, pinks and cherry-reds—evoke a tranquil atmosphere and seem to echo the colours of the countryside in which the artist lived and painted: the purity of clear skies, the gold of ripe corn and the green of meadows in spring.

Painted in an age of internecine strife and Tatar plunderings, *The Holy Trinity* was harmonious, serene and melodious, symbolising mankind's dream of a perfect world in which harmony, love and friendship would reign.

The creator of this brilliant work, the early Russian painter Andrei Rublyov, commanded enormous respect among his contemporaries, and later his name became surrounded by legend. The few facts to be found in writings of the period suggest that the great artist was born around 1370. As a youth he became a monk and spent many years in the Trinity-Saint Sergii Monastery. At that time monasteries were the centres of culture in Rus, and it was here that Rublyov received education and moral training, and also learned the art of icon-painting.

Rublyov painted his celebrated *Trinity* in memory of Sergii Radonezhsky, one of the inspir-

FIFTY
RUSSIAN
ARTISTS
14

ANDREI RUBLYOV

FOURTEENTH–
SEVENTEENTH
CENTURIES

ing minds behind the Battle of Kulikovo, who did much to help stop the civil war and unite the Russian princes in the struggle against the Tatars. The icon was kept in the *Trinity Cathedral,* built in 1411.

By this time Andrei Rublyov was already a celebrated master. In 1405 Theophanes the Greek, the monk Prokhor of Gorodets and he had decorated the *Cathedral of the Annunciation* in Moscow. Only two rows of the iconostasis in this cathedral have been preserved—the Deesis range and the festival row.

Rublyov painted seven of the festival icons —*Annunciation, Baptism, Nativity of Christ, Candlemas, Transfiguration, Raising, of Lazarus* and *Entry into Jerusalem.* They are distinguished from the works of the other masters by their gentle and harmonious tone. The scenes from the Gospels are depicted with great intimacy, spirituality and human warmth. The colours are marked by tremendous emotionality and refined beauty, with the light, gentle hues of the scenery setting off the more intense and varied shades of the characters' clothing.

One of the landmarks in Andrei Rublyov's career was his decorative work in the *Cathedral of the Assumption* in Vladimir (1408) where he worked together with his friend and colleague Daniil Chorny. The extant frescos are a fragment of an enormous depiction of the Last Judgment, which occupied the west wall of the cathedral.

By analysing the stylistic peculiarities of the frescos, scholars have established which group of figures was painted by Rublyov; they are characterised, in particular, by great artistry, and by their musical, graceful lines. The herald angel is youthfully beautiful, and St. Peter is inspired and resolute as he beckons the pious into Heaven.

The interpretation and emotional tenor of the scene of the Last Judgment are unusual: the prevailing idea—and in this one clearly senses Rublyov's own outlook—is not fear of terrible punishment but one of forgiveness. The frescos

are an integral part of the interior of the cathedral: by emphasising the flatness of the wall, they enhance the impression of lightness in the architecture.

It is supposed that the icons of the Deesis range were designed by Rublyov and painted with the help of his pupils. The language of these works is exceptionally laconic and monumental, and the forms are treated in a generalised manner, with the stress on the silhouette and solemnity of movement. The colour range is reserved and expressive, based on the decorative effect of green combined with golden-yellow and red, and of blue with cherry-red. The saints are portrayed as sages, tranquil and noble. The most expressive images are those of Christ, John the Baptist and the Apostle Paul, which were presumably painted by Rublyov himself. Of the icons in the festival row only one—*Ascension*—is attributed to Rublyov.

It was evidently at this time that Rublyov painted an icon based loosely on the famous Byzantine icon *Holy Virgin of Vladimir.* The tender colours and the fragile image of the Virgin Mary, holding close her child, express maternal love, sadness and her foreboding of her son's tragic destiny.

In 1918 three icons from a Deesis range were found in Zvenigorod—*The Saviour, The Archangel Michael* and *The Apostle Paul,* all thought to have been painted by Rublyov between 1410 and 1420.

The Zvenigorod Saviour is especially remarkable. The face of Christ is distinctive and spiritualised, with delicate, austere features. He is full of mental concentration and his gaze is direct and penetrating, expressing human kindness. There is little doubt that Rublyov embodied in this image the moral ideal of the Russian man of his time, in which peacefulness and meekness was combined with strength, courage and steadfastness of spirit.

The image of the Apostle Paul is suffused with humanity and calm wisdom, while that of the

FOURTEENTH–
SEVENTEENTH
CENTURIES

ANDREI RUBLYOV

FIFTY
RUSSIAN
ARTISTS
15

2. Illumination from *The Life of Sergii*
   Radonezhsky manuscript
3. The Holy Trinity
4. Raising of Lazarus

Archangel Michael is lyrical and full of profound poetic charm. The latter is akin to the angels of *The Holy Trinity*. At the time when *The Holy Trinity* was painted—round 1420—Rublyov was in his prime as an artist, and it is likely that another work attributed to him—*Our Saviour in His Might* (TG)*—also dates from then.

It is believed that Rublyov helped to decorate the Nativity Cathedral in the Savvino-Storozhevsky Monastery near Zvenigorod. The few

fragments of the altar partitioning that have come down to us recall Rublyov's style.

From 1424 to 1427, at the invitation of the Father Superior Nikon, Rublyov, Daniil Chorny and unknown craftsmen worked on the Trinity Cathedral in the Trinity-Saint Sergii Monastery in Zagorsk. The frescos of the cathedral have perished, and only three rows of the iconostasis, executed in different styles, remain.

The works which can be attributed to Rublyov with most certainty are *Epiphany, The Archangel Michael* and *The Apostle Paul*. These icons are distinguished by their profound content, monumental figures, beautiful silhouettes and

* The following abbreviations will be used to indicate the galleries in which works are kept: TG—Tretyakov Gallery, Moscow; RM—Russian Museum, Leningrad; H—Hermitage, Leningrad.

FIFTY
RUSSIAN
ARTISTS
16

ANDREI RUBLYOV

FOURTEENTH–
SEVENTEENTH
CENTURIES

harmonious colour spectrum, reminiscent of the colouring of the *Trinity*.

Rublyov spent the last years of his life at the Andronikov Monastery in Moscow, where he decorated the Cathedral of the Saviour. According to contemporaries, he also helped to build the cathedral. Unfortunately, none of the artist's final work has been preserved.

As far as is known, Andrei Rublyov died on 29 January 1430 in the Andronikov Monastery. The work of this artist, who had many pupils and followers, was the greatest achievement of fifteenth-century Russian painting. It reflected the leading ideas of the period when a unified Russian state was forming. Rublyov's images are profoundly humane. His elevated, poetic work was versatile, it was both tender and kind, manly and wise, and it reflected the inner crystal purity of man.

Andrei Rublyov's art is the pride of the Russian people.

4

FOURTEENTH–
SEVENTEENTH
CENTURIES

FIFTY
RUSSIAN
ARTISTS
17

DIONYSIUS

(c. 1440-1502/08)

1. Holy Virgin (Hodegitria)

Dionysius was well-known even in his youth and worked all over Muscovy. Other than this, little is known about his life.

Between 1467 and 1477 he and the painter Mitrofan decorated the *Church of the Nativity of the Virgin Mary* in the St. Pafnuty Monastery, and then he went to Moscow, where he painted the iconostasis for the Kremlin *Church of the Holy Virgin* (as the Cathedral of the Dormition was then known), built by the distinguished Italian architect Fioravanti. Later, Dionysius' biography was linked with the Monastery of St. Joseph in Volokolamsk, where he led the team of icon-painters working on the icons for the *Church of the Dormition.*

Only one of the master's early icons—*Holy Virgin (Hodegitria)* from the Monastery of the Ascension (1482, TG)—has been preserved, but it does not give a full idea of the character of Dionysius' work as it is a reproduction of a burnt Greek original. The image of the Virgin here is solemn and coldly restrained. There are two more icons by Dionysius in the Tretyakov Gallery—*Our Saviour in His Might* and *Crucifixion* (1500), in which the sources of Dionysius' art can be felt, namely, the traditions of Andrei Rublyov, adapted by the later master to the aesthetic ideals of his time. In *Crucifixion,* the figures of the saints are elegantly outlined and rather elongated—which, together with the bright colours, creates an impression of great lightness; the tragic scene acquires a calm, serene undertone. *Crucifixion* is similar in style to the frescos in the Church of the Nativity of the Holy Virgin in the Ferapont Monastery, which are among the most remarkable art treasures of Ancient Rus and Dionysius' greatest achievement.

The monastery was founded in the fourteenth century in Northern Rus by the monk Ferapont, originally of Moscow. Fortunately, the frescos have come down to us in good condition. Moreover, an ancient inscription in the church reveals that it was decorated, between the years of 1500 and 1502, by Dionysius and his sons Feodosy and Vladimir.

FIFTY
RUSSIAN
ARTISTS
18

DIONYSIUS

FOURTEENTH–
SEVENTEENTH
CENTURIES

2

The frescos in the Ferapont Monastery are all united by the theme of the glorification of the Holy Virgin, her grandeur and her mercy, and the overall conception unquestionably came from Dionysius himself. The murals cover not only the interior but also the façade, which portrays the main subject—the nativity of the Holy Virgin. The composition here unites various episodes in a smooth, calm narrative rhythm. Anna lies on a couch, surrounded by graceful servants; alongside preparations are being made to bathe the infant, while the little Mary lies in a cradle; Anna and Joachim tenderly caress their daughter. There is an intimate, lyrical element in these scenes, combined with a sense of majesty and elevation.

The theme is developed inside the church, where the frescos are arranged in four rows, entirely covering the walls and vaults. Various scenes are elaborated: *The Annunciation,* in which Mary anxiously listens to the news brought to her by the Archangel Gabriel; *The Intercession of the Mother of God,* in which, rising majestically against the background of the church, Mary shades mankind with her veil, a symbol of protection against misfortune. In the scene of *The Last Judgment* the Holy Virgin pleads with the Judge on behalf of mankind. A special place is occupied by illustrations of psalms in glorification of Mary.

Dionysius liked complex, many-figured scenes with the figures depicted in such a way as to appear especially light and elegant, with natural movements, and even his servant-girls and men-

FOURTEENTH–
SEVENTEENTH
CENTURIES

DIONYSIUS

FIFTY
RUSSIAN
ARTISTS
19

FIFTY
RUSSIAN
ARTISTS
20

DIONYSIUS

FOURTEENTH–
SEVENTEENTH
CENTURIES

dicants have a regal bearing. The artist stressed the dignity of man and the idea of the unification of the human race; he aspired to convey various experiences, but never expressed strong passions—the emotions of his characters are always restrained and noble. The construction of the scenes, though complex, is strictly balanced and polished, and the masterly drawing, with its smooth lines, gives the murals a musical character. All the scenes have a clear-cut rhythm and are like polyphonous melodies united by a single majestic, tender theme.

The greatest emotional effect, however, derives from the colouring. Dionysius was not fond of bright colours; he toned down his palette a little, making the colours lighter and thereby imparting to them greater delicacy and softness and a kind of shining purity. Pale-green, golden-yellow, pinkish, white, cherry and silver-grey hues intertwine harmoniously, and through them all runs the 'leitmotif' of azure blue. The depiction of the human figures and landscapes, which are entirely subordinated to the flatness of the walls, and the transparency of the colours help to underline the lightness of the architectural forms, seemingly pushing the walls of the church apart and making it more spacious and bright, while the severe northern countryside which surrounds the church enhances the joyful, festive impression of the painting.

Apart from the mural decorations, Dionysius and his sons also painted an iconostasis for the church. The icons are now in the museum of the town of Belozersk, the Tretyakov Gallery and the Russian Museum in Leningrad. Like the frescos, the icons are noted for their refinement and beauty; particularly beautiful is *Holy Virgin (Hodegitria)*—majestic and womanly, she proudly bears the divine infant into the world.

Dionysius' work for the Ferapont Monastery marked the culmination of his career. It is supposed that the great painter died some time between 1502 and 1508, since in 1508 the painters' workshop was headed by his son.

Dionysius' painting—a bright, exultant song in colours, glorifying goodness and beauty—was an expression of the tremendous flourishing of culture and art in the period when the young Russian state was asserting its might.

Ivan Nikitich
NIKITIN

(c. 1680-1742)

The work of Ivan Nikitin played an important role in the establishment of eighteenth century Russian portraiture as an artistic phenomenon of not merely national but also European significance. This fact became abundantly plain at the International Portrait Exhibition mounted in the Pushkin Fine Arts Museum in Moscow in 1972.

Nikitin's life is poorly documented. He was born about 1680 into the family of a priest in Moscow, and received what was for those days a good education: he could read and write Latin, knew grammar and learnt mathematics, and at one time even taught arithmetic and drawing at the artillery school in Moscow. He received his first artistic training in the typographical school at the Armoury.

Nikitin's passion for painting reached the ears of Peter the Great, who arranged for him to study under Gottfried Danauer, a painter who had come to Russia in 1711 and, like all foreigners, pledged himself to 'teach the Russian people all he knew himself'. Under Danauer, Nikitin began studying the laws of perspective and painting skills; at the same time he helped Danauer carry out commissions. Nikitin's first teacher of drawing is considered to be the Dutch etcher Adriaan Schoonbeeck.

One of the young Nikitin's first independent works is his portrait of Praskovia Ivanovna, the niece of Peter the Great (RM), which was signed by the artist and dated 28 September 1714. The work still exhibits the immobility of the late sixteenth-seventeenth century Russian *parsuna** and an inability to convey the play of light. But the likeness of this attractive girl betrays the artist's desire to attain more than mere external similarity, for he reveals, and poeticises, the inner world of his model.

Before travelling abroad Nikitin painted several more portraits, including those of Natalia Alexeyevna, Peter the Great's favourite sister

* *Parsuna* (cf. 'person'): the first Russian portraits, though they had certain features of secular art, such as individualised portrayal, were still very much under the influence of earlier paintings of saints.

1. Peter the Great on His Death-Bed

FIFTY
RUSSIAN
ARTISTS
22

I. N. NIKITIN

EIGHTEENTH
CENTURY

(TG) and of the Cossack in a red kaftan (1715, Kharkov Art Museum). They are all marked by the artist's desire for realism and by his thoughtful approach to the characterisation of each personality.

In his notebook for 1715 Nikitin wrote that he had painted 'His Majesty in profile', and there are grounds to believe that the portrait in question is that of Peter against the background of a sea battle (now in the Yekaterininsky Palace Museum in the town of Pushkin near Leningrad). The portrait had previously been considered the work of Danauer or Karavak, but it is considerably more expressive than their other paintings.

Nikitin's early portraits were enough to convince Peter of his talent, and in 1716 he and his younger brother Roman were among twenty talented artists whom the tsar sponsored to go to Italy and learn more from their colleagues there. The hopes which Peter placed on Nikitin can be seen from a well-known letter he wrote to his wife in Danzig on 19 April 1716: 'Katerinushka, my dear, I recently met Beklemishev and the painter Ivan. When they come to you, ask the King to have his portrait painted—and anyone else you like, too, especially the matchmaker, so that they might know that our people has also produced fine masters.'

The person referred to as the 'match-maker' was the Chancellor, Count Golovkin, who acted as match-maker at the wedding of Peter's niece Yekaterina Ivanovna. Nikitin painted his portrait later, in the 1720s (TG). The portrayal of Golovkin combines his individual characteristics with an expression of his importance as a statesman, who—according to the inscription on the reverse of the portrait—concluded 72 treaties with foreign governments during his life.

When Nikitin arrived in Italy, the Russian ambassador Beklemishev helped him enter the Venice Academy of Arts. About a year later the Russian 'pensioners', as they were known, moved to Florence where at Beklemishev's

request they were taken under the personal wing of the Grand Duke of Tuscany, Cosimo III Medici. Classes in painting were given by Professor Tommaso Redi of the Florence Academy of Arts, and Nikitin's artistic development was also greatly influenced by the works of the great Italian masters.

At the beginning of 1720 the Nikitin brothers returned to St. Petersburg, bringing with them letters and certificates from Beklemishev and the Grand Duke of Tuscany, which included glowing reports on their successful studies.

Peter met his 'pensioner' warmly. He awarded him the title of 'master portraitist to the Tsar's court', gave him a house not far from his palace and recommended his courtiers to have their portraits done by him. Nikitin was to be appointed director of the planned Academy of Arts. The numerous portraits painted by him upon his return from abroad speak eloquently of the maturity of his talent.

The authentication of Nikitin's works is a tricky business, for only three of them are signed. Among the portraits assigned to Nikitin is the circular one of Peter the Great (RM), one of the best portrayals of the tsar made in his lifetime. It is possible that this is the portrait mentioned by Peter in his diary for 1721: 'On Kotlin island before mass His Majesty was painted by the portraitist Ivan'.

Although this is a small-scale work, Peter comes across as a great statesman and as a man of enormous inner strength. The same understanding of the tsar's personality was seen in the official portrait of Peter the Great on His Death-Bed (1725, RM), which Nikitin was given the task of painting. Time was short, and the portrait was painted in large, fluent strokes. Both in this expressive manner of painting and in the unusual angle from which Peter is depicted (from above), one can sense Nikitin's great artistic and compositional skill and his deepfelt attitude towards his subject.

The Field Commander (1720s, RM) is a masterpiece of Russian portraiture. This is an ap-

EIGHTEENTH
CENTURY

I. N. NIKITIN

FIFTY
RUSSIAN
ARTISTS
23

2

2. Portrait of Peter the Great
3. The Peter and Paul Fortress

FIFTY
RUSSIAN
ARTISTS
24

I. N. NIKITIN

EIGHTEENTH
CENTURY

pealingly humane depiction of an anonymous associate of Peter's. He is stern and fearless, and his features bear the mark of years of tribulations. His intelligent eyes gaze intently from under his grey brows. The open composition seems to act directly on the viewer, and the simple colours are restrained and expressive.

Russia's military victories are reflected in various battle-pieces ascribed to Nikitin, e. g. *The Battle of Poltava* (1727, not preserved) and a picture of *The Battle of Kulikovo* (RM), in which the artist partly employed the composition of an etching by the Italian Antonio Tempesta—while the protagonists, of course, are taken from Russian history. A large signed work, entitled *Family Tree of the Russian Tsars* (RM), dates from 1731. Its composition is stylised and suggests a conscious return to the traditions of the seventeenth century. This is significant in the context of artist's career. Soon after Peter's death, as a result of the changes in the political situation, Nikitin's world outlook underwent substantial modification.

Nikitin grew closer to the Moscow old Russian opposition, and early in the 1730s he and his brother were arrested in connection with a pamphlet about the Archbishop of Novgorod, Theophanes Prokopovich. From Moscow they were sent to St. Petersburg, to the secret police headquarters, and were then locked up in the Peter and Paul Fortress. The investigation of their case dragged on for more than five years. Although Nikitin was guilty of very little, a decree of the Empress Anna Ioannovna in November 1737 ordered him to be 'beaten with whips and sent to Siberia to live there under perpetual surveillance'. His brother Roman was also exiled. But even in these trying times Nikitin continued to paint: at the beginning of the thirties he completed a portrait of Praskovia

Fyodorovna, the widow of Peter the Great's brother Ivan Alexeyevich (now in the Zagorsk Museum of History and Local Lore).

During the period of investigation, Nikitin painted the chief of the secret police, General Ushakov (TG), who may in return have shown the artist certain indulgences. Even in Tobolsk, where the brothers were exiled, Nikitin continued to work, and the archives point to the existence of a portrait of the Tobolsk Metropolitan Antony Stakhovsky.

The works known to us represent a mere fraction of all that was painted by this founder of Russian portraiture. He is also known to have painted Catherine the First, the daughters and grandson of Peter the Great, Alexander Menshikov and his family, the princes Golitsyn and Dolgoruky, and also iconostases and individual icons.

Just before the death of Anna Ioannovna, the Nikitins' case was reviewed and in 1742, on the orders of the regent Anna Leopoldovna, the brothers obtained permission to return from Siberia. The artist, who was seriously ill, died during the journey.

3

Bartolomeo Carlo RASTRELLI

(1675-1744)

1. Bust of an Unknown Man
2. Bust of Peter the Great
3. Anna Ioannovna with Blackamoor
   Child. Detail

Bartolomeo Carlo Rastrelli was one of several artists whose talent flourished in Russia. During the early part of Rastrelli's stay there, he profited from the times themselves, when, as Pushkin said, 'young Russia came of age with Peter's genius'. The sculptor's extraordinary gifts found fecund soil there for their development and proliferation; they were enriched, on the one hand, by the fine traditions of Russian art and, on the other, left an appreciable mark on its future course of development.

Rastrelli was born in Florence, into the family of the well-to-do nobleman Francesco Rastrelli. Noticing his artistic bent, his father sent him to a sculptor's studio, where he received an excellent first training. He could draw well and work in bronze, learned how to make casts and jewellery, obtained the skills of architectural planning, learned about construction techniques and hydraulics, and mastered the art of stage designing. But in his homeland he could find no outlet for his abilities, for the once prosperous Florence was then experiencing a serious economic and political crisis.

No commissions were forthcoming either at the papal court in Rome. Rastrelli returned to Florence, presently married a girl from the Spanish nobility and went with her to Paris, where in 1700 a son was born—the future famous architect. In 1707 Rastrelli was given the title of count in return for the gravestone he fashioned for the Marquis de Pomponne, a minister under Louis XIV, which favourably impressed the Marquis's widow and other influential figures.

The sculptor designed several gravestones, which displayed features of baroque style, complex and dynamic in composition, with many allegorical figures. French sculpture, however, was going through the period of classicism, the pronounced baroque forms of Rastrelli's creations had somewhat lost their appeal, and that is why the critics declared that the Italian had 'poor taste'. And despite Rastrelli's attempts to accommodate himself to French taste, he received no more major commissions.

FIFTY
RUSSIAN
ARTISTS
26

CARLO RASTRELLI

EIGHTEENTH
CENTURY

Louis' reign was coming to a close, and many artists were without work. Peter the Great, who had an interest in attracting artists to Russia and understood the atmosphere in France, wrote to his resident representative there, Nikita Zotov, asking him to look out for 'efficient and good' masters.

In April 1715 Zotov entered into negotiations with many artists, including Rastrelli, and on 1 May 1715 the sculptor was accepted, under contract, 'to work for three years, with his son and pupil, in the service of His Majesty the Tsar, in all arts and handicrafts of which he is capable'.

His duties were to include designing palaces, parks, cascades and fountains, making statues of marble, porphyry and other hard materials, casting sculptures of bronze, lead and iron, fashioning portraits from wax and plaster of Paris, making stamps for striking medals and coins, and finally building sets and machinery for theatrical productions. A special clause in the contract obliged Rastrelli to take on pupils.

On 24 March 1716 the forty-year-old Rastrelli arrived in St. Petersburg, and soon he took up a leading place among the sculptors of Russia. He could have spent three years abroad, but in fact remained in Russia for the rest of his life.

At first Rastrelli worked principally as an architect. He helped plan the Vasilievsky Island and build the palace at Strelna, entered his design for a senate building to a competition, made models of hydraulic machines for fountains, taught drawing at the Academy of Sciences, made sketches of fancy-dress costumes, and also sculptured. But soon the French architect Jean-Baptiste Leblond, who had come to Russia about the same time as Rastrelli and competed against him, outshone him as an architect. As a result, the versatile Rastrelli was able to display his talent only in the sphere of sculpture. Above all, he proved himself to be a marvellous portraitist. In his sculptural portraits he managed to combine baroque splendour—which was well suited to the triumphant spirit of the

Petrine period—with thoughtful insight into the human soul.

Working on his portraits, Rastrelli studied his models closely, striving to convey their most characteristic individual traits. His first important portrait was a bust of Alexander Menshikov, made in 1716. A year later he repeated the work in bronze, and in the late 1840s the sculptor Vitali reproduced the portrait in marble (RM).

Rastrelli made several likenesses of Peter the Great. During the tsar's lifetime the sculptor took a mould from him (H), reworked it and produced a perfectly faithful portrait. At the same time he made a wax bust of Peter in armour. After the tsar's death, Catherine I had Rastrelli make a life-sized, coloured waxwork figure of Peter, dressed in his own clothes (H). Both these latter works are interesting from a documentary point of view.

Rastrelli's greatest success was his bronze bust of Peter the Great (1723-29, H; another version in RM), a life-like portrait, dynamic in form and full of vigour. The sculptor made two more busts of the tsar—one in wood, for a warship, the other in gilded lead (Copenhagen Museum).

These portrait busts are monumental rather than chamber works, reflecting not only the model's individual features, but also the character of a whole epoch.

For many years Rastrelli worked on an equestrian statue of Peter. As early as 1720, at the tsar's request, he made a small model of the future monument, and in 1724 the model was ready in its final form. But it was not until twenty years later—after the sculptor's death, and with the help of his son, the architect Francesco Bartolomeo Rastrelli—that the statue was cast in bronze. The monument was finally erected in 1800 by Paul I before the Mikhailovsky Palace where it stands to this day, bearing the inscription 'To great-grandfather from great-grandson'. Though it was actually erected later than the celebrated *Bronze Horse-*

EIGHTEENTH
CENTURY

CARLO RASTRELLI

FIFTY
RUSSIAN
ARTISTS
27

2

man, this was the first equestrian statue in Russian art.

In 1741 Rastrelli completed the statue *Anna* *Ioannovna with Blackamoor Child* (RM), in which characterisation and monumental generalisation merge together. While the images of

FIFTY
RUSSIAN
ARTISTS
28

CARLO RASTRELLI

EIGHTEENTH
CENTURY

Peter and his associates express enthusiasm and the triumphant grandeur of state power (cf. the monument to Peter the Great), here, despite the superficial impressiveness and decorative refinement, there is an aura of oppressive despotism, associated with one of the darkest periods in Russian history.

Rastrelli's legacy is not confined to portraits. He did a great deal of work as a master of decorative sculpture at Strelna, the Summer Gardens and especially at Peterhof. His work also considerably influenced the art of medal-designing in Russia.

Of particular interest is the part played by Rastrelli in the design of a triumphal column, the idea for which came from Peter the Great who wished it to resemble the Trajan Column in Rome. In Peter's conception the Column in Memory of the Northern War was to immortalise the victories of the Russian army which led to the formation of the mighty Russian Empire. But after his death it became known as the Column in Memory of Peter the Great and the Northern War. The grand column, belted by bas-reliefs depicting the events of the Northern War, was to be crowned by a statue of Peter. The column was never erected, however—neither under Peter nor under any of his successors—and the model of the statue was never even completed. In 1938 the model of the column was finally reconstructed, and it is now kept in the Hermitage.

It was Rastrelli who was responsible for the architectural design of the column, and it is possible that he began work on the model and part of the bas-reliefs. But after Peter's death Catherine I transferred responsibility for the work to Andrei Nartov, a talented engraver and master turner. It is difficult to determine exactly which part of the work was executed by Rastrelli and which by Nartov, but the overall design of this unusual monument is typical of Rastrelli's work.

According to his contract, Rastrelli was to train gifted people in 'arts and handicrafts'. He tried to organise a vocational school for sculptors, but conditions proved unfavourable for systematic classes to be arranged. It is known, however, that the sculptor had many pupils, some of whom became his assistants.

Rastrelli died in 1744.

3

Anton Pavlovich
LOSENKO

(1737-1773)

Anton Losenko was born in the Ukrainian town of Glukhovo, into the family of a peasant. At the age of seven, having a good voice and musical ear, he was taken into the court choir in St. Petersburg. In 1753 he and his friends I. Sablukov and K. Golovachevsky renounced this career because their voices broke, and came under the wing of the artist Ivan Argunov.

In 1759 Argunov presented his young protégés to the tsar's court with the recommendation: '. . . these choir-boys can draw and paint, make copies of portraits and historical paintings and paint from nature. They have shown extreme diligence, and honesty in their actions.' As proof of Losenko's success, Argunov showed his picture *Tobias and the Angel* and his portrait of the court musician V. Stepanov, drawn from life. The three former choir-boys then entered the Academy of Arts, which had opened in 1758, and worked as apprentices, helping the teachers. Losenko won the favour of one of the founders of the Academy, Count Shuvalov, whose portrait (RM) he painted in 1760. There followed portraits of the poet and dramatist Alexander Sumarokov (1760, RM) and of the talented actor Yakov Shumsky (1760, RM). This latter work is particularly noteworthy. The actor's character and distinctive appearance are captured keenly, and the image is lent great life and immediacy by the device of illuminating his face and hand, making them stand out against the dark background. The golden-brown shades are harmonious and muted; the movement of the artist's brush, especially where he brings out the texture of the face and hand, is clearly perceptible.

Count Shuvalov, first president of the Russian Academy of Arts, was well aware of the need to create a national art school, with well-qualified Russian artists. This increased the president's trust in young artists. In September 1760 the most capable students at the Academy—Losenko and the future well-known architect Vasily Bazhenov—were sent abroad to study.

In Paris Losenko studied under Jean Restout,

1. Abel

FIFTY
RUSSIAN
ARTISTS
30

A. P. LOSENKO

EIGHTEENTH
CENTURY

a representative of late French academism. The first fruit of his studies was the many-figured canvas *The Miraculous Catch of Fish* (1762, RM).

The merits and demerits of the picture were evaluated by the Academy of Arts: 'In everything we find signs of good reasoning and diligence . . . and talent which promises exceptional results if he is given a chance to practise.' Having arrived at the Academy after his painting (which was dispatched to St. Petersburg ahead of him), Losenko was sent to Moscow, where he painted a well-known portrait of the 'first Russian actor'—the founder of the national theatre, a brilliant performer and teacher of many other actors—Fyodor Volkov (1763, RM). Losenko not only achieved a likeness of Volkov (that it was indeed an excellent likeness is confirmed by the descriptions of the noted Russian enlightener Nikolai Novikov), but also created a work that was quite profound for its time, disclosing the vocation and spiritual richness of the actor, who, according to Novikov, was a man of 'penetrating mind, thorough, sensible judgment and rare talent'.

In the summer of 1763 Losenko returned to Paris, where his drawings on themes from classical mythology were awarded gold medals. At this time the artist devoted much attention to the nude, and in 1764 he sent to St. Petersburg 'one painting, a colour study from life and an étude'. The works meant here appear to be the painting *Venus and Adonis* or *The Death of Adonis* (State Art Museum of Byelorussia), the study *The Apostle Andrew* (RM) and the étude *The Expulsion from the Temple* (whereabouts unknown).

In 1765 Losenko dispatched to St. Petersburg the picture *Abraham Sacrifices His Son Isaac* (RM), which is more expressive in colour than *The Miraculous Catch of Fish.*

In December of the same year the artist moved to Rome, where he lived more than three years, studying the classics to perfect his drawing skills, making drawings from the paintings of Raphael in the Vatican and elsewhere, and doing exercises in colour. The result of this work was what Losenko called 'life-size academy figures'—*Abel* (1769, Kharkov Art Museum) and *Cain* (1768, RM). Devoid of any context (the names were evidently merely a pretext for the portrayal of magnificent models), these works were important landmarks in Losenko's creative development. The tension in Cain's foreshortened figure is marvellously conveyed, and set off by the gently falling folds of the drapery. One is struck by the precise organisation of the canvas space, by the harmony of the greenish hues and by the skilfully drawn body, especially the neck and shoulders. *Cain* is one of the artist's clearest and most laconic works. The 'Roman Cycle' was completed by the picture *Zeus and Thephia* (1769, RM), commissioned by Count Shuvalov for Count Razumovsky and painted by Losenko unbeknown to the Academy.

In the spring of 1769 Losenko returned to Russia. His best works—*Cain, Abel, Justice* (based on Raphael)—were given the highest of praise.

In autumn 1769 Losenko commenced work on the painting *Vladimir and Rogneda* (RM). The subject was suggested by the Academy, leaving it up to the artist to supply the details. This picture was really the first work ever on a subject from Russian history, the background to it concerning the Novgorod prince Vladimir, who, having been refused by the Polotsk princess Rogneda, captured Polotsk, murdered the princess's father and brothers and forcibly took her as his wife.

In his picture, Losenko captures the moment when Vladimir tells Rogneda of the atrocities committed in Polotsk and says that she must become his wife. But, in contrast to historical facts, Vladimir is portrayed full of repentance, which is conveyed in his gesture, his facial expression and eyes directed towards Rogneda. The artist moralises here, striving to prove that humanity has prevailed over tyranny.

EIGHTEENTH
CENTURY

A. P. LOSENKO

FIFTY
RUSSIAN
ARTISTS
31

2. Portrait of the Actor Yakov
   Shumsky
3. Vladimir and Rogneda
4. Warriors' Heads

The main attention is focussed, of course, on Vladimir and Rogneda, whose figures are highlighted. The artist underlines the protagonists' feelings by their expressive gestures and poses, which contrast with the statuesque female figures and Vladimir's cumbrous warriors.

Vladimir and Rogneda started the national historical theme in Russian art—something which Mikhail Lomonosov and Alexander Sumarokov had called on the Academy to undertake. Moreover, it set a precedent for the interpretation of historical events from a moral position which corresponded to the most progressive views in Russian society, condemning tyranny and violence. The painting evoked a lively response from Losenko's contemporaries,

and the Council of the Academy, 'seeing the artist's outstanding talent', elected him academician and bestowed upon him the title of professor.

As professor, and subsequently director, of the Academy, Losenko did much for its students. He prepared the first Russian art textbook: *Exposition of the Proportions of Man, Based upon Reliable Study of the Proportions of Ancient Statues, . . . for the Use of Young People Learning the Art of Drawing.* Losenko's *Exposition* and drawings were used for a long time at the Academy and later at the Moscow School of Painting and Sculpture.

Losenko's work as teacher and director sapped much of his energy. It is therefore signifi-

FIFTY
RUSSIAN
ARTISTS
32

A. P. LOSENKO

EIGHTEENTH
CENTURY

cant that Etienne-Maurice Falconet interceded with Catherine II for Losenko to be given the opportunity to dedicate himself entirely to his art. ' . . .Persecuted, exhausted, saddened and fatigued by a host of academic trifles which in any other Academy are no concern of a professor's, Losenko is in no fit state to lift his brush. He will doubtless be ruined. He is the most talented of contemporary painters, but people are insensible to this fact and are sacrificing him. . . I am not alone in despairing at the fate of Losenko.'

Falconet's letter evidently had no effect on Catherine, and the promised transfer of the artist from the Academy to 'her gallery' (the Hermitage) never took place.

Losenko's last painting—*Hector's Farewell with Andromache* (1773, TG)—takes its subject from Homer's *Iliad* and asserts public-spiritedness and patriotism as exemplified by the ancients. The picture also conformed to the Enlightenment spirit of the Academy charter, which stated that 'The true and noble aim of art is to make virtue perceptible, to immortalise the glory of great people who deserve the gratitude of their country, and to fire the heart and mind to emulate'.

Anton Losenko died of dropsy on 4 December 1773. His funeral was attended by artists and actors, writers and poets. One of them, Vasily Maikov, dedicated the following lines to his friend, professor and director of the Petersburg Academy of Arts, and Russia's first historical painter.

All things thy hand did fashion are alive
And shall endure so long as life goes on,
E'en though, Losenko, death has struck thee down,
E'en though our brief companionship is gone.

Fedot Ivanovich SHUBIN

(1740-1805)

The work of Fedot Shubin, like that of all the greatest eighteenth century masters, does not belong only to its own age. Covering a broad range of genres—portrait, monumental and decorative sculpture, bas-relief—it achieves such psychological depth and plastic perfection, especially in his portraits, that Shubin can be considered one of the great masters of world art.

He was born in a fishing village in the Arkhangelsk gubernia in the north of Russia. His father, Ivan Shubnoi, a free peasant, was literate and was Mikhail Lomonosov's first teacher. The Shubnoi family worked as fishermen, ploughmen, and carved bone and mother-of-pearl.

In the winter of 1759, after his father's death, Fedot Shubnoi followed Lomonosov's example and joined a group of merchants travelling to the capital with a transportation of fish. For two years the young man carved snuff-boxes, fans, combs and other knick-knacks which sold well in St. Petersburg.

In November 1761, under the patronage of Mikhail Lomonosov and the first trustee of the Academy of Arts, Count Shuvalov, he was enrolled as a student under the name Fedot Shubin.

Shubin studied arduously and was regularly given awards and praise. In June 1766 his bas-relief *The Killing of Askold and Dir* earned him a Grand Gold Medal and 'Certificate with Sword'—which meant that he attained the first rank of officer and entered the nobility.

Shubin's academy works, including genre statuettes, have not been preserved. In recognition of his 'good success and honest, laudable behaviour' he was sent in May 1767 with a group of state-supported artists to study in Paris. Here he came under the guardianship of the Russian ambassador Dmitry Golitsyn, an enlightened, progressive man and a great connoisseur and patron of art. On the advice of Diderot, who was a friend of Golitsyn's, Shubin was assigned to study under the sculptor Jean-Baptiste Pigalle, who was famous both for his allegorical and

1. Self-Portrait
2. Bust of Prince Alexander Golitsyn
3. Portrait of Mikhail Lomonosov

FIFTY
RUSSIAN
ARTISTS
34

F. I. SHUBIN

EIGHTEENTH
CENTURY

mythological compositions and for his realistic sculptured portraits. Under his guidance, Shubin copied the works of contemporary French sculptors and antique statues and modelled bas-reliefs from pictures by Raphael and Poussin. But Pigalle made his pupil work most of all from nature. In the evenings Shubin attended a class in the art of modelling from nature at the Paris Academy of Arts, and he frequently visited the Royal Library and the studios of well-known sculptors. ' . . .There is no interesting or worthwhile place in Paris', he wrote to St. Petersburg, 'which we miss, and we spare no effort to broaden our minds.'

After three years in Paris, at the end of 1770, Shubin had the permission of the Academy to go to Rome. The next year he painted portraits of Count Shuvalov (1771, TG) and his nephew Fyodor Golitsyn (1771, TG). Also successful was his marble bust of Catherine II, despite the fact she did not sit for him. It was at this time that the Empress's favourites, Alexei and Fyodor Orlov, commissioned Shubin to paint their portraits—works which are marked by their restraint and by the realistic tendencies in the interpretation of the models.

In 1772, while travelling with the Demidov brothers—the first Russian factory-owners—in Italy, Shubin stopped at Bologna, where he completed a series of works for which he was awarded the title of honorary member of the Bologna Academy—the oldest in Europe. The following summer, before returning to St. Petersburg, Shubin and the Demidovs undertook one more journey—to London.

The sculptor's first work in his home country was a bust of Prince Alexander Golitsyn, a diplomat during Catherine's reign (1775; plaster—RM, marble—TG). This is one of Shubin's most brilliant works, an expressive image of an educated nobleman, in whom a sensitive mind merged with worldly refinement, and a sense of superiority with the tiredness of an ageing man. The folds of his garment, which underline the turn in his head and shoulders, are marvellously

fashioned. This work, which earned the praise of Falconet, gives some idea of what Shubin's contemporaries meant when they said that the marble 'breathed' under his chisel.

On 4 September 1774 the Academy of Arts awarded Shubin the title of academician for his bust of the Empress—in violation of the regulations, which stated that this title could be awarded only for historical or mythological works. This exception was possible because the court aristocracy and Catherine II herself were known to be kindly disposed towards the sculptor.

In the seventies Shubin produced a great many portraits, working quickly—at the rate of at least one bust per month. Everyone was eager to have his portrait done by the empress's favourite. Yet the sculptor's inexhaustible powers of observation and perspicacity meant that he never repeated himself, always finding new solutions based not so much on the models' external characteristics as on their mental states.

In Shubin's portraits we see the high society of St. Petersburg. Behind the superficial grace and elegance of the lady-in-waiting M. Panina (mid-1770s, TG), there are traces of coldness, imperiousness and arrogance. In his sculpture of the famous Field Marshal P. Rumyantsev-Zadunaisky (1777, RM) the artist brought out features of a strong and important personality, without in the slightest embellishing his appearance.

Quite another character is revealed in the portrait of V. Orlov (1778, TG). In the sculptor's hands, his imposing exterior—his aristocratic carriage, his opulent drapery—is charged with irony. The dull, impudent face of this ungifted man who was head of the Academy of Sciences solely due to his family ties is reproduced with merciless realism.

The bust of the rich industrialist I. Baryshnikov (1778, TG) is simple and severe in composition. Shubin saw this representative of the rising bourgeoisie as a shrewd and intelligent businessman; his individual and social features are brilliantly blended.

EIGHTEENTH
CENTURY

F. I. SHUBIN

FIFTY
RUSSIAN
ARTISTS
35

FIFTY
RUSSIAN
ARTISTS
36

F. I. SHUBIN

EIGHTEENTH
CENTURY

In the portrait of P. Zavadsky, Catherine II's State Secretary (mid-1770s, TG) one is struck by its emotionality and romantic mood—a mood intensified by the plasticity of the form and by the fast, vigorous style of modelling.

Shubin revealed the innermost workings of the soul in the remarkably poetic image of an unknown young man (mid-1770s, TG). The calm composition and soft modelling convey the young man's state of deep thoughtfulness.

In 1774-75 Shubin worked on a portrait of Catherine II and on a series of 58 round marble bas-reliefs (about 70 cm in diameter) depicting princes and rulers from Ryurik up to Elizaveta Petrovna. The bas-reliefs were intended for the Round Hall of the Chesmensky Palace and are now kept in the Armoury of the Kremlin. They were based upon descriptions of the various characters given in ancient chronicles.

Over the next ten years Shubin carried out many commissions for decorative works—statues and reliefs for the Marble Palace, sculptures for the Trinity Cathedral in the Alexander Nevsky Monastery (Lavra), a marble mausoleum for Lieutenant General P. Golitsyn. Shubin's last decorative work was a statue of Pandora to replace one of the decaying leaden sculptures of Peterhof. Its prototype was Falconet's *Woman Bathing*, which Shubin had copied in Paris.

The most noteworthy of Shubin's works of the 1780s were his busts of P. Sheremetev (1783, Kuskovo) and General I. Michelson (1785, RM), his medallion with a profile representation of Catherine II and his sculptured bust of the empress (1783, RM).

A special place in Shubin's work is occupied by his statue *Catherine II the Legislatress* (1789-90, RM). This statue was very successful, but the sculptor received no reward from the empress, nor did he obtain a post as professor at the Academy, where portrait sculpture was considered a 'low genre'.

Gradually, interest in Shubin faded. His unembellished portraits found less and less favour among his clients from the *beau monde*, who wished to see themselves depicted in ideal form. He received less commissions, and remuneration fell too. He was forced to seek help from G. Potyomkin, who wrote to the President of the Academy of Arts, I. Betskoi, asking him to employ Shubin as assistant professor in the sculpture class. The sculptor himself also applied to the Council of the Academy for a paid post. Both letters remained unanswered. Then, in 1792, Shubin addressed himself to Catherine II: 'Your Majesty, I am in poor health and must needs ask you for help . . .' Two years passed before the celebrated sculptor was installed as a professor—but still it was not a paid post. As it was, Shubin was a sick man, burdened by a large family, and all these adversities further undermined his health, but he did not stop working. The works dating from the nineties speak eloquently of the sculptor's ability to reveal his models' characters fully and profoundly. His gallery of portraits is varied: the dried-up old warrior Admiral V. Chichagov (1791, RM), the good-natured, haughty sybarite G. Potyomkin (1791, RM), the empty, self-enamoured beau Platon Zubov (1796, TG), the pedantic I. Betskoi (1790s, TG) and the dull-witted, swaggering St. Petersburg mayor Ye. Chulkov (1792, RM).

In 1792 Shubin made a portrait of Mikhail Lomonosov from memory (RM). In contrast to the others, this portrait is deeply democratic, simple in composition and form, full of intellectuality and entirely lacking in showy, official elements.

Shubin's bust of Paul I (1797, marble, RM) is a true masterpiece of portraiture. It is a complex image, comprising arrogance, cold cruelty, unhealthiness and deeply concealed suffering. Nonetheless Paul liked the work, apparently because of the signs of solemn majesty which he valued so highly.

Each year Shubin's position grew more difficult. In 1797 he turned to Paul for assistance, and a year later he appealed to the Academy 'to

EIGHTEENTH
CENTURY

F. I. SHUBIN

FIFTY
RUSSIAN
ARTISTS
37

provide at least an apartment at the state's expense, and firewood and candles'. But this request, too, was given no consideration. Shubin had no means to support his family, he was beginning to go blind, and in 1801 his house and studio—together with the works it contained—were burnt down.

These blows of fate did not force Shubin to compromise. In one of his last works—a bust of Alexander I (1801, Voronezh Regional Museum of Fine Arts)—there is a strain of cold indifference behind the emperor's affable exterior. Alexander did display charity, however, and presented the sculptor with a diamond ring. The Academy, too, was at last compelled to show some concern for Shubin, and he was given the free accommodation and candles he had begged for so long. In 1803, Alexander decreed that Shubin finally be appointed assistant professor, on the paid staff of the Academy. But his health was utterly ruined, and on 12 May 1805 Shubin died.

The sculptor's death passed almost unnoticed. His realism could not possibly meet with the approval of his titled customers. It was a tragic end to the life of a man whose art, in the words of Soviet sculptress Vera Mukhina, was the 'image of the age'.

3

Fyodor Stepanovich
ROKOTOV

(1735-1808)

1

For a long time the life of Fyodor Rokotov, the most poetic portraitist of the eighteenth century, remained a riddle. Having been very famous during his life, Rokotov was forgotten for a whole century after his death, and it was only this century that his name was restored to its rightful place in the history of Russian art.

For many years he was thought to have been of noble birth. But recently found documents have shown that in fact Rokotov was born the son of a serf, on the Vorontsovo estate near Moscow, which belonged to Prince Repnin. He is thought to have been born in 1735, and we find the first written mention of him as an artist in 1757, when the *Portrait of an Unknown Young Man in Guards Uniform* (TG) was painted. Another painting dating from this time *I. Shuvalov's Study*, known to us from a copy made by Rokotov's pupil A. Zyablov (1779, State Historical Museum, Moscow).

Count Shuvalov gave all possible support to the young artist, and it was on his recommendation that Rokotov was accepted by the Academy as a pupil in 1760. The artist's successes attracted attention and soon he became known to the Court. In 1762, as a result of his large full-dress portrait of Peter III (RM), he was made an assistant professor. Among the best works from Rokotov's early period were his *Portrait of Catherine II in Coronation Dress* (1763, TG) which served as a kind of standard from which copies were made, and his portrait of the empress' favourite Grigory Orlov (1762-63, TG).

Rokotov's full-dress portraits are beautifully decorative and skilfully drawn. Given the demands placed by the genre on the structure of each work, the artist always managed to vary the composition interestingly.

In the sixties Rokotov painted a series of informal portraits, mainly of men, which demonstrate his desire to capture both the external features and the personalities of his models. He produced expressive likenesses of the intelligent, refined aristocrat I. Orlov (RM) and

EIGHTEENTH
CENTURY

F. S. ROKOTOV

FIFTY
RUSSIAN
ARTISTS
39

1. Portrait of Ye. V. Santi
2. Portrait of A. P. Struiskaya
3. Portrait of V. N. Surovtseva

of the talented statesman and writer I. Gole-nishchev-Kutuzov, the uncle of the famous general (RM). Particularly interesting is his portrait of V. Maikov (c. 1765, TG), behind whose languid effeminacy one can sense the talented poet's acumen and ironic turn of mind. Maikov's sensitive face is painted almost tangibly, and the colour-scheme, based on reds and greens, serves further to underline the full-bloodedness and liveliness of the image. This is one of the most significant works in eighteenth century art. Rokotov had a great reputation in those days, and received so many commissions that he could not cope with them all alone. For

this reason he himself very often painted only the main part of his portraits—the face—while his assistants did the clothes and other details.

In 1775, for his copy of Giordano's *Venus, Cupid and Satyr,* made from an etching by Francesco Bartolozzi, Rokotov received the title of academician and left the capital for ever.

Moscow, which was Rokotov's destination, at that time allowed greater creative freedom than official St. Petersburg. It was there that outstanding Russian enlightener N. Novikov and the talented dramatist A. Sumarokov were working, and it was there that the well-known poet Kheraskov formed his literary circle for young

FIFTY
RUSSIAN
ARTISTS
40

F. S. ROKOTOV

EIGHTEENTH
CENTURY

people. In this enlightened, progressive environment, Rokotov's world-outlook, which was clearly in evidence in his works from the end of the sixties, took shape.

The last official commission, carried out not later than 1768, was a series of portraits of the trustees of the Moscow Foundling Hospital: I. Tyutchev (TG), S. Gagarin (RM) and P. Vyrubov (TG). Already in these works one can feel Rokotov's leaning towards simplicity even in the full-dress portrait, and in the years to come he devoted himself entirely to work on chamber portraits. It was at this period that Rokotov's own individual style and manner of painting developed. Most often he painted oval portraits, the shape of the canvas underlining the overall rhythmic construction of the works. Rokotov's figures are portrayed at varying distances, as a rule from the waist up and turning slightly. Even the model's most insignificant, restrained movements are a result of his inner state. In Rokotov's method of characterization, the expressiveness of the eyes and face are very important, his aim being not so much to give a concrete expression of the mood, but rather to create a sense of elusiveness and transience of human feelings.

Rokotov's works are marked by the refined beauty of their colour range. Usually based on three colours, they express the richness and complexity of the subject's inner world. Moreover, the artist makes distinctive use of chiaroscuro, highlighting the face and 'dissolving', as it were, the secondary details.

These features of Rokotov's art manifested themselves most fully in his female portraits, which held a special place in the art of the eighteenth century. At his peak the artist created a gallery of beautiful female images: A. Struiskaya (1772, TG), V. Novosiltseva (1780, TG), Ye. Santi (1785, RM) and V. Surovtseva (1780, RM). Each portrait is highly individual, beautiful in its own way. Like a bewitching apparition, Alexandra Struiskaya's face with its huge eyes emerges from a haze of pearly roseate hues. Her image is full of radiant purity and the intransient beauty of youth. In the portrait of V. Novosiltseva one feels her grandeur and dignity, her self-assurance and her faculty for deep thought. A pallid, delicate face, eyes slightly screwed up, looking sharply, and lips trembling with a barely perceptible smile—such is the cold, ironical Santi; her aristocracy is emphasised by a delicate combination of pinks and greens. And finally—Surovtseva, charming and feminine, with a modest Russian face and a direct, kindly look in her clear, radiant eyes.

Yet for all their individuality, Rokotov's female figures do have something in common: a complex spiritual world, a rich and beautiful inner life, and elevated human emotions. While revealing the innermost secrets of the human soul, the painter always leaves something unsaid. And this is what gives Rokotov's portraits their fascinating mysteriousness and special poetic qualities.

The lyricism of these enigmatic images was marvellously expressed by the Soviet poet Nikolai Zabolotsky in his poem *Portrait:*

Recall how from the depths of time,
Mysterious and pale,
Struiskaya, satin-robed, looked down
From Rokotov's portrayal.
Her eyes two mists,
Half-joy, half-grief,
Her eyes like twin deceits.
The union of two mysteries,
Half-ecstasy, half-terror,
A wave of reckless tenderness,
A vision of death horror.

The ideal of the man moulded by the enlightened aristocratic environment—'honour, elegance and inner dignity'—was expressed by Rokotov in his male portraits of representatives of noble intelligentsia: Surovtsev (1780, RM), the poet Sumarokov (1777, State Historical Museum, Moscow), the gifted diplomat Obreskov (1777, TG). The portrait of Obreskov is remarkable for its fine detail and deep penetration into the character of an energetic, clever, perceptive man.

EIGHTEENTH
CENTURY

F. S. ROKOTOV

FIFTY
RUSSIAN
ARTISTS
41

Rokotov's contemporary and ardent admirer N. Struisky wrote that the artist worked very quickly and lightly, 'almost playfully'. Even in old age he worked hard and with great inspiration.

Of his last years we know only that he lived continuously in Moscow. Having no family of his own, his nearest relations and heirs were his nephews.

Fyodor Rokotov died on 24 December 1808 in Moscow and was laid to rest in the Novo-Spassky Monastery.

4. Portrait of V. I. Maikov

4

Dmitry Grigorievich LEVITSKY

(1735-1822)

1

Dmitry Levitsky was one of the most important and versatile artists of the eighteenth century. His brilliant, refined portraits most fully reflected the philosophical and aesthetic conceptions of the second half of the century, and the age's belief in the power of a reason and the integrity and nobility of human nature.

Levitsky came of old Ukrainian stock and was born in Kiev. His father Grigory Levitsky was a hereditary priest who did amateur painting and etching, and it was he who taught his son the first skills of painting. An important role in the boy's development was the arrival in Kiev in 1752 of the well-known St. Petersburg artist A. Antropov to decorate the St. Andrew Cathedral. The Levitskys, father and son, got to know Antropov, and it was possible that they took part in the decoration of the cathedral, since Antropov was empowered to take on local masters as assistants.

In 1758 young Levitsky went to St. Petersburg and became Antropov's pupil. He lived in his house and for several years worked together with him. In 1762 he went with Antropov to Moscow, where he painted the Triumphal Gates erected to mark the coronation of Catherine II. Here Levitsky worked with the leading artists of the day, and there can be no doubt that the young artist benefited greatly by such contact. A year later Levitsky went his own way. Having inherited from Antropov not only painting skills but also disinterestedness, honesty and diligence, he began his independent creative career.

Levitsky's name first became known at an exhibition in the Academy of Arts in 1770, at which he exhibited six masterly portraits. One of the most interesting of these works was his portrait of A. Kokorinov (RM), the designer of the building which housed the Academy of Arts, and its first director. The portrait belonged to the typical eighteenth-century genre of the full-dress portrait, a genre which required splendour and solemnity. In this type of portrait, the apparel, gestures and

1. V. L. Borovikovsky. Portrait of D. G. Levitsky
2. Portrait of P. A. Demidov
3. Ye. N. Khovanskaya and Ye. N. Khrushchova
4. Portrait of M. A. Diakova

EIGHTEENTH
CENTURY

D. G. LEVITSKY

FIFTY
RUSSIAN
ARTISTS
43

attitude of the model, the attributes surrounding him, and the composition of the painting, with the figure in the central position, were supposed to underline the subject's high social standing. All this is present in the portrait of Kokorinov, in which a certain tranquility and serenity can also be felt, due to the restrained colour combinations. The architect's thoughtful face is painted lovingly with the stress on the human dignity and nobility of his character.

Levitsky received the title of academician, and from 1771 for seventeen years he took a class in portrait painting at the Academy of Arts.

In the seventies and eighties Levitsky was at the peak of his talent and fame, and constantly received commissions from the tsarist Court. In 1773 he painted P. Demidov (TG). The unusualness of this portrait was to some extent due to the originality of the subject's personality: Demidov was renowned for his eccentricities but at the same time he was a highly educated man, who donated enormous sums of money to the cause of enlightenment. This work is distinguished by its combination of showiness in the positioning of the figure, with the simplicity of Demidov's appearance—he is depicted in the ceremonial attitude against the background of a traditional colonnade. He is surrounded by everyday objects, such as pots of flowers and a watering-can, which are reminders of Demidov's interest in gardening. His informal dress strengthens the intimate flavour of the work.

Levitsky's search for more life and naturalness in the portrayal of people found expression in a series of portraits of girls from the Smolny Institute, founded by Catherine II with the aim of bringing up 'a new kind of woman'—well-bred and educated. Seven portraits commissioned by the empress were completed between 1773 and 1777.

In his portraits of the Smolny girls, the artist introduced the element of 'plot', showing the models in action so as best to display their character traits. The girls are portrayed performing

2

concert numbers. Ye. Nelidova, who was well-known for her artistic talent, dances and sings couplets; in her smile, her glance and her movements there is animation and cheerful coquetry. N. Borshchova dances briskly and spiritedly, while the movements of A. Levshina, a serious, dreamy girl, are smooth and slow. G. Alimova plays harp, turning to the spectator with a polite, well-mannered smile. Charming, and with a delicate, intelligent face, Ye. Molchanova recites poetry.

This series includes two double portraits—F. Rzhevskaya and N. Davydova, and Ye. Khrushchova and Ye. Khovanskaya. The latter is particularly expressive in its characterisation. The girls are acting out a pastoral scene: Khrushchova is playing a shepherd-boy, Khovanskaya a shepherdess. Levitsky bases the portraits on the juxtaposition of their individual qualities:

FIFTY
RUSSIAN
ARTISTS
44

D. G. LEVITSKY

EIGHTEENTH
CENTURY

Khovanskaya is shy, timid and a little constrained in her movements; Khrushchova is more forward, with a pert smile and a playful gesture.

Though originally he had no overall plan for the series of portraits of the Smolny girls, Levitsky succeeded in producing a unified suit, whose common theme was the charm and beauty of youth. The portraits are linked by their unity of formal devices, by the rhythm of movements, by their common constructions, and by the use of conventional theatrical or landscape background, with the human subject predominating. They are all characterised by decorative colouring and subtle use of refined tones, yet each portrait has its own distinctive colour key.

These works display Levitsky's talent for creating a decorative ensemble, intended to adorn a palace hall, and his understanding of the portrait as a large-scale compositional picture. (The whole series is now displayed in the Russian Museum, Leningrad.)

Levitsky's mastery manifested itself in many of his later canvases, especially in his *Portrait of Catherine II the Legislatress,* which he was commissioned to paint by the Chancellor A. Bezborodko (1783, RM).

The portrait of Catherine II is essentially a historical painting, in which the content is put across by a system of allegories. Such use of imagery was characteristic of the classical style, which was established at that time in the Academy of Arts. A description of the portrait by Levitsky himself has been preserved, in which he says that Catherine is depicted in the temple of the goddess of Justice; by burning poppies at the altar she 'sacrifices her own precious peace for the peace of all'; the order of St. Vladimir underlines her services to her country; the open sea visible in the distance, the Russian flag and Mercury's warder on a shield, all represent protected trade.

The moulding of the artist's views was greatly influenced by his close contact with a circle of progressive thinkers and writers (V. Kapnist, G. Derzhavin, A. Olenin and others), one of the more eminent of whom was Levitsky's friend N. Lvov. A man of exceptional education and wide-ranging abilities, Lvov constantly spoke in favour of national art and its important social role. It was he who suggested to Levitsky how he should portray Catherine II. It is interesting that in his ode *The Apparition of the Tartar Prince,* depicting Catherine, the poet Derzhavin gives poetic version of Levitsky's portrait:

From the clouds she descended
And appeared, a priestess
Or a goddess, before me;
Her white streaming dress
In silver did flow,
Her bosom was aureate,
Her crown was aglow . . .

At this time Levitsky painted a series of portraits of the Russian nobility: the writer A. Khrapovitsky (1781, RM), A. Vorontsov (late 1780s, RM), N. Lvov (1789, RM). These are very simple, small-scale works. The figure is usually portrayed in a natural attitude against a neutral, blank background. In these works Levitsky gives a sober, objective characterisation of his contemporaries, bringing out their essential physical and mental qualities and emphasising the national type.

Among Levitsky's best works is his portrait of the famous French philosopher Denis Diderot (1773, Geneva Public Library), who visited Russia on the invitation of Catherine II. Diderot is portrayed in a gown, without a wig; his old man's face is drawn with great care, and his eyes reflect his clear mind and concentration. Diderot appears to have liked the portrait, as he bequeathed it to his sister.

Levitsky's female portraits are extremely beautiful, and each has its own distinctive range of colour. The niece of the Polish king, the society beauty Ursula Mniczeck, for example, is painted in subtle shades of gold and light blue (1782, RM); in the portrait of the quick-witted Italian adventuress and singer Anna Devia Bernucci (1782, TG) the colour relationships are simpler, while her complicated toilet introduces a rather

EIGHTEENTH
CENTURY

D. G. LEVITSKY

FIFTY
RUSSIAN
ARTISTS
45

FIFTY
RUSSIAN
ARTISTS
46

D. G. LEVITSKY

EIGHTEENTH
CENTURY

'garish' element. The most attractive of the female images created by Levitsky is that of M. Diakova (1778, TG), which is tender, light and full of charm and womanliness. The poetic qualities of this portrait liken Levitsky to that other great painter of the eighteenth century, Fyodor Rokotov.

In 1787 Levitsky gave up his teaching post at the Academy. Towards the end of the century his position changed dramatically and he was no longer considered the leading artist of his times. The old master experienced great material hardships. He lived in solitude, began to get involved in freemasonry and became more and more religiously minded.

In 1807, thanks to the efforts of the conference secretary of the Academy of Arts A. Labzin, Levitsky returned to the Academy as a member of a Council. But soon he was overtaken by great misfortune: he began to lose his sight. His last work was painted in 1812.

Dmitry Levitsky died in 1822 in St. Petersburg and is buried in the Smolensk Cemetery.

4

Vladimir Lukich BOROVIKOVSKY

(1757-1825)

1. I. V. Bugayevsky-Blagodarny.
   Portrait of V. L. Borovikovsky
2. Portrait of M. I. Lopukhina
3. Portrait of Vice-Chancellor A. B.
   Kurakin
4. Portrait of A. I. Bezborodko with
   Daughters

Vladimir Borovikovsky, one of the talented and original artists of the late eighteenth and early nineteenth centuries, was born in Mirgorod, in the Ukraine.

His father was a Cossack, and almost all the members of his family served in the Mirgorod regiment. Following the family tradition, Vladimir went into military service, but having attained the rank of lieutenant he retired and devoted himself entirely to art.

The budding artist learned the first skills of painting at home. His father, uncle and brothers all did icon-painting when they were not busy with their regimental duties.

The Kiev Museum of Ukrainian Art and the Russian Museum in Leningrad both contain some icons painted by the young Borovikovsky. These early works testify to the artist's mastery of certain skills of eighteenth century icon-painting, but on the whole they are still on the level of craftsmanship. Real mastery came later, in St. Petersburg.

Catherine II's visit to the Crimea in 1787 was decisive in bringing about a change of fate for Borovikovsky.

The well-known eighteenth-century poet, V. Kapnist, then marshal of nobility in Kiev Gubernia, asked the artist to decorate one of the rooms in which Catherine was going to reside. Borovikovsky painted two large allegorical paintings—evidently with considerable skill, and he was invited to St. Petersburg. On 20 October 1787 he signed a deed on the division of property bequeathed by his father and left Mirgorod for ever.

For the first ten years the artist lived with N. Lvov, a well-known architect and a man of varied interests, keen on poetry, music and archeology. His house was a meeting-place for many eminent figures in Russian culture. Borovikovsky found himself in the company of poets whose interests and ideas were linked to the new wave in literature—sentimentalism. Karamzin's *Letters of a Russian Traveller* and *Poor Lisa* had been published, the poet Dmitriev was writ-

FIFTY
RUSSIAN
ARTISTS
48

V. L. BOROVIKOVSKY

EIGHTEENTH
CENTURY

ing his sentimental verses, and lyrical notes were to be heard in the poetry of V. Kapnist. This line in literature was reflected in the art of Borovikovsky.

In St. Petersburg Borovikovsky became a good friend of Dmitry Levitsky and possibly studied under him. From 1792 he was taught by I. Lamni, who gave him his studio when he left Russia. Here Borovikovsky lived and worked for the rest of his life. In more than thirty years of strenuous work in the capital, he painted hundreds of works. From his teachers he learned a brilliant technique, a light, transparent style, and mastery of compositional devices. At the centre of his attention was man's inner world and unique individuality.

In his portraits, the image as a whole was subordinated to his ideal of a pure, poetic personality with an elevated soul. The pose, the positioning of the hands and the landscape were all a kind of setting for the model's face. Borovikovsky developed a distinctive style, in which softly playing mother-of-pearl shades and a smooth surface like porcelain were combined with precision of drawing and classically severe lines.

One of the artist's best early works is his delightful portrait of O. Filippova (1790, RM), the wife of one of Borovikovsky's friends—an architect, who helped construct Kazan Cathedral. She is depicted against the background of a garden, in white morning dress, a pale rose in her hand. The image of the young woman is devoid of any trace of affectation or coquetry. Her facial features are distinctive; the almond shape of her eyes, the way her nostrils are drawn and the mole over her upper lip all lend particular charm to her face, which bears an expression of almost childlike tenderness and dreamy thoughtfulness.

In the late eighteenth century the art of the miniature portrait was very widespread—a genre which combined lyricism and great intimacy (miniature portraits were commissioned in memory of near and dear ones) with decorative qualities. Borovikovsky worked

in this genre at various periods, but particularly in his early years.

The distinctive content of Borovikovsky's art led him to work out new, more varied portrait forms. He did many double portraits and showed a propensity for small-scale, chamber works.

Such, for example, were his portraits of 1794, including *Lizanka and Dashenka* and *Khristinia, the Peasant Woman of Torzhok* (c. 1795, TG), all portraying serfs owned by N. Lvov. These portraits certainly exhibit the same idyllic notes that can be "heard" in the study of Ye. Arsenieva (mid-1790s, RM) and in the well-known portrait of *Catherine II Walking in the Park at Tsarskoye Selo* (mid-1790s, TG).

The portrait of Catherine II, walking with her favourite dog in the park, is unconstrained, even intimate. The image of the empress is not devoid of sentimentality, but what is important is that Borovikovsky portrays her not as a 'goddess on Earth' but in a normal domestic situation. It is significant that Alexander Pushkin was later attracted to this image: it was as just such a benevolent, majestic ruler that Catherine had to appear to the heroine of his story *The Captain's Daughter,* the inexperienced, innocent, trusting Masha Mironova, who seeks the empress's aid and patronage.

One of Borovikovsky's most mature lyrical works was his portrait of Maria Lopukhina (1797, TG). The young woman's attitude is relaxed and simple, yet refined and elegant. The harmony of the image results from the whole artistic structure of the work: the flowing lines, the movement of her hand, the rhythm of the trunks and branches of the trees in the shady park, the subtlest nuances of light and shade, and the gentle blue, mother-of-pearl colours, reminiscent of the magical sounds of a clavichord.

This portrait left a mark on the poetry of the nineteenth century in the form of a poem by Yakov Polonsky:

> *Long since she passed away: no more those eyes,*
> *No more that smile which tacitly expressed*
> *The suffering of her love and her sad thoughts.*
> *But her beauty Borovikovsky has preserved.*

EIGHTEENTH
CENTURY

V. L. BOROVIKOVSKY

FIFTY
RUSSIAN
ARTISTS
49

FIFTY
RUSSIAN
ARTISTS
50

V. L. BOROVIKOVSKY

EIGHTEENTH
CENTURY

3

EIGHTEENTH
CENTURY

V. L. BOROVIKOVSKY

FIFTY
RUSSIAN
ARTISTS
51

Her soul, in part, is therefore with us still,
And this her gaze and this her body's charm
Will fascinate indifferent generation,
                                    teaching them
To love, to suffer, to forgive and to be silent.

4

Borovikovsky's male portraits were no less typical of the age. There is the serious, rather sullen aspect of D. P. Troshchinsky, Catherine II's State Secretary (1790s, RM), to whom the artist was attracted because of his uncommon intelligence and abilities. F. A. Borovsky is depicted as a courageous man, covered with the glory of Suvorov's campaigns; his stern, energetic face is portrayed with great realism (1799, RM).

Official, full-dress portraits hold a special place in eighteenth-century Russian art, and Borovikovsky is no exception. Both in his work and in Levitsky's, the full-dress portrait, whose main function was to glorify the subject's social station, laid special emphasis on man's inner world. This can be seen in the portraits of the Persian Prince Murtaza-Kouli-Khan (1796, RM) and of the 'diamond prince' Vice Chancellor A. B. Kurakin, known as the 'peacock' because of his arrogance and love of ostentatious luxury (1801, TG), and also in the well-known portrait 'in dalmatic and purple' of Paul I (1800, RM), which was commissioned for the conference hall of the Academy of Arts.

Borovikovsky, then, was equally at home with such monumental, commissioned portraits, and with lyrical, intimate works.

In the early years of the nineteenth century the artist took part in the decoration of the Kazan Cathedral which was then being built. He painted ten icons.

Borovikovsky was a charming person, gentle of character. His pupils—among the favourites was Alexei Venetsianov—lived in his house like members of the family. His relations constantly turned to him for help: he sorted out their quarrels and supported them morally and materially.

Borovikovsky died in his sixty-eighth year, asking to be buried 'without ceremony'. Venetsianov wrote in a letter to a friend: 'That great and respected man Borovikovsky has passed away, he has ceased to adorn Russia with his works and to torment those who envied him . . . I am going to write his biography.'

Many decades passed before much public interest was shown in this great artist, but an exhibition in 1905 at which more than a hundred of his portraits were displayed helped to bring him into the public eye. After the October Revolution, works which had been scattered around stately homes and private collections found their way into museums and galleries and now give a fair idea of the rich legacy of this outstanding master.

Mikhail Ivanovich
KOZLOVSKY

(1753-1802)

1

Though an artist of great versatility, it was particularly in sculpture that Mikhail Kozlovsky made a name for himself.

He was born into the family of a military musician. The boy's precocious talent for drawing prompted his parents to send him to the Academy of Arts. Here he entered the sculpture class and was taught by Nicolas Gillet, a French artist who trained many talented sculptors of that time. Apart from sculpture which he attacked with great enthusiasm, Kozlovsky was also very keen on drawing, and when it came to choosing which to specialise in he vacillated for a long time.

In 1772 Kozlovsky was awarded a first class gold medal for his programme bas-relief *Prince Izyaslav in the Field of Battle* (plaster, in the Scientific Research Museum of the USSR Academy of Arts), the theme of which was taken from Russian history. Here he succeeded in creating a dynamic scene: the characters poses are full of expression, their gestures are exaggeratedly emotional. The artist had not at this stage achieved the severe, restrained style which was to characterise his mature period.

Winning a Grand Gold Medal for his diploma work *The Return of Svyatoslav from the Danube* (1773), Kozlovsky graduated from the Academy of Arts and set off for Italy to continue his education. His horizons were widened, and his work profited, by the knowledge he gained here of works of classical art and by his close study of canvases by Renaissance artists. Of the work he completed in Rome, however, apart from some drawings done with enormous verve and perfection, nothing has come down to us. In 1780 the Marseilles Academy of Arts awarded him the title of academician—a fact which testifies to the popularity of his works abroad.

On his return home, Kozlovsky worked on the decoration of many architectural monuments: bas-reliefs, for example, for the Concert Hall at Tsarskoye Selo (architect: Giacomo Quarenghi) and for the Marble Palace in St. Petersburg (architect: Antonio Rinaldi). He also

1. V. I. Demut-Malinovsky. Portrait
of M. I. Kozlovsky
2. The Vigil of Alexander of Macedon

EIGHTEENTH
CENTURY

M. I. KOZLOVSKY

FIFTY
RUSSIAN
ARTISTS
53

made a marble statue of Catherine II, represented as Minerva (1785, RM). It is an idealised, majestic image of the empress and legislatress. Catherine liked the statue and Kozlovsky obtained permission to travel to Paris 'to further his knowledge in his art'.

In 1790 in Paris the sculptor fashioned his statue *Polycrates* (RM). The theme of man's striving for freedom which this work expressed, reflected the revolutionary events in France which Kozlovsky witnessed. The master portrayed the most intense moment in the sufferings of Polycrates, bound by the Persians to a tree. Never before had the sculptor attained such expressiveness and drama in conveying complex

human feelings, or such forceful imagery. He was aided in this by his excellent knowledge of anatomy and by working with models.

In 1794 Kozlovsky was made an academician; later 'in recognition of his talents', he was appointed professor, and in 1797—senior professor. His importance as a teacher at the Academy was extremely great. As an excellent graphic artist and a sensitive, attentive teacher, he commanded love and respect all around. A whole series of talented young sculptors emerged from his studio, including S. Pimenov, I. Terebenev and V. Demut-Malinovsky.

In the late 1780s and 1790s the sculptor was at the peak of his talent. At this period he was

FIFTY
RUSSIAN
ARTISTS
54

M. I. KOZLOVSKY

EIGHTEENTH
CENTURY

3. Monument to A. V. Suvorov
4. Polycrates
5. Theseus Deserting Ariadne

EIGHTEENTH
CENTURY

M. I. KOZLOVSKY

FIFTY
RUSSIAN
ARTISTS
55

attracted by the heroic themes full of patriotic fervour. In 1797 he carved the marble statue *Yakov Dolgoruky Tearing Up a Royal Decree* (RM). It is significant that the artist took his theme here from recent Russian history. He was drawn by the image of Peter the Great's associate, who was not afraid to tear up an unjust tsar's decree—which laid impossible burdens on the impoverished peasantry—in the tsar's presence. The figure of Dolgoruky is full of determination and steadfastness. His face is angry and stern. His right hand holds a torch, his left the scales of justice. At his feet are a dead serpent and a mask—symbols of treachery and pretence.

Kozlovsky also took subjects from the Homeric epics and Roman history. An important place in his art is occupied by his work on the figure of Alexander of Macedon (1780s, RM). In the statue *The Vigil of Alexander of Macedon* the sculptor represented an episode from the training of the future leader's will. The young man's body is handsome and perfect, his movements nimble and smooth. The silhouette of the statue is well thought-out, with distinct, expressive contours.

Kozlovsky based a series of sculptored and graphic studies on Homer, the most successful of which was the marble statuette *Ajax Protects the Body of Patrocles* (1796, RM) on the theme of manly friendship and devotion. The tense movement of Ajax's figure, his broad stride and the vigorous turn of his head all reveal his resolution and willpower. The scene derives a sense of drama from the contrast between the lifeless immobility of Patrocles' body and the strong muscular Ajax.

Almost all of Kozlovsky's later works were marked by a spirit of heroism and valorous struggle. In the bronze group *Hercules on Horseback* (1799, RM), this was a symbolic expression of the military genius of Suvorov. The outstanding general is represented as the young Hercules, astride a galloping steed, and this figure is expressive and imposing. In a

sense, this group was a preliminary stage in the sculptor's work on his masterpiece—the monument to the great Russian general Alexander Suvorov.

It was with great zeal that Kozlovsky embarked on this project in 1799. The sketches now kept in the Russian Museum testify to the long, complex search that led to the final solution. Only in the final versions did the artist arrived at the idea of representing Suvorov as the 'god of war' with a sword and shield in his hands. In order to glorify the strength and courage of the Russian general, Kozlovsky resorted to allegory, creating an idealised, generalised image of a warrior. It contains no concrete features of Suvorov's own personality, for the whole point of the monument was to express the general's bravery, resoluteness and inflinching will. He is caught in the middle of an energetic but restrained movement, swiftly, lightly taking a step forward. He holds a sword high, in readiness to strike. With his shield he protects the crown and the papal tiara. His head is turned sharply to the side, and his open, youthful, proud face speaks of his unruffled courage. Seen from the front, the statue is marked by solemnity, tranquility and monumental clarity. From the right the warrior's attacking movement is particularly striking, while the viewer on the left is most clearly aware of the figure's firmness and confident power. The pedestal, designed jointly by Kozlovsky and A. N. Voronikhin, is a harmonious part of the overall conception: the solid rhythmically proportioned form of the round granite column is in marked contrast to the light, graceful figure of the hero.

The monument was unveiled on 5 May 1801, on the Field of Mars in St. Petersburg, not far from The Engineers' Castle. In 1820, due to the reconstruction of the buildings on the Field of Mars, it was moved to the embankment, to the square named after the Russian general. The Suvorov monument marked the apex of Kozlovsky's career, and its construction was the greatest event in Russian artistic life of the period.

FIFTY
RUSSIAN
ARTISTS
56

M. I. KOZLOVSKY

EIGHTEENTH
CENTURY

Another of Kozlovsky's finest achievements, and one of the most beautiful decorations of the fountains at Peterhof, was his *Samson*, the central statue of a sculptural ensemble jointly constructed by many of Russian's best sculptors—Shubin, Martos, Shchedrin, Prokofiev, Gordeyev and others. But the most important of those involved was probably Kozlovsky, whose

5

work provides the compositional key to the sculptural complex of the Grand Cascade. Once again the artist resorted to symbolism: Samson personifies Russia, while the lion represents defeated Sweden. This allegorical imagery was understood by everyone in the eighteenth century. Samson's mighty figure is shown in a complex twisted position, full of tensity and motion.

Kozlovsky's *Samson* is one of the world's finest pieces of decorative sculpture. The ensemble of the Peterhof fountains, destroyed by the Nazis in the Second World War, has now been restored. And it is adorned once again by the statue *Samson Rending the Lion's Jaws*—a copy of Kozlovsky's work, made in 1947 by the Leningrad sculptor V. A. Simonov.

Kozlovsky's last works were gravestones, full of heartfelt sorrow, for P. I. Melissino (1800) and S. A. Stroganova (1802, 'Necropolis, of the Eighteenth Century', the Leningrad Museum of Town Sculpture).

The sculptor's life came to an abrupt end just as he had reached the peak of his talent. He died on 18 September 1802 at the age of forty-nine.

Ivan Petrovich MARTOS

(1752-1835)

Ivan Martos was born in the village of Ichne in the Chernigov region of the Ukraine. At the age of twelve he was sent to the Academy of Arts, where for eight years he studied sculpture under Nicolas Gillet and drawing under Anton Losenko.

Graduating from the Academy with a gold medal, he went to Rome to further his education. Here the young artist made a thorough study of ancient art, especially classical sculpture and architecture.

On his return to St. Petersburg Martos became a teacher at the Academy and steadily climbed the ladder of promotion: first he became an academician, then professor, and later he was appointed rector of the Academy.

Even the young sculptor's earliest works show signs of artistic maturity. Among these works was the marble bust of Nikita Panin (1780, TG). Striving to endow the image with importance and grandeur, Martos depicted Panin in classical apparel, successfully using a frontal positioning of the figure.

At this period Martos began working in the field of sculptured tombstones, an entirely new sphere of Russian representative art. And it was in this field that Martos excelled. The tombstones which he carved in 1782—for S. S. Volkonskaya (TG) and M. P. Sobakina (Museum of Architecture at the USSR Academy of Building and Architecture)—are veritable masterpieces of Russian sculpture. Sobakina's stone is marked by musical lines, beautiful rhythms and a very expressive composition. The figures of the mourner and the genius of death at the base of the pyramid are the embodiment of sincere sorrow. Despite the complex positioning of the figures and the abundance of drapery, the composition is perceived as a harmonious whole. On the tombstone for S. S. Volkonskaya is depicted a solitary mourning woman, full of restrained sorrow. The laconic clear imagery of this monument, the fine low relief work and the delicate treatment of the marble make this one of the most accomplished examples of Russian sculpture.

FIFTY
RUSSIAN
ARTISTS
58

I. P. MARTOS

EIGHTEENTH
CENTURY

These works were so successful that Martos began to receive a large number of commissions, as a result of which he carved gravestones for N. A. Bryus (1786-90, Museum of Architecture at the USSR Academy of Building and Architecture), N. I. Panin (1790), Ye. S. Kurakina (1792), A. F. Turchaninov (1796), A. I. Lazarev (1803) and Ye. I. Gagarina (1803; all are in the Leningrad Museum of Town Sculpture). These stones vary in composition and method of execution; the earlier ones tend to be lyrical and intimate, while the later ones are rather monumental, sometimes tragic.

The most outstanding of the sculptor's later works was his tombstone for Ye. Kurakina. The mourning woman lying on the sarcophagus seems to have fallen asleep in tears, her head resting on her crossed arms. The complicated foreshortening and the intense restless rhythm in the heavy folds of her garments enhance the impression of tragedy. The sincerity and depth of the weeper's suffering are utterly convincing in this statue, and at the same time her figure is marked by majestic power and inner energy. In this work Martos rose to the heights of real monumental art. As one of his contemporaries put it, the sculptor could make the marble 'weep'.

Martos's skill and prodigious output rank him among the greatest artists of his time. There was barely a single important commission for sculptural work in which he did not participate. He did stucco decorations for the palaces at Tsarskoye Selo (now the town of Pushkin) and Pavlovsk, and modelled a statue of Actaeon for the Grand Cascade at Peterhof.

At the beginning of the nineteenth century building was begun on the Kazan Cathedral in St. Petersburg, and Martos was one of the artists who decorated it. His contribution included the bas-relief on the Biblical theme of the wandering of Jewish people *(Moses Divines Water in the Wilderness)* on the attic of east wing of the colonnade, and the statue of John the Baptist, situated in a niche of the portico. The bas-relief exemplifies Martos's excellent understanding of the relationship between a decorative relief and the architecture of a building as a whole. The great length of the composition required mastery in the construction of the figures, and the sculptor coped perfectly with the difficult task of conveying the array of emotions and inner states of people racked by thirst.

Martos achieved true fame as a result of his monument to Minin and Pozharsky in Moscow. His work on this monument coincided with the war of 1812, and with the resulting rise of patriotism and national awareness in the country. The idea of raising a monument to these heroes of seventeenth-century Russian history came considerably earlier, however. In 1803 Vasily Popugaev, one of the active members of the Free Society of Lovers of Literature, Science and Art (the most progressive educational organisation of the time), proposed that a nationwide subscription be raised and that the money thus collected be used to erect a monument to the 'Russian plebeian' Minin and Prince Pozharsky. Martos set about this work with great enthusiasm. 'Which of the celebrated heroes of olden days,' he wrote, 'has surpassed the courage and exploits of Minin and Pozharsky?' In his conception, which became clear even in the first sketches, Minin and Pozharsky were to form a unified group, joined by the emotions and patriotism. Admittedly, their standing figures—with their cloaks blowing and rather affected gestures—were still theatrical and pompous. Later sketches stressed the importance of Minin, his activity and steadfastness, 'Here Minin was the main active force,' wrote S. Bobrovsky, one of the members of the Free Society of Lovers of Literature, Science and Art.

In 1808 the government ran a competition, in which Martos was challenged by other sculptors such as Shchedrin, Prokofiev, Demut-Malinovsky and Pimenov. But Martos's design won first place. Compared to his sketches, in which the images of the heroes still showed traces of melodrama and the composition lacked unity, the monument in its final form is austere and

EIGHTEENTH
CENTURY

I. P. MARTOS

FIFTY
RUSSIAN
ARTISTS
59

FIFTY
RUSSIAN
ARTISTS
60

I. P. MARTOS

EIGHTEENTH
CENTURY

EIGHTEENTH
CENTURY

I. P. MARTOS

FIFTY
RUSSIAN
ARTISTS
61

solemn. The two figures are closely linked not only emotionally but also compositionally. Minin immediately draws the viewer's attention because of his purposefulness and fervour; his image is at once restrained and full of tremendous inner power and activity—a combination achieved by the powerful modelling of the figure. Both the broad, sweeping gesture of his right hand, pointing towards the Kremlin, and his expressive vertical stance affirm the dominating position of Minin in the composition. Pozharsky is also full of resolution and readiness to undertake a great feat. Accepting the sword from Minin's hand, he rises a little from his seat, ready to follow him. Pozharsky's face is inspired, bearing traces of recent sufferings but at the same time courageous. In their outward appearance, Martos emphasised their typically Russian national features, successfully combining elements of classical and Russian dress in their costumes.

The monument was originally erected near the Arcade (Gostinny dvor) opposite the Kremlin wall. Its unveiling in 1818 was a major event. 'During this grand ceremony,' wrote the newspaper *Moskovskie vedomosti,* 'the concourse of people was incredible: all the shops, the roofs of the Gostinny dvor . . . even the Kremlin towers were covered with people anxious to enjoy this new and unusual spectacle.'

In this work the artist managed to express ideas and feelings that concerned wide sections of the Russian public. The figures of these heroes of Russian history were perceived as contemporaries and their exploits were reminders of the events of the recent war against Napoleon.

Meanwhile, Martos had done several other works, quite diverse in character. In 1812, for example, he made a statue of Catherine II, and in 1813 he drew sketches of the four evangelists for the Kazan Cathedral. The sculptor's creativity continued to flourish in the years to come. Besides teaching at the Academy of Arts, in the 1820s he produced several large monumental works: monument to Paul I in Gruzino, to Alexander I in Taganrog (1828-31), to Richelieu in Odessa (1823-28) and to Lomonosov in Arkhangelsk (1826-29). Documents have revealed that Martos also worked on a monument to Dmitri Donskoi but this project appears never to have been completed.

The artist's capacity for work was impressive. 'I cannot be idle,' he wrote. Those who knew Martos remarked upon his industry, selflessness and extreme modesty. In a report to the Minister of Public Education, the president of the Academy Olenin wrote of him: 'In his modesty Martos has never burdened the government with requests on his own behalf, and he receives wages from the public purse no greater than many pupils of his pupils receive.'

Martos lived a long, industrious life, wholly given over to the service of art.

1. A. G. Varnek. Portrait of I. P. Martos
2. Tombstone for M. P. Sobakina
3. Monument to Minin and Pozharsky
4. Tombstone for S. S. Volkonskaya

Orest Adamovich KIPRENSKY

(1782-1836)

1

Orest Kiprensky, the great portraitist of the early nineteenth century, was born in the Oranienbaum district of Petersburg Gubernia, on an estate belonging to the landowner A. S. Diakonov. The future artist was entered in the register of Koporye church as the illegitimate son of the peasant girl Anna Gavrilova, who a year after the birth of her son was married to the landowner's manservant Adam Schwalbe.

In 1788 Kiprensky was sent to the school run by the Academy of Arts and nine years later he entered the class of historical painting, which was usually reserved for pupils who displayed some ability. His teachers were the professor of historical painting G. I. Ugryumov and the master of plafond and decorative painting Gabriel-François de Doyen.

The artist won his first gold medal in 1805 for the historical canvas *Dmitri Donskoi on Sustaining Victory over Mamai* (RM). But it was not historical painting that brought him fame.

As early as 1804 Kiprensky painted one of his most talented works—a portrait of his father, Adam Schwalbe (RM). The portrait is impressive because of its remarkable maturity, its deep understanding of human nature, and the level of mastery attained at such an early stage in the artist's career. We see a self-willed man, full of dignity and spiritual strength. The work is realised in warm colours with free, sweeping brushwork, built on contrasts of light and shade.

This brilliant portrait impressed Kiprensky's contemporaries. In 1830 it was displayed at an art exhibition in Naples and, as the artist himself wrote, 'the Academy here concocted the following ideas . . . some considered the portrait of my father a Rubens masterpiece, others thought it was a Van Dyck, while a certain Albertini went as far as Rembrandt!'

The artist's early works included a *Self-Portrait* (1808, RM). The easy-going, elevated character of this inspired image, and the distinctive style of painting and composition, were clear signs of a new attitude to portraiture.

NINETEENTH
CENTURY

O. A. KIPRENSKY

FIFTY
RUSSIAN
ARTISTS
63

1. Portrait of Ye. S. Avdulina
2. Portrait of A. K. Schwalbe
3. Self-Portrait

3

Both the personality and the work of the artist were suffused with the spirit of the liberal first decades of the nineteenth century. Kiprensky was a romantic artist, the first of the portraitists to catch the tenor of the age and to poeticise the value and beauty of man's spiritual wealth. 'Who said that feelings deceive us?' he wrote in an album of drawings.

The year 1808 saw the start of Kiprensky's friendship with the well-known collector and art patron A. R. Tomilov, whose house was one of the centres of artistic life of the first quarter of the nineteenth century.

It was around this time that artist painted portraits of A. R. Tomilov (1808, RM), I. V. Kusov (1808, RM), A. I. Korsakov (1808, RM) and also another *Self-Portrait* (c. 1809, TG).

On 27 February 1809 Kiprensky left for Moscow, where he was to help Ivan Martos complete his work on the monument to Minin and Pozharsky. In Moscow the artist's contacts widened. In Rastopchin's salon and at Mme Muravyova's house, he met the poets K. N. Batyushkov, P. A. Vyazemsky, V. A. Zhukovsky, S. P. Marin, and also Denis and Yevgraf Davydov. He was enormously influenced by the atmosphere of such meetings and creative discussions, by Rastopchin's private art gallery (which had something like 300 exhibits, including pictures by Velazquez, Van Dyck and Tintoretto) and by the pre-war mood of Russian society.

Abounding in impressions, Kiprensky's life in Moscow was conducive to intensive artistic activity. 'Kiprensky is half-crazed by his work and

FIFTY
RUSSIAN
ARTISTS
64

O. A. KIPRENSKY

NINETEENTH
CENTURY

by his imagination,' wrote Rastopchin to the conference secretary of the Academy of Arts, A. F. Labzin.

Among the best works of the Moscow period, 1809-1812, are portraits of A. A. Chelishchev (1810-11, TG), Ye. P. Rastopchina (1809, TG) and Ye. V. Davydov (1809, RM). In his full-dress portrait of Ye. V. Davydov, a hero of the 1812 war decorated with the gold sword for his bravery, Kiprensky strove to depict a man of a progressive turn of mind, a forerunner of new social forces in Russia. The attraction of the portrait lies in the nobility, dignity and emotional elevation of the character.

In March 1812 Kiprensky returned to St. Petersburg. For several of his portraits—including those of Ye. V. Davydov, Prince Oldenburgsky, I. A. Gagarin and A. I. Kusov—he was awarded the title of academician of portrait painting.

Kiprensky reached his peak as a portraitist at the time of the 1812 war. 'The Patriotic War gave us our Curtiuses, Scaevolas and Regulu-ses,' wrote a veteran of that war, P. Svinyin. As though in a rush to record the heroes of the war, Kiprensky made numerous pencil drawings. A series of graphic portraits depicted the artist's friends: the brothers M. and A. Lanskoi, General Chaplits, the home guards A. P. Tomilov and P. A. Olenin, the poets K. N. Batyushkov, I. I. Kozlov and V. A. Zhukovsky, and the fable-writer I. A. Krylov.

He also produced a series of pencil portraits of children and young people, which are marked with joyful sense of purpose and by the general harmoniousness that typified Kiprensky's work of that period. Such were the portraits of N. Kochubei, Petya Olenin, the peasant boys Andryusha and Moska, the Kalmyk girl Bayausta, the future Decembrists N. M. Mura-vyov and A. P. Bakunin. Kiprensky's drawings made an invaluable contribution to the development of world graphic portraiture.

Some of Kiprensky's best paintings also date from this time—including his masterly portrait of D. N. Khvostova (1814, TG).

In mid-May 1816, having received the title of Adviser to the Academy of Arts, he was given state support to travel to Italy thanks to the endeavours of his friends, especially the writer Zhukovsky.

During his years in Italy (1816-1823) the artist continued to work intensively. However, his mood and to some extent his works of this period were affected by the hostile attitude towards him of the civil servants in the Russian embassy in Rome, who kept an eye on their pensioners, and by the upheavals of the revolution in Italy. Among his best works of these years were his portrait of A. M. Golitsyn (*c.* 1819, TG), his pencil portrait of S. S. Shcherbatova (1819, TG) and his famous *Self-Portrait* of 1819 , which was commissioned by the Florence Academy for the Uffici Gallery.

This *Self-Portrait* brings out new traits of the painter's work. Here, nothing remains of the sparkling immediacy and thirst for life that were the keynote of his earlier self-portrait. The world around him had lost its joyful attraction and was daubed in sombre hues. Kiprensky was acutely aware of the dichotomy between ideals and reality.

In July 1823 Kiprensky returned to his homeland, which was going through a period of cruel reaction under the auspices of the chairman of the Military Department Arakcheyev. Arakcheyev and the Minister Guriev were made honorary members of the Academy of Arts. 'The Academy,' wrote Kiprensky on his return to St. Petersburg, 'has grown mouldy.'

The suppression of the Decembrist Uprising in 1825 threw Kiprensky into a state of grief and disillusion. There is no information available on the artist's attitude to the Decembrists' secret society, but he did meet many of them at the house of the officer of household cavalry D. N. Sheremetiev, and was on friendly terms with some of them. He was most certainly deeply moved by their fate, as was a considerable part of Russian society.

NINETEENTH
CENTURY

O. A. KIPRENSKY

FIFTY
RUSSIAN
ARTISTS
65

4. Portrait of A. S. Pushkin
5. Faun with Pipe

FIFTY
RUSSIAN
ARTISTS
66

O. A. KIPRENSKY

NINETEENTH
CENTURY

Despite his cold official welcome in Russia and serious inner crisis, Kiprensky's mastery in no way flagged. His portrait of the poet Alexander Pushkin (1827, TG) was his greatest achievement in the field of portraiture. It was painted at the request of Delvig, a poet and friend of Pushkin, between May and July 1827, while the latter was on a short stay in St. Petersburg. Pushkin liked the portrait and acquired it after Delvig's death. He dedicated the following lines to Kiprensky:

Loved-one of light-winged fashion—
Though neither French nor English born—
You re-created me, magician,
The crystal muses' chosen one.

There was a general feeling of indignation at the fact that Kiprensky, who had made such impressively realistic drawings and paintings of participants in the 1812 War, was not asked to paint portraits for the official 1812 War Gallery. Alexander I passed over other Russian artists too, and gave the commission to the English artist George Dawe.

'I went to Italy,' wrote Kiprensky, 'with the sole purpose of bringing to Russia the fruits of a more mature talent, but instead, on my return I was covered in the envy of my adversaries. Ignoring this envy, I always strode firmly onwards, knowing that sooner or later time always reveals the truth.'

At the end of the twenties he again left for Italy. His marriage to his former pupil and inspiration Maria Falcucci failed to brighten up the last years of his life.

Orest Kiprensky died on 5 October 1836 and was buried in Rome.

'The celebrated Kiprensky has died,' wrote the artist A. A. Ivanov from Italy. 'He was the first to bring fame to a Russian name in Europe ... Kiprensky was never decorated and never granted favours by the Court—and all for the simple reason that he was too noble and proud to seek such things.'

Silvestr Feodosiyevich SHCHEDRIN

(1791-1830)

Silvestr Shchedrin, the greatest Russian landscape-painter of the early nineteenth century, was the most striking exponent of the realist aspirations of the time.

The Shchedrin family, like the Bryullov and Ivanov families, was a kind of artistic dynasty. Silvestr Shchedrin was born in St. Petersburg. His father, Feodosy, was a well-known sculptor, professor and assistant rector of the Academy of Arts. And his uncle Semyon, a professor of landscape-painting, gave the young Silvestr his first lessons. 'I remember being taken to the Hermitage by my uncle when I was still young', Shchedrin recalled later. 'I walked past most of the pictures and only stopped to look at Canaletto.'

Shchedrin's first successful art lessons in the family were soon backed up by training at the Academy. From 1800 his teachers were M. M. Ivanov, F. Ya. Alexeyev, whose main interest at that time was in painting views of St. Petersburg, and the architect Thomas de Thomon, who taught him the laws of perspective.

In 1811 Shchedrin graduated with a gold medal. His graduation piece was the landscape *View from Petrovsky Island in St. Petersburg,* which conformed totally to the classical spirit. However, the young artist's interest in depicting concrete, rather than 'invented', views soon asserted itself in his first large-scale works: *View of Tuchkov Bridge From Petrovsky Island* (1815, TG) and *View of the Stock Exchange From the Bank of the Neva* (1817, RM).

In 1818 Shchedrin was among the first four pensioners to be sent to Italy. His travel notes and his letters home, written with gentle humour, reveal the artist's lively mind and powers of observation.

Having settled in Rome, Shchedrin set about painting views of the city. He was attracted by the Colosseum, his approach to which was far from classic. 'The Colosseum,' Shchedrin wrote, 'ordered me to paint its portrait.' Contemporaries noted that in this 'portrait of a building' the real-life 'model', with its powerful architectural

FIFTY
RUSSIAN
ARTISTS
68

O. A. KIPRENSKY

NINETEENT
CENTURY

forms and distinctive stonework, was excellently conveyed.

In the picture *New Rome. Holy Angel Castle* (1825, TG) the artist reveals the beauty in simple and ordinary things. The grand structures of the Holy Angel Castle and St. Peter's Cathedral become part of the general city scene. Shchedrin tried to convey the play of light on the rocks and walls, on the greenery and the boats—light which united all these objects, sometimes making them shine or sparkle, sometimes concealing or emphasising their contours. He softened the highlights on the water and made the shadows transparent and airy. The buildings give the impression of being wrapped in air. In this painting Shchedrin passed from heavy, dark-brown shades to light silvery-greys. 'With great difficulty I have extricated myself from these dark shades,' he wrote to the sculptor S. Galberg.

In a small, iridescent landscape *Lake Albano in the Outskirts of Rome* (1823-24, RM), the water gleams with silver, while the verdure seems airy and suffused with pink sunlight. Light acts like a magician, transforming everything. This painting is one of Shchedrin's masterpieces.

The artist's seascapes are particularly poetic. He was enraptured by Naples and its surroundings. On his first trip there from Rome, which lasted from June 1819 to the spring of 1821, Shchedrin lovingly described the colourful life on the seafronts, the merry-making and carnivals, and the scenery of southern Italy . . .

'. . . Once again I am staying on the Santa Lucia Embankment—the best spot in the whole of Naples. The view from my window is magnificent: Vesuvius a stone's throw away, the sea, mountains, picturesquely situated buildings, people constantly in motion, walking and working—what better place for a landscape painter!'

In *View of Naples* (1819, TG) Shchedrin depicted himself among the townsfolk on the busy embankment. The artist was often to be seen with the fishermen and peasants in the coastal villages. A jolly, sociable person, he was on amicable terms with the local population, and portrayed them in numerous pictures. '. . . Within few days I acquired a host of friends—farmers retired soldiers and others . . . These peopl were so fond of me that having discovered whe I usually arrived they came ahead of time not t miss me . . .'

At this time Shchedrin made friends with Ka Bryullov and Konstantin Batyushkov—it wa with the latter that he stayed while in Naple Together with Orest Kiprensky he began wor on a portrait of A. M. Golitsyn.

Having ultimately settled in Naples in Jun 1825, Shchedrin undertook trips to Sorrent Capri, Vigo and Amalfi. His landscapes and sea scapes ranked among the finest *plein air* paint ings anywhere at that time, especially the serie which included *On the Island of Capri* (182 TG), *The Small Harbour at Sorrento* (182 TG) and *The Large Harbour at Sorrento* (182 TG). Nature here accords with man, whose na tural and contemplative life takes its course i the 'happy moments of being'.

The unusual composition of the seascape (the closed line of the sea-shore) not only len them an intimate, chamber-work quality, but a so likens them to open loggias.

Arbour Covered with Vines (1828, TG) an *Grotto at Sorrento* (1829, TG) rely on the con trasts between the shaded area and the sunl open countryside. The midday sun penetrate the dense greenery of the olives and grapev nes, picking out the people's figures and patche of vegetation amid the shadow.

In his later period, Shchedrin moved awa from chiaroscuro tonal painting in favour heightened colour range, as is clearly illustrate by *Small Harbour in Sorrento. Evening* (182 TG) and *Moonlit Night at Naples* (1828, TG

Shchedrin gained popularity in Italy and h landscapes sold well. Meanwhile the dates of h stay abroad had long since expired. He was p off by the thought of a future in the formal a mosphere of the St. Petersburg Academy Arts. But he did not entirely abandon thought

NINETEENTH
CENTURY

O. A. KIPRENSKY

FIFTY
RUSSIAN
ARTISTS
69

3

of returning home: 'I am most displeased by your advice not to go to Russia,' he wrote to S. Galberg.

Despite a serious, progressing illness, the artist did not lose his *joie de vivre* and sense of humour. His last letters from Italy were full of hopes for a recovery and for a return home. But he never did return to his native country.

In October 1830 he died, and a monument by S. Galberg was erected on his grave in Sorrento.

Silvestr Shchedrin gave his own lyrical interpretation of the scenery of Italy—something that eluded many of his contemporary Italians. His landscapes contained that poetic affirmation of the beauty of simple things which was so characteristic of Russian portraiture and genre-painting of the first half of the nineteenth century.

1. K. P. Bryullov. Portrait of S. F. Shchedrin
2. Lake Albano in the Outskirts of Rome
3. New Rome. Holy Angel Castle

Alexei Gavrilovich
VENETSIANOV

(1780-1847)

1

One of the founders of the Russian genre painting, Alexei Venetsianov, was born into a not particularly well-off merchant family in Moscow. His father traded in fruit-bushes. There is evidence that he also dealt in pictures, and this may have helped awaken the young Venetsianov's interest in art. The future artist had his first lessons in drawing in a private Moscow boarding-school.

It was when he came to St. Petersburg in 1807 that he began to take painting seriously. He was taught by Vladimir Borovikovsky, in whose studio he worked until 1810. At the same time he studied and copied works of classical art in the Hermitage.

Venetsianov's earliest works included portraits of A. I. and A. S. Bibikov (1805-09, RM). His interest in portraiture was not accidental—it was in this genre that most innovations were made in the early nineteenth century. The young artist's successes were immediately noticed. The majority of his early portraits were done in pastel, a technique little used by Russian artists. They are unassuming, simple works, totally lacking in showiness.

In 1811 Venetsianov painted one of his best early works, *Self-Portrait* (RM), for which he was awarded the first academic title—associate of the Academy—and shortly afterwards, for his *Portrait of K. I. Golovachevsky, Inspector of the Academy of Arts, with Three Pupils* (1811, RM), he was made an academician. Such early, sudden recognition of the artist was due entirely to the merits of his works. His *Self-Portrait,* painted in restrained shades of olive, stood out from self-portraits by other artists of the time because of its impartiality and naturalness. The portrait of Golovachevsky is in a more traditional line, and suffers from being rather didactic, but nonetheless the treatment of the images is winningly cordial and warm.

Also at this period Venetsianov did some interesting work in the field of graphic art. He attempted to start up Russia's first satirical magazine—*Journal of Caricatures, 1808*—in which he hoped, by means of drawings, to 'improve

NINETEENTH
CENTURY

A. G. VENETSIANOV

FIFTY
RUSSIAN
ARTISTS
71

1. Self-Portrait
2. Portrait of K. I. Golovachevsky,
   Inspector of the Academy of Arts,
   with Three Pupils
3. Harvesting in Summer
4. The Nobleman

morals and educate society in the best traditions'. But the very first issue of this publication was suppressed by the government. The reason for the ban is thought to have been an etching to accompany Derzhavin's ode *The Nobleman,* the significance of which far exceeded that of mere illustration. The satirical portrayal of an obese, indolent nobleman, and the sympathetic depiction of his suppliants—a wounded soldier, a widow and child—made this etching extremely topical and socially poignant.

Venetsianov returned more than once to satirical etchings. During the Patriotic War of 1812 he produced a series of topical sheets. In his etchings *The French Coiffeur* and *French Education*, for instance, he lampooned the Gallomania of the Russian nobility.

The artist found his real vocation, however, neither in graphics nor in the art of portraiture which had brought him fame. His talent lent itself to quite a different area. Venetsianov was fully aware of this, and half-way through his career he found the strength to give up working as a portraitist. On one of his portraits we find a remark: 'Venetsianov hereby renounces portrait-painting, March 1823.'

FIFTY
RUSSIAN
ARTISTS
72

A. G. VENETSIANOV

NINETEENTH
CENTURY

At the beginning of 1819 the artist had gone to the small estate of Safonkovo in Tver Gubernia. Here, at the age of forty, he more or less went back to square one. He was fascinated by the common people, by serfs and peasants who had heroically fought Napoleon's troops and who retained their human dignity and nobility despite the yoke of serfdom. And although from time to time he did still do some portraits, Venetsianov's main interest from the 1820s on was in genre art.

This new stage in the artist's work was not merely the result of fortuitous circumstances in his private life, however. The beginning of the nineteenth century was a time when all the progressive members of Russian society were striving to bring about a transformation of the country and the enlightenment of the people. It was then that a society was set up in St. Petersburg with the noble aim of spreading literacy among the common people. This was the prevailing atmosphere in which Venetsianov's art took a new turn. Rural life provided him with a wealth of material and opened up a new world—the world of the beautiful, lyrical Russian countryside.

Venetsianov's first pictures in the new genre—the pastels *Beet-Picking* (c. 1820, RM) and *The Reaper* (1820, TG)—eloquently testify to the fact that he was making a conscious effort to achieve realistic authenticity, considering the painter's main goal 'to represent nothing otherwise than as it is in nature . . . to obey nature alone, without adding the manner of any artist'.

Central to Venetsianov's work is the painting *The Threshing-Floor* (1821, RM), on which he worked for more than three years. Depicting a commonplace scene, the artist gives an extremely realistic impression of the enclosed area, which is illuminated by a flood of light pouring in from either side. However, the desire to record everything precisely 'as it is in nature' led to a certain dryness and immobility in the portrayal of the human figures.

The Threshing-Floor was the first in a series of works on peasant themes. As portrayed by Venetsianov, the Russian peasants are people filled with beauty and nobility of mind, with moral purity and inner integrity. In his desire to poeticise Russian man and to affirm his dignity, the artist tended to idealise the life and work of the peasantry, without showing the actual hardships of serf labour. But the very fact of treating 'low' —from the point of view of official aesthetics— theme of peasant life is worthy of notice. Like no other artist in the first half of the nineteenth century, Venetsianov asserted his right to depict the common folk who worked the land.

His talent really flourished in the twenties and thirties, when he produced such masterpieces as *Ploughing in Spring, Harvesting in Summer* (both 1830s, TG), *Children in the Field* (early 1830s, RM) and several sketches.

The working peasants in Venetsianov's canvases are beautiful and full of dignity. In *Ploughing in Spring* the theme of work is interwoven with those of motherhood and the beauty of the Russian countryside. The artist's best and most accomplished genre work—*Harvesting in Summer*—is marked by a lyrical, epic perception of life. While in the first picture Venetsianov depicted a spring landscape with vast expanses of fields, leaves just appearing on the trees, and light clouds in the blue sky, in the second he allows one to feel the height of a Russian summer—a time of toil in the villages—with shining golden cornfields and a scorching sky. Both canvases are painted in bright, clear colours.

One of Venetsianov's most poetic works, full of serenity and peace, and love of man and nature, is the small painting *Sleeping Shepherd-Boy* (1823-26, RM). The smooth, calm rhythms of the plains, the gently sloping hillsides covered in slender young trees, solitary firs, a low-banked stream—all these dear, familiar motifs the artist found in his native countryside. In Venetsianov's paintings the landscape is not merely a background but plays an active role in conveying moods and in the overall conception.

NINETEENTH
CENTURY

A. G. VENETSIANOV

FIFTY
RUSSIAN
ARTISTS
73

In 1824 an exhibition of Venetsianov's paintings in St. Petersburg evoked an enthusiastic response in Russian progressive circles. 'At last we have an artist who has used his wonderful talent to depict things purely Russian, to describe the things all around him, which are so close to his heart and to ours . . .' wrote P. P. Svinyin, the founder of the Russian Museum in St. Petersburg.

In the years that followed Venetsianov painted many portraits of peasant girls—*A Peasant Girl, Peasant Girl with Mushrooms in the Wood, Pelageya* (1820s, RM), *Girl with Embroidery, Peasant Girl with Cornflowers* (1830s, TG) and others. For all their differences, these works are united by the artist's aspiration to express his new ideas about beauty in art, about popular beauty, inspired and noble.

These works did not bring Venetsianov recognition in official circles, however. The Academy of Arts did not conceal its distaste for this artist who was drawn towards things they considered base and bound up with the common people. He longed to teach at the Academy, to be able to pass on his knowledge and experience to young artists. 'But I am for ever denied the possibility of obtaining any kind of post at the Academy of Arts,' he wrote bitterly. His hopes of teaching 'thousands of hopefuls' came to fruition only later, when at his own expense he opened an art school for peasants in the village of Safonkovo. The list of talented and original artists discovered and trained by Venetsianov

4

included N. Krylov, Ye. Krendovsky, A. Tyranov, S. Zaryanko, G. Soroka and many others. Several of them he managed to release from serfdom. His pupils expanded and in many ways deepened the themes and images of their teacher, enriching genre painting with new content.

Venetsianov continued to work prolifically in the 1840s. Among his best works from this period were *Sleeping Girl* (Gorky State Art Museum), *Fortune-Telling* (RM), *Girl with Accordion* (Gorky State Art Museum) and *Peasant Girl Embroidering* (TG). He had many more plans, but his sudden death in 1847 left them unrealised.

Venetsianov's importance in the history of Russian art is extremely great. He was one of the first artists who dedicated themselves to the portrayal of the peasantry and who declared genre painting to be a fully fledged, important sphere of art. His canvases contained popular images, full of inspiration and human dignity.

Stepan Stepanovich
PIMENOV

(1784-1833)

1

Stepan Pimenov, one of the great Russian sculptors of the early nineteenth century, was born the son of a humble St. Petersburg customs official. Having discovered in him the makings of an artist, his parents sent him at the age of eleven to the Academy of Arts, where he soon distinguished himself by his exceptional abilities and diligence. The talented young sculptor's works frequently won awards. In 1801, for example, he gained a silver medal for 'modelling from nature' and the next year he received a gold medal for a bas-relief entitled *Jupiter and Mercury in the Guise of Wayfarers Visiting Philemon and Baucis.*

'Pimenov's distinguishing features,' wrote his contemporaries, 'are his powerful passionate composition and spirited, sweeping modelling.' Pimenov took part in a competition in 1802 to carve a memorial tombstone to his favourite teacher and professor at the Academy, Mikhail Kozlovsky (plaster, RM), who had recently died. The competition was won by Vasily Demut-Malinovsky, whose bas-relief composition fulfilled the conditions laid down for the competition. Pimenov received the Second Gold Medal, but as regards artistic perfection and poetic embodiment of the subject his work was in no way inferior to that of Demut-Malinovsky. Pimenov did not go in for a complex allegorical representation. The tombstone is simple and majestic. In it, the muse of sculpture is represented as a beautiful young woman, thoughtful and sad. Her head is lowered, her eyes are closed, and the hand holding a hammer hangs limply. The contours of the inclined figure are smooth and beautiful. With its perfect composition and clear conception, this work was a striking manifestation of the young sculptor's exceptional giftedness.

In 1803 Pimenov graduated from the Academy with a Grand Gold Medal for his diploma work *The Killing of Two Varangian Christians Who Refused to Bow Down Before Perun.* Then, together with Demut-Malinovsky who had also graduated, he set about the interesting task of making sculptural decorations for Kazan

1. Portrait of S. S. Pimenov by unknown artist of early 19th century

NINETEENTH
CENTURY

S. S. PIMENOV

FIFTY
RUSSIAN
ARTISTS
75

Cathedral which was then being built (1801-11). The cathedral was designed by the architect A. N. Voronikhin, and the responsible task of decorating it was given mainly to sculptors of the older generation—Martos, Shchedrin, Prokofiev and Gordeyev. A special resolution of the Council of the Academy of Arts spoke of the 'adoption of all measures to ensure that the work on the Kazan Cathedral does honour to the Academy and to the artists themselves'. Pimenov produced two statues for the main façade: one of Prince Vladimir (1804-07), the other of Alexander Nevsky (1811). Prince Vladimir is portrayed as an intrepid fighter, energetic and strong. His face is severe and concentrated, his attitude free and independent. With a broad gesture of his right hand he grips a cross, while his left hand holds a short sword. The sculptor had undoubtedly studied Russian national types, and this can be seen in his treatment of Vladimir. With its heroic qualities, its clear imagery and plasticity, the statue is one of the best examples of early nineteenth century monumental sculpture. On the strength of this piece, Stepan Pimenov was elected academician.

Alexander Nevsky is portrayed quite differently from the resolute, wilful Vladimir. The celebrated military leader is seen just after having sustained a victory. He has laid down his shield and removed his armour, and looks to the skies in gratitude. Though this is a common motif in sculpture, Pimenov's image is not ostentatious or theatrical. Alexander Nevsky appears as a grand, wise, worthy man. The soft, generalised moulding of his face conveys his inner state well. Both this statue and that of Vladimir were cast by the famous Russian master V. P. Yekimov.

The work of Pimenov and other sculptors who decorated the Kazan Cathedral was highly rated by their contemporaries. 'The successful construction and decoration of this Cathedral,' wrote A. Pisarev, 'shall turn the attention of all Europe to the artistic geniuses of Russia and shall usher in the epoch of successful Russian art in this enlightened age.'

After the inauguration of the Kazan Cathedral Pimenov was awarded a diamond ring. His success did not escape the notice of the Academy of Arts, and he was made an assistant professor with teaching responsibilities. Meanwhile, he and Demut-Malinovsky were intrusted with the task of producing sculptures for the Mining Institute, the premises of which were also designed by A. N. Voronikhin. Here Pimenov's talent as a monumentalist really shone through: his sculptural ensemble *Hercules and Antaeus* (1809-11), with its powerful plastic forms, harmonised beautifully with the majestic solemnity of the building and with the massive columns of the high portico.

The sculptor based this work on an ancient myth, according to which Antaeus derived strength from the Earth-Mother and so long as he remained in contact with it was invincible. In order to be conquered, Antaeus had to be separated from the earth. Pimenov conveys here the tensest moment in the struggle—Hercules has lifted Antaeus and has him in his clutches, his own mighty figure seemingly rooted to the ground. Antaeus resists furiously and tries to free himself, but his body is already weakening. His head and hand thrown back in exhaustion indicated that his strength is sapping away. The muscles of the wrestling figures are marvellously sculptured, and one can feel that Pimenov had an excellent knowledge of human anatomy. The drama and acuteness of the struggle do not, however, undermine the general solemnity and equilibrium of the sculptural group. This is achieved by means of the integrated composition, the monumental forms, the consummate modelling and the expressive silhouette. Transferred to Pudozh stone by the best stone-cutter of the time Samson Sukhanov, *Hercules and Antaeus* was rapturously applauded by Petersburg art-lovers. A bronze cast of the model was exhibited in the Russian Museum.

In 1811 Pimenov, Shchedrin, Terebenev and Demut-Malinovsky were invited to design sculptures for the Admiralty which was being

FIFTY
RUSSIAN
ARTISTS
76

S. S. PIMENOV

NINETEENTH
CENTURY

constructed to the plans of A. Zakharov. The statues sculptured by Pimenov (it is known that in 1812 alone he carved 16 figures from Pudozh stone) included allegorical representations of Fire, Air and Summer, plus colossal statues of Asia and America and the rivers Dnieper and Neva, intended for the upper colonnade of the tower. Unfortunately, Alexander II had them destroyed in 1860.

Pimenov's work at the beginning of the nineteenth century was exceptionally versatile. While on the one hand producing monumental works, he also worked in the field of small decorative sculpture. In 1809 he was asked to supervise the sculptural section at the Petersburg porcelain factory (now the Lomonosov Factory). Here he designed a series of sculptural groups and also supervised the production of services. The best known of the pieces created by Pimenov at the factory was the so-called Guriev service with figures of Russian girls and boys in national costumes.

In his small china genre statuettes dating from this period, Pimenov embodied types from the simple Russian peasantry. The best of these figurines are *Girl with Yoke* and *Boy-Water-Carrier* (1810s RM), which strongly recall the works of Venetsianov. The sculptor's last works at the porcelain factory—the ensembles *Russian Troops Crossing the Danube* and *Russia's Protection of Moldavia and Walachia* (1829)—were a response to the events of the Russo-Turkish war of 1828.

Pimenov's most prolific period, the 1820s, was linked with the name of the architect Carlo Rossi, with whom the sculptor collaborated on his best monumental-decorative works. Their cooperation started in 1817, when Pimenov made models of soldiers for the façades of the pavilions of the Anichkov Palace in St. Petersburg. The next year Rossi invited him to help decorate two large palaces which were under construction—the Yelaginsky and the Mikhailovsky. For the Yelaginsky Palace Pimenov made models of decorative statues intended for the faça-

des of the kitchen wing: bas-reliefs and decorated columns for the orangery, haut-relief figures for the vestibule. In the exterior of the Mikhailovsky Palace (which now houses the Russian Museum) Pimenov was responsible for the sculptured composition of the winged figures of Glory, the trophies in the tympana of the main façade and numerous reliefs over the ground-floor windows. Inside the palace all that remains of Pimenov's decorations are the caryatides in the gallery and the bas-reliefs in the White-Columned Hall.

Together with Demut-Malinovsky, Pimenov helped decorate the building of the General Staff in St. Petersburg, whose triumphal arch was conceived by Rossi as a memorial to the victories of 1812-14 Patriotic War. The sculptural group which crowns the arch—a fine example of the synthesis of architecture and sculpture—became the pride of Russian monumental art. Designed to be observed from various angles and from a great distance, it is noted for its beautiful, clear-cut silhouettes and universalised forms.

Pimenov went on to sculpture decorations for the two large structures which constitute the ensemble of the Alexandrinsky Theatre—for the Public Library he made statues of Homer and Plato, and for the theatre a model of Appolo's chariot.

The artist's last monumental works were for the Narva Triumphal Gates, built by the architect V. P. Stasov (1827-34). The Narva Gates were erected in St. Petersburg on the site of old wooden gates which had fallen into decay. They were an unusual monument to Russian arms, which had secured victory in the 1812-14 War, and to the courage and glory of the Russian army. The sculptor produced a statue of a hero, which stands between columns in front of the wall of the pylon: the figure of a warrior, dressed as an early Russian epic hero, embodies courage, strength and quiet confidence. For the chariot which sits atop the arch, Pimenov sculptured a figure of Glory (1832).

NINETEENTH
CENTURY

S. S. PIMENOV

FIFTY
RUSSIAN
ARTISTS
77

2

3

4

2. Girl with Yoke
3. Arch of the former General Staff
4. Hercules and Antaeus
5. Sculptured group on the Arch of
   the former General Staff

FIFTY
RUSSIAN
ARTISTS
78

S. S. PIMENOV

NINETEENTH
CENTURY

5

For many years Pimenov taught at the Academy of Arts, performing his duties with great devotion. In 1814 he received the title of professor, but in 1830 Nicholas I had him dismissed 'for independence and boldness of opinion'. The talented sculptor, a master monumentalist who had decorated many of the architectural monuments of St. Petersburg, was forced to give up the work he loved in his prime.

The cruelty of Nicholas I and the constant fault-finding of official circles were, it seems, one of the reasons for the sculptor's early death. He died in 1833 at the age of forty-nine.

Vasily Ivanovich
DEMUT – MALINOVSKY

(1779-1846)

Vasily Demut-Malinovsky occupies one of the leading places among the masters of Russian monumental sculpture of the first half of last century. His works echoed the heroic epoch of the 1812 War and were close to the thoughts and feelings of the Russian people. He was born the son of a wood-carver, in St. Petersburg. His first contact with art came in his early childhood, when he used to watch his father at work, and in 1785 he was sent, a six-year-old boy, to the Academy of Arts.

In 1799, for the bas-relief *An Angel Leads the Apostle Peter out of the Dungeon*, Demut-Malinovsky was awarded a second-class gold medal, and the following year he won a first-class gold medal for bas-reliefs which he and some other artists made for Rastrelli's monument to Peter the Great. That year he also graduated from the Academy. Two years later his work was judged best in a competition to design a memorial tombstone for M. I. Kozlovsky. Its musical lines, classically severe silhouette and rhythmic expressiveness were what distinguished this bas-relief allegorical composition, which was executed with genuine grace and delicate lyricism. The sculptor managed to find expressive artistic means to convey his powerful emotions and sorrow over his dead teacher.

'This monument,' wrote one student on the sculptor's work, 'contains everything that was developing in Demut-Malinovsky's talent —simplicity and seriousness of thought, and a feeling for and understanding of the beauty of the human body, that cornerstone of classical art.'

In 1803 Demut-Malinovsky was sent with a group of graduates from the Academy to continue his studies in Italy. Here he combined concentrated individual work with a study of western-European art and the architecture of ancient Rome. A host of drawings from nature, copies from the classics and compositions on mythological themes appeared in his albums. In Rome he began work on a bas-relief *Hercules and Omphal*. He also devoted much time and

1. M. I. Terebenev. Portrait of V. I. Demut-Malinovsky

FIFTY
RUSSIAN
ARTISTS
80

V. I. DEMUT-MALINOVSKY

NINETEENTH
CENTURY

2. Pluto's Abduction of Proserpina
3. A Russian Scaevola

2

energy to the art of working marble—an art which he mastered to perfection by the end of his stay in Italy.

Demut-Malinovsky returned to Russia in 1806. Everything he had created abroad perished en route and he now had the prospect of producing new works. His study for a statue of *The Prophet Elijah* earned him the title of acad-emician. The sculptor's main work on his return to St. Petersburg consisted in designing decorations for the Kazan Cathedral and the Mining Institute which were both under construction. For the Cathedral he made a statue of the disciple Andrew and for the Mining Institute a sculptural group entitled *Pluto's Abduction of Proserpina*, based on ancient mythology. Pluto

NINETEENTH
CENTURY

V. I. DEMUT-MALINOVSKY

FIFTY
RUSSIAN
ARTISTS
81

is carrying the resisting Proserpina away to the underworld. With her left hand she tries to fend off her abductor, while with her right she touches her head in despair. At their feet lies a three-headed dog, the legendary guardian of Hades. The group is alive with vigour and movement, but at the same time it is majestic and monumental. The statue's powerful forms and rather heavy proportions are determined by its intended position and function. Along with Pimenov's group, it was erected in front of the massive portico of the Mining Institute and harmonises, both in scale and proportions, excellently with the building. Demut-Malinovsky's bas-relief friezes are also in keeping with the architecture and do not mar the overall smoothness of the wall. The design of the Mining Institute was a good example of the synthesis of architecture and monumental sculpture which was so typical in Russian town planning of the early nineteenth century.

In cooperation with Voronikhin, Demut-Malinovsky helped decorate one of the most beautiful interiors of the palace at Pavlovsk—the lantern room' with its caryatids (1808). In 1812-14 he worked with Pimenov on the sculptural decorations for the Admiralty, which was put up at that time.

The most stunning product of the patriotic wave that swept the country in the Patriotic War was the statue *A Russian Scaevola* (1813, RM). The idea for this work was suggested by an actual fact: a Russian peasant who escaped from captivity preferred to chop off his hand than remain branded—a mark of slavery. This event reminded contemporaries of the feat of the legendary Roman youth Mucius, who in the year 507 B.C., in front of the emperor Porsenna, who had besieged Rome, put his hand in the altar flame as proof of his pledge to kill the enemies of his native land. Shaken by the boy's courage, the emperor freed him and lifted the siege of the city. The youth, who had sacrificed his right hand, became known as Scaevola, or 'left-hander'. In his statue Demut-

Malinovsky depicts the Russian peasant just when he has raised the axe. The twist of his torso, the energetic swing of his arm and the severe expression on his wilful face all add up to an image of tremendous inner determination, courage and nobility. Following the traditions of the time, the artist presents the figure almost naked, draped in near-classical style. In his treatment of the image, however, he sought to emphasise national Russian features: notice, for example, the broad-shouldered, stocky figure of the peasant—a far cry from classical models—and the hero's open face, framed by a short beard and curly locks of hair. Never before in Russian monumental sculpture had such an imposing image been created of an ordinary man from the people. For this work Demut-Malinovsky was made professor in 1813.

One of the master's early works in the field of tomb sculpture was his monument for the grave of Ye. I. Baryshnikova (Museum of Architecture at the USSR Academy of Building and Architecture). In 1814 he executed a memorial tombstone for A. N. Voronikhin ('Necropolis of XVIII Century', Leningrad Museum of Town Sculpture). But Demut-Malinovsky's most fruitful work was done in the sphere of monumental decorative sculpture. Here he worked in close collaboration with Stepan Pimenov, starting in 1820-21. Their first important joint venture was concerned with the decoration of the Yelaginsky Palace in St. Petersburg, where Demut-Malinovsky designed the sculptures for the Oval Hall and the Dining Room.

Demut-Malinovsky's contribution to the Mikhailovsky Palace included a frieze between the columns of the portico, which comprised forty-four individual reliefs, and a large sculptural group on the attic of the building facing the Mikhailovsky Gardens. In the interior of the palace he was responsible for the grand, elegant main staircase.

It was with great enthusiasm that Demut-Malinovsky and Pimenov set about the creation of sculptures for the arch of the General Staff

FIFTY
RUSSIAN
ARTISTS
82

V. I. DEMUT-MALINOVSKY

NINETEENTH
CENTURY

building. The design was a joint effort and it is sometimes hard to decide exactly which artist the individual details of the composition belong to. From the reports of the Academy of Arts, however, it is known that Demut-Malinovsky sculptured the chariot in the Victory group on the arch and also the figures of a young warrior and two horses.

Later the sculptor helped decorate the building of the Public Library: his creations included a statue of Minerva over the pediment, figures of Demosthenes, Hippocrates and Euclid and a sculptured frieze. For the Alexandrinsky Theatre he produced statues of Terpsichore and Erato, which have unfortunately not been preserved. Later, he and Pimenov again collaborated on the design of the Narva Triumphal Gates, built by the architect Stasov to mark the victory of Russian arms in the 1812-14 Patriotic War. Demut-Malinovsky's share included the chariot in the Glory group, figures of warriors and two horses. The sculpture of the Narva Gates is marked by restraint and simplicity and is devoid of allegorical imagery which was so characteristic in monumental decorative works of the period.

The long-standing partnership between these two outstanding sculptors was brought to a close by Pimenov's death in 1833.

In his last years Demut-Malinovsky expended much care and energy in moulding stucco decorations for the interiors of the Winter Palace and for the building which housed the Academy of Arts. In 1833 he was awarded the title of honorary professor, and in 1836, after the death of Ivan Martos, he became rector of the department of sculpture at the Academy of Arts.

After Martos Demut-Malinovsky was the best known and most popular sculptor of the first half of the nineteenth century, and he received many commissions. His works in the field of monumental sculpture are very interesting. His monument to Catherine II in the village of Troitsky-Kainardji (1833-34) was conceived as a hymn to Russian arms, which had triumphed over Turky. His last major work was a monument to the Russian national hero Ivan Susanin in Kostroma (1838-46).

The sculptor died on 16 July 1846, but his name lives on in the beauty and grandeur of the architectural ensembles of St. Petersburg.

Fyodor Petrovich TOLSTOY

(1783-1873)

1. Self-Portrait

Fyodor Tolstoy, one of the most interesting and original artists of the first half of last century, was born in St. Petersburg into the family of the head of the War Commissariat, and—as was customary then—was immediately registered as sergeant to the Preobrazhensky regiment. His parents, who envisaged their son becoming a military man, sent him to the Polotsk Jesuit College and then to the Naval Corps. The boy's artistic abilities were discovered very early, and while still studying at the Naval Corps he began to attend the St. Petersburg Academy of Arts. Gradually his desire to become a professional artist grew stronger, but to do that he would have to retire from the service, give up his military career and face the fury of his parents and family and a break with his relatives and friends. Only great courage and his boundless love for art allowed him to take this step. In 1804 he sent in his papers, and a life full of privations and difficulties began for the young artist.

At the Academy of Arts Tolstoy studied sculpture under professor I. P. Prokofiev and also became friendly with Orest Kiprensky, whose guidance helped him in drawing plaster-casts.

Tolstoy copied antique statues and studied ancient history with gusto, fascinated by the customs and mores of the people of the distant past. His deep and sincere love for classical art, which emerged in his youth, would stay with him for the rest of his days. His remarkable talent and diligence quickly led to success. His first works were drawings and bas-reliefs on classical themes: in 1806, for example, he made the drawings *Alexander of Macedon's Trust in the Physician Philipp, The Judgement of Paris,* and *The Struggle of Hercules* (RM). For the wax bas-relief *Alexander of Macedon's Triumphant Entry into Babylon* (1809, H) Tolstoy was elected honorary member of the Academy of Arts.

Tolstoy worked in almost every sphere of art —in model designing, sculpture and graphic art, and later in painting and decorative art. His early works, haut-reliefs in rose wax—*Boy Un-*

FIFTY
RUSSIAN
ARTISTS
84

F. P. TOLSTOY

NINETEENTH
CENTURY

der a Shawl, Children Bathing (both 1808-09, Kalinin Picture Gallery), *Psyche* (1808-09, H)—exhibit a high level of professionalism. The figure of Psyche is distinguished by its beautiful lines, smooth contours and gentle, expressive modelling. Tolstoy's contemporaries were impressed by his knowledge of natural forms and by his superb mastery of the secrets of wax modelling.

A quite unusual aspect of his early period was his wax portraits—small profile representations executed in fairly low relief in light-coloured, yellow or rose wax on a black board or glass. While in his early portrait bas-reliefs the sculptor sought to express the workings of his subject's minds (portrait of A. F. Dudina, portraits of Tolstoy's brothers), in his later works he tended rather to generalise and typify the images, exercising great freedom in his choice of artistic devices (cf. portraits of K. A. Leberecht and P. A. Tolstoy).

Tolstoy's early work as a medal-designer was done entirely under the auspices of the St. Petersburg Mint, where he was appointed in 1810. A medal, in his view, ought to be clear and accessible, 'so that everyone can immediately understand the occasion for its being minted'.

'I proposed to design the medals required of me,' wrote Tolstoy, 'in the classical Greek manner, this being the best in the fine arts, strictly reflecting the customs, costumes, locality and country of the time and the persons involved in the events to be depicted on the medal . . .'

His first medal, *In Memory of Chatsky's Educational Work,* which conformed to the best traditions of classicism, appeared in 1809, and in 1813-17 he produced many more medals, including one to be awarded to pupils at the Academy. All of them had a strict composition, beautiful contours, smooth rhythms and precise drawings. In his long, arduous years in the field of medal-designing, Tolstoy developed a doctrine of 'what and how to learn in order to become a medal-artist rather than a medal-master'.

Real fame came to the artist after he created a series of medallions on themes from the 181? War against Napoleon. 'I am a Russian and I am proud of that name,' he wrote during the war. 'Wishing to participate and share in the glory of my countrymen, I ventured upon an undertaking which would trouble even the greatest artist. But the hitherto unheard of glory of our days can inspire even a mediocre talent to enter the gates of the future. I decided to convey to posterity all the shades of emotions felt by me, and wished to tell the people of the future that in our day everyone felt as I did, and everyone was happy to bear the name of a Russian.'

It is important to point out that Tolstoy carried out this work—for more than twenty years—not at the request or orders of some highly placed personage, but motivated purely by his own genuine patriotism. He celebrated the military actions not in portraits of generals but in figures which symbolised the Russian troops and people's volunteer army. He carefully studied the details of battles, read the descriptions by military experts and talked to war veterans. The drawings and sketches which have been preserved allow one to follow the creative process behind each composition and show that the laconic, expressive qualities of Tolstoy's artistic idiom were the fruit of extensive searches and painstaking labour. He achieved his goal that 'everyone who looks at the finished medal should recognise the event being illustrated without resorting to the inscription'.

Tolstoy's medallions are very diverse both in subject-matter and treatment. The majority of them concern the most important battles of the Patriotic War, and all are firmly rooted in real life and history, interpreted with sincerity and emotion.

The medallions became widely known not only in Russia but also abroad, and Tolstoy was elected as a member to almost all the European academies of arts. His artistic peak coincided with his most active period of political and civic activity. Like many progressive people of his time, Tolstoy longed for sweeping changes in

NINETEENTH
CENTURY

F. P. TOLSTOY

FIFTY
RUSSIAN
ARTISTS
85

2. Psyche Admiring Her Reflection
   in a Mirror
3. Family Portrait

3

the social order. In 1816 he joined the free-ma-sons, and later he took part in the organisation of so-called 'Lancaster schools', the aim of which was to spread literacy among the popula-tion.

Tolstoy's social activities led him in 1818 to join a secret society—the Union of Prosperity, of which he became one of the leaders. He did not wholly go along with the Decembrists, but he did not lose his convictions, his daring and his broadmindedness. This can be clearly seen from two memoranda which he submitted to Nicho-las I in 1826 in which he bravely defended the dignity of the human personality, harshly criti-cised the senseless drills and discipline of the

cane in the army, and angrily condemned serf-dom and bureaucratic extravagances. He was most active in his attempts to achieve freedom for the Ukrainian poet T. G. Shevchenko.

But the artist's involvement in public affairs did not cause him to desert his art. In 1816 he made four wax bas-reliefs illustrations for Hom-er's *Odyssey* (TG). These works represent an invaluable part of his sculptural legacy. His fine understanding and knowledge of the antique world, his great insight into Ancient Greek life which fascinated him so, enabled him to reconstruct pages from history with lyrical charm and realism.

FIFTY
RUSSIAN
ARTISTS
86

F. P. TOLSTOY

NINETEENTH
CENTURY

4

Apart from medallions and bas-reliefs, Tolstoy produced several sculptures. In 1822 he modelled a *Head of Morpheus* (terracotta, RM), in 1839 a *Bust of Nicholas I* (marble, RM) and in 1848 a *Head of Christ* (plaster of Paris, RM; marble, TG). In 1849 the Council of the Academy of Arts confirmed him in the post of professor, in recognition of his services to sculpture.

An important place in his artistic legacy is occupied by his illustrations to Ippolit Bogdanovich's poem *Dushenka* (Psyche). For thirteen years he worked on these drawings (1820-33, TG), which were later used to make engravings. In these drawings, the brilliant use of the line

—which characterised all his work—manifested itself particularly clearly. The line or contour, was for Tolstoy the main means of artistic expression. In his hands the line is elastic and precise, sometimes stronger, sometimes weaker, creating a full impression of depth and materiality in his figures and objects. The varying character of the lines allowed him to solve plastic and spacial problems with extreme concision. Tolstoy's illustrations to *Dushenka* were his finest graphic achievement.

Fyodor Tolstoy was also renowned as a designer of sets for ballets and operas. In 1838 he designed the scenery and costumes and did a large number of drawings of individual dance

NINETEENTH
CENTURY

F. P. TOLSTOY

FIFTY
RUSSIAN
ARTISTS
87

steps for the ballet *The Aeolian Harp,* and in 1848 for the ballet *The Echo.*

Tolstoy considered sculpture, medal-designing and graphic art his main spheres of activity, and it was to them that he directed most of energy. In his rare free hours he used to cut silhouettes from black paper; this he did for himself and his friends, quite independently of prevailing tastes and of the demands of the Academy and official commissions. The silhouettes vividly reflected his realistic aspirations and interest in the surrounding world. He also painted several pictures: *Family Portrait* (1830, RM), *Embroiderings. In the Rooms* (TG) and *View of the Markoville Summerhouse in Finland* (1855, TG).

Fyodor Tolstoy died on 13 April 1873, at the age of ninety. His life was long and industrious, and he left a glowing legacy. Created over a hundred years ago, his works are still very much alive today.

4. Family Portrait
5. People's Volunteer Army. Medallion

5

Karl Pavlovich
BRYULLOV

(1799-1852)

1

2

Karl Bryullov was a son of academician of ornamental sculpture Pavel Bryullov. He was born in St. Petersburg and at the age of nine became a pupil at the Academy of Arts, where his older brothers were already enrolled.

Many leading artists of the time—A. I. Ivanov, A. Ye. Yegorov, V. K. Shebuyev—noticed Bryullov's rare abilities at an early age. According to one of his friends he left the Academy with 'handfuls' of awards and all the minor and major silver medals. His teachers were not at all pleased, however, by those of the young artist's works which violated the strict academic rules.

A competition painting *Narcissus Admiring His Reflection in the Water* (1819, RM), for example, was judged to show 'reprehensible fantasy', and the young Bryullov was blamed for depicting a classical character against a non-classical background. Moreover, the artist had 'upset' the purity of the ideal form by 'daring' to show a shadow from one of the trees falling on Narcissus' leg. But, supported by his teacher A. I. Ivanov, Bryullov did receive a second-class gold medal and, consequently, the chance to compete for a first-class gold one (*The Appearance of Three Angels to Abraham by the Oak of Mamre*, 1821, RM).

In August 1822 Karl and his brother Alexander set off for Italy as beneficiaries of the newly founded Society for the Encouragement of the Artists. The road to Rome took them via Riga, Berlin, Dresden, Venice, Padua and Bologna. The artists had been warned by special instructions against the revolutionary feelings that were ripening in Russia and had seized France and Italy, and also against becoming too keen on the 'low genre', i. e. genre painting. In addition, they were instructed as to which of the theorists had to be followed: the list included Leonardo da Vinci, Vazari, Raphael, Winkelmann, Mengs and Visconti.

Bryullov's work in Rome commenced with a study of Raphael's Vatican frescos and antique sculpture. What appealed to him in the work of the great painters of the past—Raphael, Titian,

NINETEENTH
CENTURY

K. P. BRYULLOV

FIFTY
RUSSIAN
ARTISTS
89

Rembrandt—was their verisimilitude. 'The first thing I acquired on the trip,' he wrote to his elder brother Fyodor, 'was a realisation of the pointlessness of mannerism.'

Notwithstanding the Society's warnings, Bryullov applied himself avidly to genre painting, and produced his *Italian Morning* (1824, whereabouts unknown), *Girl Picking Grapes in the Environs of Naples* (1827, RM) and *Italian Midday* (1827, RM). All these pictures are full of the joy of living. Bryullov saw beauty in the profusion of sensations in life, in the immediacy of human feelings, in simple, everyday things. His view of the tasks of art manifested itself clearly in *Italian Midday*. A young Italian woman is plucking a bunch of grapes amid dense greenery. The gentle outline of her head, shoulders and arms, the colour on her cheeks and the dazzle of her moist eyes all sparkle with the joy of existence, with a full-blooded awareness of life and with a sense of being at one with nature. The sun's rays pierce the foliage of the vineyard, flitting over the girl's arms, face and clothes; the

atmosphere is one of a vital link between man and nature.

The old aesthetic canons were shaken in their foundations. The Society for the Encouragement of Artists was obliged to remark to Bryullov: 'Your model was of pleasant, rather than of elegant proportions . . . the aims of art in general must be to portray reality in its most elegant form.' To which Bryullov replied: '. . . the artist has the right to deviate from conventional beauty of forms and to seek variety in those simple natural forms which are often even more pleasing to the eye than the austere beauty of statues.'

The artist's delight in the beauty of nature and in the free manifestation of human emotions roused his interest in the small chamber portrait and in the picture portrait. He painted *Self-Portrait* (c. 1833, RM), portraits of A. P. Bryullov (not later than 1841, RM) and G. G. Gagarin (c. 1833, RM), and water-colour portraits of the Olenins, and *Countess O. P. Fersen on a Donkey* (1835, RM); his large group-portraits of Prin-

FIFTY
RUSSIAN
ARTISTS
90

K. P. BRYULLOV

NINETEENTH
CENTURY

5

cess Yelena Pavlovna and her daughter (1830, RM), Yu. P. Samoilova with Giovannina Paccini and an Arab boy (not later than 1842, USA) and the famous picture portrait *A Lady on Horseback* (1832, TG) received a particularly warm reception.

Bryullov's striking talent, good education and independent outlook (cf. his break with the Society for the Encouragement of Artists and his refusal to wear the Order of Vladimir, which he was awarded by Nicholas I) attracted the attention of his contemporaries. It is not surprising that his studio on the Via Corso in Rome was a popular meeting-place.

Bryullov's friends included the composer Mikhail Glinka and A. K. Tolstoy, the brothers Turgenev, Zinaida Volkonskaya, Yu. P. Samoilova and Vasily Perovsky.

The artist's most important work was *The Last Day of Pompeii* (1833, RM) which dealt with the tragedy of Roman city that perished when Vesuvius erupted (first century A. D.).

Bryullov took six years to complete this canvas, having studied documents relating to the destruction of Pompeii, Pliny's letters to Tacitus and other historical and archeological materials, and also having visited the excavations at Herculaneum and Pompeii.

The action in the picture develops swiftly and occupies an enormous area. The whole city is in confusion; the deep-red sky torn by cold arrows of lightning, the sharp contrasts of light and shadow, and the running people, even now, in this tragic moment of their lives, are classically beautiful. Bryullov succeeded in conveying the most valuable thing in people—love of one's neighbour.

NINETEENTH
CENTURY

K. P. BRYULLOV

FIFTY
RUSSIAN
ARTISTS
91

1. Portrait of the Sisters O. A. and
   A. A. Shishmareva
2. Portrait of the Singer Pauline
   Viardot
3. Portrait of M. A. Lanchi
4. Portrait of A. N. Strugovshchikov
5. The Last Day of Pompeii
6. The Temple of Apollo the Epicu-
   rean
7. Self-Portrait

Current events troubled the artist. He was acutely aware of the anxious, often tragic life around him, in which people inspired by worthy ideals crossed swords with the forces of reaction and perished. The destruction, confusion and dynamism of this painting all mirrored an age which the writer Nikolai Gogol styled 'an age of crises felt by everyone'.

But Bryullov had not yet broken with the traditions of classicism . . . Idealisation of nature, canonical positioning of the figures, conventional light and colour—all this is present. But the new is making startling inroads—as seen in the mass character of the scene, in the absence of the obligatory main hero, in the dynamic quality of the picture as a whole and, most important, in the artist's interest in man's inner world and his desire to show the complexity of feelings.

In the autumn of 1833 Bryullov opened the doors of his studio, and soon *The Last Day of Pompeii* began its triumphant tour of exhibitions all over Europe, from Rome and Milan to Paris and St. Petersburg. Its success was enormous.

Gogol wrote about the painting: 'His figures are beautiful, for all the horror of their position.' Pushkin went into ruptures over the artist and dedicated a poem to him. The head of the Italian art school Vincenzo Camuccini declared Bryullov a 'colossus' of an artist. Sir Walter Scott, who visited his studio, called his creation an epic. Bryullov was elected honorary member of the Academies of Milan, Bologna, Florence and Parma. In Paris he was awarded a gold medal. The painting was greeted ecstatically by progressive circles in Russia: among those who

FIFTY
RUSSIAN
ARTISTS
92

K. P. BRYULLOV

NINETEENTH
CENTURY

appreciated their fellow-countryman's talent were Lermontov, Baratynsky, Zhukovsky, Belinsky, Herzen and Glinka.

Before returning to his homeland to take up a post as professor at the Academy of Arts, Bryullov set off on an 'artistic expedition' with V. P. Davydov to Greece, Turkey and Asia Minor. A master of drawing, sepia and watercolour, Bryullov produced a suit of studies of Greece.

On the invitation of Grigory Gagarin, a representative of the Russian Embassy in Constantinople, Bryullov sailed to Constantinople on the brig *Themistocles,* captained by the later famous Admiral V. A. Kornilov. The watercolour portrait of Kornilov and the Greek landscape are among the best examples of Bryullov's graphic art.

On 25 December 1835 the artist returned to Moscow, and in May 1836 he went to St. Petersburg. Pushkin, with whom Bryullov made friends in Moscow, wrote to his wife: 'Bryullov is with me now. He is going to Petersburg, reluctantly, afraid of the climate and of being tied down.'

His life in St. Petersburg was not easy or independent. His professorship at the Academy degenerated into an official 'service', always under the eye of the tsarist Court, with commissions for church icons and portraits of the tsar's family, and with the difficult work on the historical canvas *The Siege of Pskov (Osada Pskova)* which turned, as he put it, into 'distress from Pskov' *(Dosada Pskova).*

But his friendship with Pushkin, Zhukovsky, Krylov and Glinka, and his acquaintanceship with Gogol, Belinsky, Lermontov, Baratynsky and Dargomyzhsky, helped him on to new successes.

The portrait gallery of his contemporaries which Bryullov produced in St. Petersburg (he painted about eighty portraits) is the most pre-cious part of his legacy. Full-length portraits, in which he had excelled in the twenties and thirties, were also very important in his Petersburg period. Among the best are those of V. A. Perovsky (1836, RM), Ye. P. Saltykova (1841, RM), the sisters Shishmareva (1839, RM), and, especially, the picture portrait *Countess Yu. P. Samoilova Leaving the Ball with her Adoptive Daughter Amazilia Paccini* (no later than 1842, RM). This last work has an unusual allegorical meaning. In the background is depicted the emperor in a sultan's costume, and a courtier dressed as the god of commerce Mercury points to a girl in a white veil, personifying innocence. The masquerade is associated here with the falseness and emptyness of the *beau monde.* Contrasted with it in the portrait are the images of the proud and independent Countess Samoilova and the pensive, tender Amazilia Paccini.

Bryullov achieved especial success in realist psychological portraiture. His likenesses of the writer N. V. Kukolnik (1836, TG), the poet V. A. Zhukovsky (1838, TG), and the fable-writer I. A. Krylov (1841, TG), the poet and translator A. N. Strugovshchikov (1840, TG), the archeologist A. M. Lantchy (1852, TG) and himself (*Self-Portrait,* 1848, TG) are all gems of Russian portraiture. The critic Belinsky wrote of them: 'To be able to paint a faithful likeness is to be endowed with a certain talent, but that is only the half of the story . . . Let your friend have his portrait done by Bryullov, and it will appear to you that a mirror reflects his image less faithfully, because this will be not merely a portrait, but a work of art, which captures not only external similarity but the whole of his soul as well.'

Self-Portrait, painted when he was ill, is a kind of autobiography of the artist.

In the spring of 1849 Bryullov went abroad for the sake of his health. He died on 23 June 1852 in the village of Marciano near Rome.

Ivan Konstantinovich AIVAZOVSKY

(1817-1900)

1. A. V. Tyranov. Portrait of I. K. Aivazovsky
2. The Brig *Mercury,* after Her Victory Over Two Turkish Ships, Meets a Russian Squadron
3. The Ninth Wave

The work of Ivan Aivazovsky, who won worldwide fame in his own lifetime, can be regarded as a single epic poem of the sea, remarkably integrated in its perception of the world. A retrospective view of his work was given by the Soviet artist Martiros Sarian: 'His art is the affirmation of man and humanity and the negation of despotism and violence. Aivazovsky was an artist who thirsted for and glorified freedom.'

He was born in Feodosia in the Crimea, the son of an Armenian merchant. Even as a child he displayed artistic ability, and particularly liked to draw ships and the sea. The young artist's talent came to the attention of the city architect Koch, who helped find him a place at the Simferopol grammar school (1830) and then in the Petersburg Academy of Arts, where he joined the class of the landscape painter M. N. Vorobiov (1833). The critics responded positively to Aivazovsky's first painting *Study of the Air over the Sea* (1835, TG), which was displayed at an Academy exhibition. In 1837 he was awarded a first-class gold medal for three seascapes, in particular the splendid *Calm Sea,* and before he went abroad he was commissioned to paint views of several Crimean towns. It was at this time that he painted views of Yalta, Feodosia, Sevastopol and Kerch and pictures entitled *Moonlit Night* and *Storm.* In the Crimea Aivazovsky met admirals M. P. Lazarev, V. A. Kornilov and P. S. Nakhimov, had an opportunity to study the construction of warships, took part in a sea landing on the Caucasian coast, and painted his first battlepiece— *Troops Landing near Subashi.* During the operation near Subashi he also met M. M. Naryshkin, A. I. Odoyevsky and N. N. Lorer, Decembrists, who had been degraded to the ranks. The new Crimean works were successfully exhibited at the Academy of Arts, and in 1840 Aivazovsky was given a chance to travel to Italy.

In Rome he studied and copied works by past masters, did studies from nature and also worked on compositions from memory. All

FIFTY
RUSSIAN
ARTISTS
94

I. K. AIVAZOVSKY

NINETEENTH
CENTURY

along he enjoyed success. His picture *Chaos* was accepted for the Vatican museum. He had a great many admirers: artist and theorist Alexander Ivanov spoke of his rare faculty for depicting the sea; the engraver Francis Jourdain claimed that Aivazovsky was the founder of the genre of sea-scape in Rome and that after him 'imitation Aivazovskys' began to appear at exhibitions; the English seascape-painter Daniel Turner dedicated an enthusiastic sonnet to him after seeing the picture *The Bay of Naples by Moonlight* (1839, Feodosia, Aivazovsky Picture Gallery). In 1843 Aivazovsky embarked on a journey around Europe with an exhibition of his paintings. 'Rome, Naples, Venice, Paris, London and Amsterdam conferred upon me the most flattering awards,' the artist recalled. One of these awards was the title of academician—from the Amsterdam Academy of Arts. At home, the St. Petersburg Academy also made him an academician.

In 1845, with an expedition led by F. P. Litke, Aivazovsky visited the coast of Turkey and Asia Minor. Shortly after returning to St. Petersburg he again left for Feodosia. 'This feeling or habit is second nature to me,' he wrote. 'I enjoy spending winter in St. Petersburg, but at the first breath of spring I am assailed by homesickness and I am drawn to the Crimea and the Black Sea.'

Having built a house and studio there, Aivazovsky finally settled down in Feodosia for good, though almost every year he took his exhibitions to St. Petersburg and other Russian towns, and occasionally abroad. He painted thousands of works that testified to his knowledge of the fickle moods of the sea—sometimes raging in furious grips of a storm, sometimes bright and transparent in light sunny haze, sometimes mysterious with a streak of moonlight quivering on the quiet waves. Aivazovsky was a constant observer of the elements at sea and made a huge number of sketches then using these drawings—and with the help of his wonderful memory and great gift for improvisation he could paint a whole canvas in a single day. The

artist A. A. Rylov recalled that Aivazovsky once painted a view of the Black Sea in two hours, in front of students in Kuinji's studio at the Academy. The artist expressed his creative credo in the following words: 'A person who is not endowed with a memory that retains impressions of nature may make an excellent copyist, a living camera, but he will never make a real artist. The brush cannot catch the moments of the living elements: it is inconceivable to paint lightning, or a gust of wind, or a splashing wave, from nature. The subject of a painting takes shape in my memory as the subject of a poem does in a poet's.'

The well-known picture *The Ninth Wave* (1850, RM) belongs to Aivazovsky's mature period. It conveys the strength that can be brought out in man by the elements: shipwrecked sailors are seen encountering the dreaded ninth wave. An elevated romantic feeling is put across by the colouring—by the contrasts in the saturated dark-greens of the waves and the haze around the rising sun, and by the tinges in the foam of the tumultuous sea. The rich light and colour effects in this painting are evidently the same as were in Aivazovsky's earlier works which astounded art-lovers on his travels in Europe.

Over the years the artist became more restrained in his rendering of the colour effects of nature, but he never lost his interest in the sea. *The Wave* (1889, RM) is dominated by an overwhelming, rearing mass of water, the colour of which is comprised of elusive half-tones of grey and light-blue. And in old age he painted the enormous canvas *Amid the Waves* (1898, Feodosia, Aivazovsky Picture Gallery) which wonderfully conveys the motion of the sea. There is poetry, however, not only in his dramatic storm portrayals, but also in his calm seascapes—for example, in *The Black Sea* (1881, TG), about which the artist Ivan Kramskoi wrote: 'The painting shows nothing but water and sky, but the water is a boundless ocean, not stormy, but swelling, severe and infinite, and the

NINETEENTH
CENTURY

I. K. AIVAZOVSKY

FIFTY
RUSSIAN
ARTISTS
95

3

sky—if that were possible—is even more infinite. This is one of the grandest pictures I know!'

Aivazovsky was also important as a painter of battle-scenes. As 'Painter to the Naval Staff' (he was given this title in 1844) he depicted episodes from the defence of Sevastopol, and several times he treated the heroic feats of the Russian Navy. 'Every victory of our troops on land or sea,' he wrote, 'gladdens my heart as a Russian and urges me to depict it on canvas.' The Russian Navy deeply appreciated the efforts of its chronicler. In the autumn of 1846 even before he painted the battle-piece *The Battle of Navarin* and *The Battle of Chesmen* (1848, Feodosia, Aivazovsky Picture Gallery), during an exhibition timed to mark his tenth year as an artist, a squadron of six warships under the command of V. A. Kornilov called in Feodosia to celebrate the occasion. Aivazovsky was granted the free-

dom of Feodosia, and he was buried with military honours.

Aivazovsky responded in his work to contemporary political life, for example, to the movement led by Giuseppe Garibaldi and to episodes from the struggle of the Greek people against Turkish rule. He died on 19 April 1900 while working on the picture *A Turkish Ship Blowing Up*.

Aivazovsky did much to help provide amenities for the city of Feodosia. Due to his efforts, the city gained an Archeological Museum, a school, a club, and in 1880 a picture gallery. Artists such as Lagorio, Kuinji, Bogayevsky and Voloshin benefited greatly by the gallery and by Aivazovsky's own studio. After his death the picture gallery was bequeathed to the city, and it now contains the largest collection of the master's works.

Alexander Andreyevich IVANOV

(1806-1858)

1. S. P. Postnikov. Portrait of A. A. Ivanov
2. Boys at the Bay of Naples

The artist, thinker and theorist Alexander Ivanov, in the words of the writer Nikolai Chernyshevsky, 'belonged in his aspirations to that small élite of geniuses who are decidedly people of the future'.

Alexander Ivanov was born in St. Petersburg. His father Andrei Ivanov, was a professor of historical painting. In 1817 Alexander joined the Academy as an 'external pupil' and—unlike the regular pupils—continued to live at home. He had his first success with the picture *Priam Begging Achilles for the Body of Hector* (1824, TG). The subject is taken from Homer's *Iliad* and the picture, which was painted when Ivanov was eighteen, won him a gold medal.

The artist completed his student years with a programme work on a Biblical theme: *Joseph Interprets the Prisoners' Dreams* (1827, RM). Ivanov was awarded a first-class gold medal. However, the ideas which were clearly expressed in the picture—of man's defencelessness in the face of tyranny, and the flouting of the concepts of justice and lawfulness—caused dissatisfaction among the Academy's ruling circles. The depiction on the dungeon wall of an Egyptian execution was seen as a direct allusion to the execution of five leaders of the Decembrist uprising. True, the Academy officials could find no real proof of such an analogy and tried to hush up the whole episode, but still Ivanov had to produce a new diploma work in order to obtain the right to go to Italy. In the spring of 1830, having completed a small work entitled *Bellerophon Sets Out on a Campaign against Chimaera,* Ivanov finally was given an opportunity to travel to Italy at the expense of the Society for the Encouragement of Artists.

The start of his stay in Rome, however, was overshadowed by the news of his father's retiral—dismissed from the Academy of Arts, on Nicholas I's orders, after thirty-two years of service. 'Born in the fetters of the monarchy,' wrote Alexander Ivanov from Italy 'I have often seen my *confrères* tormented, I have seen the haughtiness of the aristocracy and the emp-

NINETEENTH
CENTURY

A. A. IVANOV

FIFTY
RUSSIAN
ARTISTS
97

ness of those who occupy important positions . . . I have always heard my relations complaining of the injustices of their superiors, whose power intimidates and enslaves them.'

But his personal sufferings did not dampen his belief in the power of art to transform man spiritually. In Italy he studied Classical and Renaissance art and particularly admired the Venetian frescos. In response to all this, he produced one of his most poetic works—*Apollo, Hyacinth and Cypress Making Music and Singing* (1831-34, TG). This painting was a hymn to lyricism, warm friendship and creative inspiration.

From the very start of his stay in Italy Ivanov was constantly on the look out for a theme that might totally engross him.

It was while he was still working on *Apollo, Hyacinth and Cypress* that he conceived the idea of a large-scale painting about the appearance of the Messiah. As a kind of 'trial run' for this work, he painted a two-figure composition on a theme from the Gospels: *The Appearance of Christ to Mary Magdalene* (1834-35, RM). The picture was successfully exhibited in Rome and then was sent to St. Petersburg Academy of Arts. Ivanov was consequently awarded the title of academician.

The artist was becoming more and more absorbed by the idea of the moral regeneration of mankind. 'The world abounds in evil . . . Art has forgotten to keep pace with social ideas,' he wrote from Italy.

Over a period of twenty years Ivanov worked on his huge canvas *Christ's Appearance to the People* (1837-57 TG). The artist's notes show that he conceived the picture as a historical work. 'In this painting I must portray people from different estates, people who are inconsolable as a result of the debauchery and oppression of secular governmental figures and as a result of atrocities committed by the Judaic kings themselves, ingratiating themselves with the Romans to ensure their place on the throne . . . I must show their timidity and fear of

the Romans, and their feelings that show through, their desire for freedom and independence.'

The subject for the painting was taken from the Gospels. On the bank of the River Jordan, where the ceremony of baptism has just taken place, John the Baptist addresses the people with words of hope, pointing to the figure of Christ walking on the hillside. The excitement caused by John's words has a great effect on the people. Behind him are the future apostles of Christ—the impetuous John, the grey-haired Andrew and the doubting Nathanael; on the other side are Pharisees, Romans and others. At John the Baptist's feet are two seated figures—a patrician and his slave. On the tortured, furrowed face of the slave there is a semblance of a smile: 'For the first time joy showed through the suffering to which he was accustomed,' wrote Ivanov.

In that it showed the great and noble beauty of the human spirit, and in its penetration of human suffering, the image of a slave was a true revelation in Russian and world painting.

The artist saw in this Biblical legend a chance to express his dream of freedom: '. . . the day of humanity has dawned, the day of moral perfection.' And the moral perfection of people should turn the world which 'abounded in evil' into a world of universal harmony.

The artist's dream of transforming society may have been utopian, given the acute social contradictions of the age, but it did adumbrate the ideas of progressive thinkers of the next generation. Ilya Repin said of the painting: 'Its idea is close to the heart of every Russian. It depicts the suppressed people, longing for freedom, crowding after a fervent preacher.'

The painting of this enormous canvas (40 m²) was preceded by extensive preparatory work. Ivanov made more than 600 preliminary études, sketches and drawings. These études proved to be a wonderful school in realism for the following generation of artists, too.

The best of them is the étude of the head of

FIFTY
RUSSIAN
ARTISTS
98

A. A. IVANOV

NINETEENTH
CENTURY

John the Baptist (TG and RM), in which the broad, sweeping manner of painting, based on contrast of cold and warm tones, increases the emotional effectiveness of the image.

Ivanov's searching and realistic aspirations manifested themselves most strongly in the preliminary landscape studies. He studied every detail of his picture and tested it against nature —from the stones, grass and colour of the soil to 'the distant landscape, hidden in luxuriant olives and covered by the morning vapours of the earth'.

The more closely he looked at nature, the more riches he discovered in it. The single object exists in a whole, infinite space. The treatment of distance, the integrated depiction of nature as a multitude of linked parts, became the main aspect of Ivanov's landscape painting. *Póntos Marsh* (RM), *The Bay of Naples at Castellammare* (TG) and *The Via Appia at Sunset* (TG) are captivating because of their epic grandeur and simple composition.

Working on his études in the open air, Ivanov set himself the complicated task of showing the interaction of sunlight and colour.

Particularly noteworthy are his famous landscapes with 'boys bathing', in which he succeeded in conveying the link between his models and the landscape: *Boys at the Bay of Naples* (TG), *Seven Boys in Coloured Clothing and Drapery* (RM), *Étude of Nude Boy* (RM). These works are considered masterpieces of Russian and world landscape-painting.

The work on études required enormous concentration, inventiveness and capacity for work. But Ivanov's sponsorship by the Society for the Encouragement of Artists was over and both the Society and the Academy were persistently urging him to return home. 'The thought of returning knocks the palette and brushes from my hands,' he wrote. He knew only too well what was happening in Nicholas I's Russia from letters and meetings with friends. In Italy he made friends with Gogol and Herzen and the scientist Sechenov.

The eventful 1840s, the revolutionary tremors in Italy, Ivanov's own reflections on the social conditions of life and his friendship with people who were linked with a new stage in the development of Russian culture—all this brought about a *volte-face* in Ivanov's world-outlook. In autumn 1857 he went to London to meet Alexander Herzen and to discuss with him the latest views on religious and cultural events in Europe and Russia. 'We have gone far . . . in our thoughts, in the sense that faced with the latest decisions of literary scholarship the basic idea of my painting is almost completely lost . . . and I barely have the spirit to improve on it.'

Ivanov's disillusion about the universal significance of the picture to which he had devoted his best years did not break him. The desire to 'found a new station of art' inspired him to further plans, in particular the creation of a monumental mural.

The mural was to have comprised a unified series of 500 works. The artist managed to complete about half of the planned studies, done in gouache, water-colour, sepia or pencil. Ivanov wished to express, in poetic imagery, popular traditional tales which were refracted in various ways in the Biblical stories. By juxtaposing Biblical legends with the myths of the Greeks, Egyptians and Assyrians, he tried to divine their common basis. His comprehension and conception of religious subjects was quite novel at that time.

In essence, these Biblical studies restated the theme of the heroic personality and the people—the theme that runs through the whole of Ivanov's work.

In the spring of 1858 Ivanov returned to St. Petersburg. His masterpiece, *Christ's Appearance to the People*, and the numerous études for it, exhibited in the halls of the Academy of Arts, drew a cold reception. The artist was the butt of much bitter and unjust criticism. But Ivanov did find some worthy friends in his homeland—the art critic Vladimir Stasov and Nikolai Chernyshevsky, with whom he shared his plans, dis-

NINETEENTH
CENTURY

A. A. IVANOV

FIFTY
RUSSIAN
ARTISTS
99

cussed the possibilities of starting a new Russian artistic school and of setting up educational institutions for young artists, and dreamed of travelling over Russia and painting new national historical canvases.

Alexander Ivanov's life came to an abrupt end in July 1858, when he died of cholera. Alex-ander Herzen wrote an obituary for the journal *Kolokol (The Bell);* Ivan Kramskoi, too, wrote with profound sorrow about Ivanov, predicting the enormous effect that the moral power of his art would exert on future generations of artists.

3. Christ's Appearance to the People

FIFTY
RUSSIAN
ARTISTS
100

NINETEENTH
CENTURY

Pavel Andreyevich
FEDOTOV

(1815-1852)

1

It was by an unorthodox route that Pavel Fedotov, officer of the household troops in the Finland regiment, became an artist. Born in the outskirts of Moscow, the son of a retired lieutenant, his childhood was spent in poverty. The boy would sit for whole days on a hay-shed, observing all that was going on in the neighbouring yards and streets. These first childhood impressions left their mark on Fedotov's creative work: 'The store of observations made at the very start of my life,' he wrote later, 'constitute the basis for my talent.'

His father wanted to see him in a military career, and at the age of ten he was sent to the Moscow Cadet Corps. This was the start of years of monotonous and wearisome training. But it was then that the boy's artistic bent revealed itself. His first essays—portraits of friends and caricatures—proved successful. On finishing the Cadet Corps in 1833, Fedotov was appointed to the household troops of the Finland regiment in St. Petersburg, where he served for ten years (1834-44). Nicholas I's army was plagued by endless reviews and manoeuvres and a mania for parades. As a distraction from the boredom and monotony, Fedotov read a lot, studied languages, took an interest in music and wrote poetry; but as before his main hobby was painting and drawing. At around this time he started attending evening classes at the Academy of Arts. His pencil brought to life scenes of senseless, exhausting drills; the themes of his drawings and water-colours were military exercises and camp service.

The more time and effort Fedotov put into his artistic hobby, the more clearly he realised that he would have to choose between painting and a military career. He was forced to give even more thought to the matter by a letter from the well-known fable-writer Ivan Krylov, who, having been impressed by the talent of the young officer, strongly advised him to give up military service and 'dedicate yourself to your true calling—the depiction of the life of the people'. Fedotov had already considered going into retire-

1. Self-Portrait. A Page from an album
2. The Major's Marriage Proposal

NINETEENTH
CENTURY

P. A. FEDOTOV

FIFTY
RUSSIAN
ARTISTS
101

2

ment and now the idea would not leave him in peace. But only someone possessed of great courage and, above all, self-confidence, could renounce a secure position and doom himself to an indigent existence. So Fedotov asked Karl Bryullov, whose fame had spread all over Europe, to give his assessment of his works. Bryullov studied Fedotov's works and gave the young artist his 'blessing'. His parting words —'Keep at it—a firm will, constancy and hard work can get you anywhere'—had a remarkable effect: Fedotov took to his art with redoubled energy, striving to increase his output.

But it was still some years before Fedotov retired. On the difficult path of selfless service to art he had to face poverty, privations and loneliness. With his faithful batman Korshunov he moved into small, cold rooms on Vasilievsky Island in St. Petersburg and began a life dedicated to art, 'giving myself neither mercy, nor leniency, nor rest!'.

Drawings galore! Fedotov drew everywhere —at the market-places, at the trading rows, in government departments and on the street. But these were not the creations of an impartial observer. With every drawing Fedotov commented on life, fighting stagnation and bureaucratism, exposing the morality of Nicholas's dignitaries. His drawings, which resemble quick, light sketches, convey objects and figures with

FIFTY
RUSSIAN
ARTISTS
102

P. A. FEDOTOV

NINETEENTH
CENTURY

remarkable precision; together, they make up a kind of artist's diary.

The drawing *The Embankment of Vasilievsky Island in Winter* is marked by the simplicity and trueness to life of its composition, while there is a biting satirical flavour to *The District Official, The Chief and His Subordinates, Cold and Shivering People,* and *How People Sit Down* (RM). From this multitude of disparate observations which he mounted in albums, Fedotov went on to produce complete works. Thus was born the idea for a series of *Morally Critical Scenes from Everyday Life,* done in sepia: *First Morning for a Deceived Young Man; Living at Someone Else's Expense; Old Age of an Artist Who Married Without a Dowry; Relying on His Talent; Fashion Shop; The Mouse-Trap; Fidelka's Illness and Death* and *Christening-Party* (1840s, TG).

The diverse themes of these drawings, their sharp criticism, their scope and their technical brilliance are all grounds for considering the series one of the most important for the artist's creative development. But these works are not entirely faultless: they suffer from overcrowded compositions, 'wordiness', and an inability to isolate the main point from what is of secondary importance—the action is sometimes so complex that the artist, for fear of not being understood, supplies the drawings with an explanatory text. Yet working on the sepias gave Fedotov a great deal: he gained experience both of life and art and gathered material for new works.

Fedotov's first complete oil-painting was *The Fresh Cavalier* or *An Official the Morning After Receiving His First Award* (1846, TG). In this everyday subject, the artist managed to express many typical phenomena of Russia under Nicholas I. The comic situation is generalised and thus acquires great power. The Fresh Cavalier is made to personify the vices of contemporary society: bureaucratism and bribery, moral impoverishment and callousness. The celebrated Russian critic Vladimir Stasov wrote of the hero of the painting: 'He is truculent and merciless, and capable of ruining whomsoever and

whatsoever he desires without the slightest flutter on his face. Evil, self-conceit, a petty, vulgar life—all this is present in the face, pose and figure of this inveterate bureaucrat, in his dressing-gown and bare feet, with his curl-papers and his award pinned to his breast.'

In 1847 Fedotov painted *The Fastidious Bride* (TG), based on Krylov's fable of the same title. The characters are described with ruthless satire: the old maid, her bridegroom—a fashionably dressed hunchback—and the overjoyed parents. The work is a brilliant example of Fedotov's painting skills. The years of intensive work had not been in vain: the artist had learned to convey the material texture of objects with great virtuosity—from the sheen of mahogany and the rippling of the bride's silk dress to the gilding on the frames and the soft nap of the carpets.

Composition was becoming one of the most important expressive factors in Fedotov's work, serving to bring out the main idea and concentrate the attention on the chief protagonists. Thus, in *The Aristocrat's Breakfast* (1849, TG), the tense pose of the upper-crust fop shown in the centre and the hurried movement of his hands, hiding a slice of bread from the unexpected guest, betray the pettiness and insignificance of this aristocrat who has squandered his fortune.

When Fedotov showed his pictures to the sick Bryullov, the famous artist was enraptured by them. 'Congratulations,' he said, 'you have outstripped me.' Such was his admiration for Fedotov as a genre painter.

The painting that brought Fedotov widespread fame was *The Major's Marriage Proposal* (1848, TG).

A year earlier Fedotov had written a poem entitled 'The Major's Marriage, or Improving One's Circumstances' about a major who decided to put himself on a surer financial footing by marrying a rich merchant's daughter. The painting which followed developed the theme. The artist takes us into the merchant's house, where

NINETEENTH
CENTURY

P. A. FEDOTOV

FIFTY
RUSSIAN
ARTISTS
103

3. N. P. Zhdanovich at the Piano
4. Policeman and Cabby
5. The Young Widow
6. Encore! Encore!
7. The Young Man with a Sandwich

FIFTY
RUSSIAN
ARTISTS
104

P. A. FEDOTOV

NINETEENT
CENTURY

the family is getting ready to receive the suitor. An ordinary, undistinguished episode from merchant-class life takes on universal meaning in this painting. Fedotov was not merely ridiculing the merchant's vanity, the major's profit-seeking, the bride's airs and graces or the mother's coarseness. The object of his criticism was the morality of people of different classes, people who turned marriage into a profitable exercise, into a deal. It was a condemnation of the seamy side of everyday life which astonished nobody in the Russia of Nicholas reign. Looking at the action depicted in *The Major's Marriage Proposal*, it was not hard to realise that what was going on was a shameless, horrifying trade in people. 'It was another tragedy,' wrote Stasov, 'threateningly looking out from behind a jolly, amusing screen.'

Fedotov's talent manifested itself with enormous power in this painting. Its composition is remarkably lively, natural and simple. The *dramatis personae* are closely linked with one another, so that we can almost read a narrative of the life, morals and mores of a merchant family. The figures are characterised particularly aptly by their gestures.

In conceiving this picture, Fedotov was guided above all by life. But the main thing was not petty details but the search for the typical and the expressive. The images created by him are the result of thoughtful selection and synthesis of characteristic traits inherent in a particular social type.

Fedotov's works made a huge impression on his contemporaries. They could sense the artist's innovatoriness both in his treatment of quite new themes, in his critical attitude to reality and in his new creative method which allowed genre painting to attain the level of socially significant art.

By the end of the forties Fedotov was an accomplished master, an artist with an established world-outlook and an individual creative face. He worked at a feverish pace. Ideas for new pictures tumbled into his head one after the other,

but not all of them were fated to be realised. The final, most difficult period in his life was setting in. It was the middle of Nicholas's dark reign with its terror and cruel censorship. Any display of critical thinking led to persecution and prohibition . . . 'The people could have learned a great deal,' the artist wrote at that time, 'but the censorship prevents it.' Soon the journal *Sovremennik* (The Contemporary), on which Fedotov collaborated, was closed down. His *Morally Critical Scenes* were never published. Lithographs of his pictures were banned too. The artist found himself in a hopeless material situation and his family was forced to sell their house to pay debts.

Fedotov had renounced a great deal—a military career, wealth and personal happiness—for the sake of art. He firmly and unhesitatingly stuck to his chosen path, and, despite the hardships, he continued to work tirelessly.

In the last years of his life Fedotov turned to portrait-painting. His portraits revealed new facets of his talent—a deeply poetical, emotional approach to his subject. In an effort to unveil the mental states of his subjects, Fedotov usually depicted them in their customary environment, caught in the middle of some action. This gives his portraits a genre character. The best of them is that of N. P. Zhdanovich (1849, RM).

In 1852, one of Fedotov's first dramatic pictures appeared—*The Young Widow* (TG). With tremendous empathy, the artist tells of the bitter fate of a woman left without a husband and expecting a baby. She stands deep in thought, resting against the sideboard. Her belongings have been sealed up to cover the debts left by her husband. At first glance lyrical, this painting proves to be as acute and significant as Fedotov's early canvases. Here too he uncloaked a world of violence and tyranny, where a weak, unprotected person can so easily perish.

The idea for the painting was suggested by the fate of Fedotov's widowed sister, who was left

NINETEENTH
CENTURY

P. A. FEDOTOV

FIFTY
RUSSIAN
ARTISTS
105

with two small children on her hands after her husband's death.

At almost the same time as *The Young Widow,* Fedotov painted two more magnificent pictures: *Encore! Encore!* (1850-51, TG) and *The Gamblers* (1852, State Museum of Russian Art, Kiev). Both works, in essence, are on the same theme—the spiritual bankruptcy inflicted on Russian life by Nicholas's regime. Never before had Fedotov achieved such power of social accusation, such sharpness of critical thought.

The artist's manner of painting was now more spirited and sweeping, and colour more important as a factor of lighting. It is the idea behind *Encore! Encore!* that dictated the picture's emotional, tense colour range—the combination of the reds and browns of the interior and the cold, intense blue square of sky at the little window. This work was the climax of the artist's creative development, one of the masterpieces of Russian realist painting of the nineteenth century.

Fedotov's life ended tragically. He died at thirty-seven in a psychiatric hospital.

'Fedotov is dead,' wrote the critic Stasov, 'having brought into the world only a tiny grain of the wealth with which his nature was endowed.

But that grain was of pure gold and bore great fruits.'

7

Vasily Grigorievich PEROV

(1834-1882)

1

1. Self-Portrait
2. Troika

2

Among the *Peredvizhniki* (organisers of mobile exhibitions)* who devoted their talent to the 'muse of wrath and sorrow', a special place was occupied by Vasily Perov.

Perov was born in Tobolsk, the illegitimate son of the public prosecutor G. K. Kridener—an enlightened, free-thinking man who received exiled Decembrists in his home. The boy showed a love for art at a very early age. Having received a rudimentary education from his mother, and then from the reader at the local church, in 1846 the young Perov entered A. V. Stupin's art school in Arzamas, after which he continued his education at the Moscow School of Painting and Sculpture. The young artist's world-outlook was influenced by many things —by mixing with other pupils, who came from all over, by his close friendship with the artists I. M. Pryanishnikov and I. I. Shishkin, by his classes with teachers who continued the traditions of Venetsianov, and by his love of literature, especially Nekrasov, Turgenev and Tolstoy.

His years of study were hard ones: he had nowhere to live and no money. He almost gave up the School and left Moscow, but then his fate took a happier turn. Upon hearing of the young student's impecuniosity, one of the teachers at the School, Ye. Ya. Vasiliev, decided to put him up in his own flat.

In 1856 Perov had his first success: for the drawing *Head of a Boy* he received a second-class silver medal, and for the picture *The Police-Officer's Arrival at the Inquest* (1857, TG) he was awarded a first-class silver medal. From the outset of his career, the artist kept firmly to genre painting, continuing the traditions of democratic realism begun by Pavel Fedotov.

In 1861, already an accomplished master of genre painting, Perov graduated from the School, receiving a first-class gold medal for the painting which brought him fame—*Sermon in*

* The *Peredvizhniki* is discussed in detail on p. 112.—*Ed.*

NINETEENTH
CENTURY

V. G. PEROV

FIFTY
RUSSIAN
ARTISTS
107

the Village (TG). This early work clearly exhibits what were to become the artist's distinguishing marks—a sharp satirical flavour and apt characterisation, clear composition and gentle, muted colours.

Developing the same theme, Perov completed *A Village Easter Procession* (1861, TG), one of the most daring and accusatory works of Russian painting. In this picture, the artist showed the joyless life of a miserable Russian village of the sixties, with all its indigence and ignorance. He condemns the drunkenness and outrageous behaviour of the village clergy—but the painting is not merely anti-clerical, its meaning is much deeper. Perov lays bare the dark sides of Russian reality and expresses criticism of the socio-political system. When the picture was exhibited in St. Petersburg it engendered a lively debate: some were heartily on the artist's side, praising his boldness and artistic mastery, while others—notably the clergy and officialdom—were extremely indignant. Presently the picture was removed from the exhibition and banned from being shown to the Russian public. The art lover and collector Pavel Tretyakov, who bought it for his gallery, received a letter from the artist Khudyakov, who wrote, '. . . There are rumours to the effect that you will soon be asked to explain to the Holy Synod what rights you think yon have to buy such immoral pictures and put them on public display. . . Perov might well end up in Solovetsky Monastery instead of Italy!'

In 1862 Perov painted another canvas—*Tea-Drinking at Mytishchi* (TG)—in the same anti-clerical mould as the earlier works. Here he sharply criticised social inequality and exposed the hypocrisy and parasitism of the clergy. The work was occasioned by the artist's personal impressions from a trip to the town of Mytishchi, where he observed such scenes more than once.

In January 1862 Perov was sent abroad at the expense of the Academy of Arts. He visited many museums in Berlin, Dresden and Paris and studied the works of the old masters. He also spent a great deal of time in the poor quarters of Paris, attended popular festivities and fairs and strolled in the environs of the city. The paintings executed at this time illustrate the everyday life of the lower classes in Paris, street musicians, beggars, ragmen and simple Parisians. They include *The Blind Musician* (1863, TG), *A Savoyard* (1863-64, TG), *Parisian Fête* (1863, TG) and *Street Scene in Paris* (1863, TG).

Life abroad weighed heavy on Perov and he longed to go home. Before two years were up he wrote to the Council of the Academy of Arts and asked permission to return home early: '. . . In two years of living abroad, for all that I wanted to, I have been unable to produce a single picture that was to my satisfaction. My insufficient knowledge of the character and moral life of the people makes it impossible to bring any of my works here to a successful conclusion. I consider it less useful to devote myself to the study of a foreign country for several years than, were it possible, to study and treat the boundless wealth of subject-matter to be found both in town and country life in our motherland.'

Perov was given permission to return home. He was deeply affected by his fresh encounter with Russian reality and with the poverty and misery that reigned in Russia after the notorious 'emancipation' of the serfs. The main motif of his work now became sympathy with the bitter lot of the working people. But the orientation of his works remained the same, and they lost none of their former denunciatory power and public-spiritedness.

Among the best works from this period were *Funeral Procession* (1865, TG), *Troika* (1866, TG), *The Drowned Woman* (1867, TG) and *At the Last Inn* (1868, TG). All of them stand out because of their depth of content, vivid imagery and emotional power.

One of the most moving of these works is *Funeral Procession*. Head down, a little horse is drawing a sled with a wooden coffin, covered with bast matting, over a winter field. The dead man—husband, father, breadwinner—is ac-

FIFTY
RUSSIAN
ARTISTS
108

V. G. PEROV

NINETEENTH
CENTURY

companied on his last journey by his family. As the critic Vladimir Stasov wrote, 'Coldness, wasteland, backwoods besprinkled with snow, oblivion and eternal obscurity: any one of a million little birds may as well have frozen on the road, unknown to anybody, and with nobody interested in its life or in its death—such is the content of this picture.' From the concrete situation portrayed Perov managed to rise to a universal image of the grim fate of the Russian peasant. There is nothing superfluous in the painting: the composition is well thought-out and the rhythmical repetition of the lines are of great importance, lending the picture a lament-like quality. The dismal winter landscape and the low, grey, leaden sky intensify the mood of forlornness that suffuses the scene. *Funeral Procession* has always been one of the most popular works of this 'poet of sorrow', as the artist M. V. Nesterov called Perov.

Perov achieved even greater emotional power and artistic laconicism in *At the Last Inn*—a work suffused with profound grief and solitude. The mood is created above all by the landscape. Somewhere on the horizon, where the road disappears, glows a yellow strip of diminishing winter twilight. Sombrely silhouetted against it are the stone towers of the town gates, crowned with double-headed eagles. In no other work did Perov attain such expressive colouring and such broad, free brushwork.

In *Troika* Perov spoke out against the inhuman exploitation of child labour in a capitalist town, against the social injustice that doomed children to a hungry and beggarly existence.

The theme of the city is heard even more loudly in *The Drowned Woman*. Perov himself witnessed the tragedy depicted here. In his original study for the painting the artist painstakingly recorded all that he saw—a crowd of people, a policeman asking those present whether they recognise the unknown woman. In the final version only two figures remain —the body of the drowned woman and the policeman, who is indifferent to everything. A cold, light mist is rising from the river, and through the haze can be seen the silhouette of the Moscow Kremlin; it is quiet, early morning. The poetry of nature awakening makes even more poignant the tragedy of a life cut off too early.

In the painting entitled *The Arrival of a Governess at a Merchant's Home* (1866, TG) Perov turned to the fate of women. We see a governess, a modest, intelligent girl, timidly and embarrassedly presenting herself to the merchant's family, who brazenly and unceremoniously look her up and down. In his powerful characterisation of merchant-class figures and in his cutting satire, Perov is akin to the dramatist Ostrovsky, who also exposed the oppressive world of the merchant class.

In Perov's works of the second half of the nineteenth century, according to Stasov, Russian art emerged 'in all the grandeur of its real role: it portrayed life, it "explained" it, and it passed sentence on it'.

In 1869 in Moscow, Perov got together with the group of artists who subsequently founded the Society of Peredvizhniki. In 1871 the Society's first exhibition opened in St. Petersburg, and its exhibits included Perov's *The Hunters Take a Break*, *The Angler* and his portraits of Alexander Ostrovsky and Ye. Timasheva. From this time on the artist's life was bound up with the Society, and for seven years he was member of its board. Also at this time, he began teaching at the Moscow School of Painting and Sculpture, and tried his hand at writing. He wrote several stories, such as 'Aunt Maria'; 'Under the Cross'; 'In Real Life; Fanny under No. 30' and others, in which he told the story of how many of his pictures were created.

In the seventies Perov produced fewer and fewer works with a social message. Instead, the accent moved on to gently humorous genre paintings showing characteristic scenes from Russian provincial life. *The Fowler* (1870, TG), *The Angler* (1871, TG), *The Hunters Take a*

NINETEENTH
CENTURY

V. G. PEROV

FIFTY
RUSSIAN
ARTISTS
109

3

Break (1871, TG) and *The Botanist* (1874, TG) all fall into this category.

The interest in man which was always present in Perov's art found its deepest expression in the portraits of his contemporaries. In the main, these were portraits of peasants. The artist was attracted by people with vivid personalities and a rich inner world. *Gloomy Fomushka* (1868, TG) is a peasant who has clearly had a hard life, full of drudgery and humiliation, but he has retained his human dignity. Even more penetrating in its psychology is the portrait of *The Wanderer* (1870, TG).

Perov's portraits of eminent cultural figures,

painted in the early seventies, bear comparison with the best works of Kramskoi and Repin. Perov's portraits are remarkably simple, sincere and realistic; they are natural in composition and austere and sparing of colour. The playwright Alexander Ostrovsky (1871, TG) is portrayed in a simple domestic surrounding. The portraits of the doctor V. V. Bessonov (1869, TG), the poet Apollon Maikov (1872, TG), the writer Ivan Turgenev (1872, TG) and the lexicographer Vladimir Dal (1872, TG) are all painted with extreme delicacy and sincerity. But the finest of all his portraits is undoubtedly that of Fyodor Dostoyevsky (1872, TG). His

FIFTY
RUSSIAN
ARTISTS
110

V. G. PEROV

NINETEENTH
CENTURY

4

not only Perov's best, but one of the best in the whole of Russian painting,' wrote Kramskoi.

Some of Perov's portraits are sharp and satirical. As an artist of great integrity, he remained truthful even when carrying out official commissions. In his portrait of the merchant I. S. Kamynin (1872, TG), for example, he could not help expressing his own attitude to this typical representative of the 'realm of darkness': the vivid individual image is used to reveal social features characteristic of the merchant class as a whole.

In the last years of his life Perov worked prolifically, and turned to a new genre—historical painting. He planned a trilogy about the Pugachov rebellion, but only managed to complete several studies for the last part of the trilogy —*The Judgment of Pugachov* (1879, RM). Other of his plans also remained in the draft stage—for example *The Siege of Pskov* (1879), *Pimen and Grigory* (1879), *Mikhail Tverskoi in the Tatar Horde* (1876) and *The Torture of Boyarynya Morozova*. The artist's last work was the large, many-figured painting *Nikita Pustosvyat* (1881, TG).

Vasily Perov was only 48 when he died, on 10 June 1882. His importance in the history of Russian painting is enormous. He had something new to say in many genres, but his real vocation was genre painting, to which he devoted all his talent and the best years of his life. In this genre he took up social problems of inestimable importance, expressing the most progressive ideas of the time.

bent back and head drawn into his shoulders and his large, strong, nervous hands clasped around his knees bespeak a man who has known much suffering but has preserved great inner strength. The writer's head is wonderfully drawn—especially the sensitive, emaciated, pale face with its high brow and sharp, dark eyes. The expressiveness of the portrait is aided by the greyish-brown colour range, relieved only by the red flecks on his black tie. 'This portrait is

3. At the Last Inn
4. Portrait of F. M. Dostoyevsky

NINETEENTH
CENTURY

FIFTY
RUSSIAN
ARTISTS
111

Ivan Nikolayevich KRAMSKOI

(1837-1887)

1. N. A. Yaroshenko. Portrait of I. N. Kramskoi

Ivan Kramskoi has a place in the history of Russian culture as a talented portraitist, historical and genre painter, theorist, teacher and fervent opponent of dogmatism in art, and as one of the leaders of the Society of Peredvizhniki.

He was born in the village of Novaya Sotnya, near Ostrogozhsk in Voronezh Gubernia; he was the third son of a town council clerk. After his father's death, the twelve-year-old boy could no longer continue his education, and his artistic interests, which manifested themselves very early, found no support among those near to him. His fortunes changed quite by chance, after he was recommended as a retoucher to a visiting photographer in Ostrogozhsk, Ya. Danilevsky. In October 1853 Kramskoi left his native village with Danilevsky and after itinerating around various Russian towns finally found himself in St. Petersburg. Here he found employment with the capital's best photographer, Denier. His new friends, young artists, spotted his talent for drawing and advised him to study. In the autumn of 1857 he was accepted by the Academy of Arts.

Kramskoi's years of study coincided with the rise of social-democratic thought in Russia. The spread of the ideas of the revolutionary democrats–Chernyshevsky, Pisarev, Dobrolyubov, Herzen—struck a chord in the hearts of the young non-aristocratic intelligentsia, including the students at the Academy of Arts. A group of talented young people formed around Kramskoi, who even in Ostrogozhsk had been fascinated by the articles of the critic Belinsky.

Almost every evening young people gathered in Kramskoi's flat on Vasilievsky Island. In this little flat, something like a new Russian Academy was growing up, as yet small, but which would later develop into a large 'Artists' Artel'.

Meanwhile, the Academy maintained its former positions, but the bases of the old aesthetics were crumbling under the weight of new demands. The antagonism between the aspirations

FIFTY
RUSSIAN
ARTISTS
112

I. N. KRAMSKOI

NINETEENTH
CENTURY

of Kramskoi's group and the traditional academic system led to open conflict in the autumn of 1863. Fourteen competitors for a gold medal refused to paint pictures on the required theme —'Feast at Valhalla'—and asked to be allowed to choose their own subjects. When the Academy Council turned down their request, they left the Academy, headed by Ivan Kramskoi. The artists were put under secret surveillance and the press was forbidden to mention them.

1863 saw the establishment of the Artists Artel; its leading figure was Kramskoi, the initiator of the first art exhibition outside Petersburg (in Nizhny Novgorod). The young artists' protest found a sympathetic response in democratic circles. Kramskoi gave warm support to the Moscow artists (G. G. Myasoyedov, V. G. Perov, I. M. Pryanishnikov) who were founding the *Peredvizhniki* Society which for many decades following the signing of its Regulations in 1870 united Russia's leading artists, and became a synonym for Russian realist art.

A sensitive, highly principled man, Kramskoi was one of the leading figures in the *Peredvizhniki* Society and became the intellectual father of a whole generation of artists.

Kramskoi believed that 'only a sense of social purpose can give an artist strength and multiply his powers, only a mental atmosphere that is dear to him and healthy can inspire and elevate him, and only confidence that the artist's work is needed and appreciated by society can help those exotic plants called pictures to ripen'.

Kramskoi always demanded a high level of formal perfection. 'Without ideas there is no art, but at the same time without vivid, striking painting there are no pictures, but merely good intentions.'

The most valuable part of Kramskoi's artistic legacy is the portraits of his contemporaries, including pencil portraits of M. M. Panov (1860, Dnepropetrovsk Art Museum),

G. G. Myasoyedov (1861, RM), N. A. Koshelev (1866, RM) and N. D. Dmitriev-Orenburgsky (1861, RM). In the sixties he painted his wife, Sofia Kramskaya. The most expressive of all the portraits painted at this time was the oval *Self-Portrait* (1867, TG)—a vivid image of Kramskoi the man, artist and teacher 'Just look at him!' wrote Ilya Repin. 'What eyes he has! You can't get away from them, even though they are small and set deep in their hollow sockets, grey, shining.'

Simplicity, modesty, humaneness and perspicacity—the things that Repin saw in Kramskoi—were all characteristic traits of his personality and work. In the seventies and eighties he achieved great success not only in portraiture, but also in genre and historical painting.

At the First *Peredvizhniki* Exhibition his picture *The Mermaids* (1871, TG) attracted a lot of attention, while the big event at the Second Exhibition was his large painting *Christ in the Wilderness* (1872, TG), in which he used the well-known Biblical subject to comment on the drama of human life. In a letter to the writer Vsevolod Garshin, Kramskoi wrote that he had resorted to hieroglyphics, to the Gospel story, because for him Christ was a symbol of a man with a high sense of social duty. Even earlier, with the appearance of Alexander Ivanov's famous painting, the Gospels lost their canonical meaning, and progressive Russian artists used religious themes in their work as a means of assessing contemporary life.

'Influenced by a variety of things,' Kramskoi wrote to Garshin, 'I have come to a very distressing understanding of life, and I clearly see that there is a moment in every man's life . . . when he is in doubt: whether to go to the right or to the left. This, then, is not Christ. Or rather, I don't know who it is. It is an expression of my own ideas . . . Christ is alone and tormented by doubts: should he go to the people, teach them,

NINETEENTH
CENTURY

I. N. KRAMSKOI

FIFTY
RUSSIAN
ARTISTS
113

2

uffer and perish, or should he yield to tempta-ion and give it all up . . .'

Not surprisingly, the reactionary press greet-d the picture with hostile criticism. Kramskoi vas accused of distorting the image of Christ nd of expressing anti-religious feelings. The rogressive generation, however, perceived it as call to civic action. Lev Tolstoy wrote to Pa-el Tretyakov: 'This is the best Christ I know.'

Kramskoi spent the summer of 1873 with his amily near Kozlovka-Zaseka in Tula Guber-nia. Here he received news of the death of his young friend, the landscape-painter Fyodor Va-siliev. Kramskoi had shown constant concern for him and more than once he had asked Tre-tyakov to subsidise the dying artist on the secu-rity of his paintings. The loss of a close friend undoubtedly affected the emotional structure of Kramskoi's unusual picture *Inspection of an Old Manor-House* (1873-80, TG). That same sum-mer he wrote to Tretyakov: 'I am doing my best to paint a portrait of Count Tolstoy, who turns

FIFTY
RUSSIAN
ARTISTS
114

I. N. KRAMSKOI

NINETEENTH
CENTURY

out to be my neighbour: his estate at Yasnaya Polyana is only five versts from here.' In fact, he painted two portraits—one for Tretyakov, the other for Tolstoy himself (1873, TG). Struck by the integrity of Tolstoy's character, Kramskoi wrote, 'I remember the pleasure of my first meeting with a man in whom all individual judgments are firmly linked to his general precepts, like spokes to a hub . . . For the first time I confronted a rare phenomenon—maturity, culture and an integrated character.' Tolstoy also had a sympathetic attitude towards the artist. Moreover, Kramskoi served as the prototype for the artist Mikhailov in the novel *Anna Karenina*.

Kramskoi's portrait of Tolstoy was commended by their contemporaries. 'Of all the portraits of Tolstoy, including those by Repin, Ghe and others, Kramskoi's is one of the most successful at expressing the brilliant writer's complex, powerful character.'

At Kozlovka-Zaseka Kramskoi also painted a portrait of his friend Ivan Shishkin with a portable easel (1874, TG), and some years later he executed another (1880, RM), which is considered one of the most successful of the famous landscape-painter. For Pavel Tretyakov, Kramskoi painted a gallery of figures from Russian cultural life: Ivan Goncharov (1874, TG), Yakov Polonsky (1875, TG), Pavel Melnikov-Pechersky (1876, TG), Sergei Aksakov (1878, TG), Mikhail Saltykov-Shchedrin (1879, TG), Pavel Tretyakov (1876, TG).

One of the best works of this period is the picture-portrait *Nekrasov at the Time of 'The Last Songs'* (1877, TG). Kramskoi eagerly accepted the offer to paint a portrait of the sick Nekrasov. Sometimes he had to work in short bursts of ten or fifteen minutes, as the writer's health was rapidly deteriorating. Kramskoi succeeded in bringing out the contrast between Nekrasov's physical malaise and mental lucidity, creating a noble image of the citizen-poet, a man with a warm heart and great willpower, one of the leading representatives of the democratic intelligentsia of the 1870s.

The common folk are also well represented in Kramskoi's portrait gallery. 'The people,' he wrote, 'are an inexhaustible source of creative inspiration.' Some insight into the artist's attitude to this theme can be gained from his portrait *Forest Warden* (1874, TG), which portrays a wilful, indomitable character. With reference to this portrait, Kramskoi wrote: 'The point of my étude was to depict one of those types (and they do exist in the Russian people) who have an understanding of social and political aspects of the people's life and who have a deep-seated dissatisfaction, which borders, in critical moments, on hatred.'

Quite different—light and gentle—is the image of Mina Moiseyev (1882, RM), a well-known narrator of folk tales.

Kramskoi did not restrict himself to portrait painting. He also produced many multifigured narrative pictures. Upon finishing *Christ in the Wilderness,* he began a painting with the title *Laughter*. It remained unfinished, but it shows the artist's continuing preoccupation with the idea of the conflict between the noble, bold man who lives for the good of others, and human self-interest. 'This laughter has persecuted me for several years now. It's not hard to be good because it's hard, but because people laugh.'

The last years of the artist's life were extremely burdensome. With deep sorrow he wrote: 'I have fought honestly all my life, and only now, at the very end, have I grown tired.' In the eighties he worked simultaneously on two paintings: *Unknown Woman* (1883, TG) and *Inconsolable Grief* (1884, TG). The latter was in many ways autobiographic: two of Kramskoi's children had died.

Despite the misfortunes of his final years, Kramskoi believed in his strengths, and his artistic ideals remained unchanged. 'I have confidence in Russian art: I know that sooner or later it will gain wide respect.'

Kramskoi kept on working to the very end. He died while painting a portrait of Doctor Rauchfuss, on 25 March 1887.

INETEENTH
CENTURY

I. N. KRAMSKOI

FIFTY
RUSSIAN
ARTISTS
115

'Rest in peace, mighty man,' wrote his fa-
ourite pupil and friend Ilya Repin. 'Having
limbed out of the insignificance and grime
f the backwoods, without a penny or outside
id, with only your ideals and aspirations, you
uickly became the leader of the most talented
nd educated young people at the Academy
f Arts. With tremendous energy you founded
vo artistic associations, one after the other,
ejecting once and for all the outmoded clas-
cal authorities and demanding respect and
ecognition for national Russian art. You are
orthy of a national monument, as a Russian
tizen and artist!'

Christ in the Wilderness
Nekrasov at the Time of 'The Last Songs'
Woman in Tears

FIFTY
RUSSIAN
ARTISTS
116

NINETEENT
CENTURY

Nikolai Nikolayevich GHE

(1831-1894)

1

Nikolai Ghe was born in Voronezh. When h
was three months old his mother died, and soo
after his father, a retired officer, went with h
family to Kiev and thence to Podolsk Guber
nia where he bought an estate. It was her
that Ghe's childhood was spent. He was brough
up by his grandmother and a serf nanny. Even a
a boy he had developed the kind, gentle natur
which always attracted people to the artist.

From 1841 Ghe studied for six years in Kiev
at first at a private boarding-school, then at th
grammar-school, and it was here that he bega
to take a serious interest in drawing. In 1847 h
entered the mathematics department of Kie
University and after a year transferred to St. Pe
tersburg University. Two years later he left uni
versity and joined the Academy of Arts, firml
convinced of his vocation. While revering th
Academy as a temple of art, however, he di
criticise the academic methods of teaching
Among the professors, Ghe singled out Ka
Bryullov, whose creative independence and de
sire to deviate from accepted canons he valued
He acclaimed Bryullov's painting *The Last Da
of Pompeii,* the influence of which can be dis
cerned in many of Ghe's early works, includ
ing his diploma piece on a Biblical subjec
Saul with the Medium at Endor (1856, RM).

In this painting the artist depicted Saul col
lapsed in horror before the menacing shadow c
the prophet Samuel, who has predicted death t
the King of Israel. Ghe uses typical mid-centur
devices to convey the dramatic scene: exaggera
ted gestures, bright local colour. The pictur
demonstrates that Ghe had completely master
ed the Academy-approved methods of compo
sition, drawing and modelling of form. For thi
work he received a first-class gold medal and
scholarship to travel abroad.

In 1857 the artist went abroad—to Germany
Switzerland and France, and then settled i
Italy, where he became interested in classica
history and drew several studies with very dra
matic plots: *The Death of Virginia, The Love o
the Vestal Virgin,* etc. But soon he realised tha

NINETEENTH
CENTURY

N. N. GHE

FIFTY
RUSSIAN
ARTISTS
117

2

the events and heroes he was depicting were alien to him. He became firmly convinced that an artist can paint 'only what is really dear to him, only that which he holds sacred in his heart'.

Ghe got into his stride with the painting *The Last Supper* (1863, RM). The well-known Gospel story is reinterpreted here as a human drama. Christ is portrayed deep in thought, tragically shocked by the recreancy of one of his apostles. The other apostles are also perturbed; each is individually characterised—the noble, refined John and the rather coarse, temperamental Peter. The monolithic group of Christ and the apostles is contrasted with the solitary, sombre figure of the traitor Judas Iscariot, who is forsaking his former friends. The idea of the struggle between good and evil is not only expressed in the composition. It is reinforced by the contrast of light and shade. At the same time, this contrast lends tension to the scene, with its 'fiery' colour-scheme based on the correlation of red and green. In *The Last Supper* Ghe picked up the philosophical and moral line in Russian art begun by Alexander Ivanov. Both artists were idealists. Both regarded Christianity as the way to establish justice on Earth and as the path to man's moral perfection. And both were interested in the moral aspect of the legend about Christ.

FIFTY
RUSSIAN
ARTISTS
118

N. N. GHE

NINETEENTH
CENTURY

Nikolai Ghe had an unusual method of working. He did not make preliminary sketches but pictured a whole scene at once in his mind and then looked for a model, transforming it to fit his plan. For Christ he used a photograph of Herzen; for John the wife of the artist A. P. Zabel posed; and Peter is modelled on the artist himself (it is remarkable that at the age of 32 he saw himself as he was to become thirty years later).

The picture was given a hostile reception by the reactionary press while it was applauded by the progressive intelligentsia. Ilya Repin wrote: 'Not only here in Russia but—I would go as far as to say—in the whole of Europe, in all periods of Christian art, there has never been anything on this subject to equal this picture. If it was interesting for the enlightened public, then it was even more instructive for artists because of its newness, its bold composition, its expression of a great drama and its overall harmony. This painting can happily be hung alongside the very greatest works of art.' As a result of this work, Ghe was elected to the Academy of Arts.

After a short stay in St. Petersburg Ghe returned to Florence where he spent another six years working on subjects from the Gospels. The most impressive of these works were *The Heralds of the Resurrection* (1867, TG) and *Christ in the Garden at Gethsemane* (1868, RM).

In Italy the artist also painted a series of landscapes, including *Transportation of Marble* (1868, RM) and *Marble-Cutting at Carrara* (1868, State Museum of Russian Art, Kiev). Both are characterised by the artist's interest in reproducing light and air effects, by the purity and saturation of colour, and by the juxtaposition of contrasting colours to convey bright illumination. However, Ghe regarded landscape as a subsidiary genre, essential for the study of nature but of no independent importance.

Several portraits also date from this period, notably of people who were close to Ghe: for example, *Portrait of the Artist's Wife and Son*

(1859, RM) and, of particular interest, a portrait of Alexander Herzen (1867, TG). The portrait of Herzen is painted with great sympathy for the writer, who was spiritually akin to the painter and highly regarded by him. It is a deeply psychological work with a simple composition: Herzen's brightly illuminated face stands out against a dark background. One is aware of a complex inner world, intelligence and subdued sadness. The artist smuggled the canvas back to Russia.

While living abroad, Ghe was well informed about artistic events at home. In 1867 he made the acquaintance of the artist Grigory Myasoyedov and together they conceived the idea of a society of artists. In 1869 Ghe returned to Russia and, living in St. Petersburg, actively collaborated with Kramskoi in organising the Society of *Peredvizhniki* It was in this period that Ghe's work came closest to the democratic realism of the *peredvizhniki*. This can be seen, for example, in his producing a painting on a subject from Russian history—*Peter the Great Interrogates Tsarevich Alexei* (1871, TG; facsimile by the artist in RM). In this psychological picture the drama unfolds purely through the characterisation of the protagonists. The action takes place in the Monplaisir Palace. At the table sits Peter, his resolute and wrathful glance turned on his guilty son, who stands before him, his head bent forlornly. 'Anyone who has seen these two simple, ingenuously positioned figures,' wrote Saltykov-Shchedrin, 'must confess that he was a witness to one of those stunning dramas which can never be erased from the memory.'

In this painting Ghe displayed an understanding of the dialectical historical development of the struggle between the reactionary and the progressive. The drama of father and son outgrows the sphere of personal relations. By bringing together the world-outlooks of both, the artist exposed the meaning of that turbulent, critical age, and also linked the image of Peter with the vital idea of his own time—readiness to sacrifice the personal for the sake of the interests of society.

NINETEENTH
CENTURY

N. N. GHE

FIFTY
RUSSIAN
ARTISTS
119

3

Ghe strove to convey the historical atmosphere authentically and made a special journey to Peterhof, from where he, in his own words, 'brought back the whole background of the picture in my memory'. He studied the portraits of Peter and Alexei in the Hermitage and also legal documents relating to the case of the tsarevich. Such a method of working on a historical theme was new in Russian art, and Ghe became one of the founders of realist historical painting.

In the seventies and eighties the artist concentrated mainly on portraiture, his aim being to record the outstanding figures of his time for posterity. He was interested not in the changing states of his models but in conveying their per-manent qualities. He was attracted by people in full possession of their faculties, people of intelligence and energy. The faces he painted were full of expression, the composition of his portraits was lucid and simple, the colouring austere: cf. for example, the portraits of Mikhail Saltykov-Shchedrin (1872, RM) and Lev Tolstoy (1884, TG).

Later Nikolai Ghe came into disagreement with the *peredvizhniki* Like them, he considered protest against the ugly forms of reality and against the suppression of the human personality to be the basis of art, but the purpose of art was, for him, to express an ideal, perfection. Ghe saw the meaning of art in the fact that it

FIFTY
RUSSIAN
ARTISTS
120

N. N. GHE

NINETEENTH
CENTURY

4

phical meaning of the work—the eternal conflict between goodness and love, on the one hand, and callousness and indifference, on the other —is expressed more straightforwardly. The structure of the painting rests on the outer contrast between the fat, self-satisfied Pilate and the tormented Christ, dressed in tatters.

In Ghe's last works, the image of Christ underwent an evolution. Ghe wanted to shock people with the sufferings of Christ, to make them think about the vital questions of life, about moral problems. His choice of subjects was telling: *The Judgment of the Sanhedrin* (1892, TG), *Golgotha* (1892, TG), *Crucifixion* (1894, TG).

The small work *Golgotha* is extremely powerful in its expression of suffering. The expansive brushwork, the fragmentary composition, the generalised form and the sharp lines all contribute to the heightened expressiveness of the image. In his final works Ghe paved the way towards the new art of the turn of the century.

In 1882 the artist met and became friends with Lev Tolstoy. The writer's views, and his understanding of Christianity, largely coincided with those of Ghe. Ghe's painting, however, was more or less unaffected by Tolstoy's doctrine of 'non-resistance to evil'. The active, passionate character of the artist's work was not compatible with meekness and resignation. His works always protested against the suppression of the individual and expressed faith in man. He said, 'I know nothing better than man and I shall always believe: all my joy, my happiness, my knowledge—everything comes from people.'

Nikolai Ghe died in 1894 on his farm in Voronezh Gubernia.

could show 'the difference between what we should be and what we are'. The truths promulgated by art should, in Ghe's view, be eternal, and not linked to a particular concrete circumstance. In the sphere of form, too, Ghe's searchings often proved incomprehensible to the *peredvizhniki*.

In 1875, due to material difficulties, Ghe left St. Petersburg for ever, and from then on he lived on a farm in Voronezh Gubernia. The last period in his art was devoted almost exclusively to themes from the Gospels. He sought more acutely expressive imagery and greater emotionality in his works.

In *What Is Truth?* (1890, TG), the philoso-

NINETEENTH
CENTURY

FIFTY
RUSSIAN
ARTISTS
121

Ivan Ivanovich SHISHKIN

(1832-1898)

Ivan Shishkin was born in the small provincial town of Yelabuga. His father, a merchant of modest means, was a great lover of antiquity. In an effort to foster his son's interest in history he took him to the archeological excavations of the ancient Bulgarian kingdom on the Volga, where he was helping the Moscow professor K. Nevostruyev. In 1844 the boy was sent to Kazan grammar-school, where he soon found friends with whom he could draw and discuss art. The set-up of the grammar-school, however, was an obstacle to his aspirations and inclinations, and after the summer holidays of 1848 he did not go back to the school—'so that I would not become a clerk', as he put it. Shishkin's autobiography gives some idea of his activities as a young man, having freed himself from the 'grammar-school with its narrow-minded formalism'.

In 1852 Shishkin entered the Moscow School of Painting and Sculpture and received a good grounding under the guidance of A. N. Mokritsky. From 1856 to 1860 he continued his studies at the St. Petersburg Academy of Arts under S. M. Vorobiov (whom, it should be said, he already outstripped as an artist). The young artist's successes, which earned him gold and silver medals, upheld the hopes expressed by his former tutor Mokritsky when Shishkin was entering the Academy: 'We have lost an excellent, talented pupil, but we can expect, with time, to see him turn into an excellent artist if he continues to study with the same love at the Academy.' Shishkin's aspiration for 'authenticity, similarity and a portrait—like quality in the representation of nature' was already in evidence in the early work *View of the Environs of St. Petersburg* (1856, RM).

In 1858-59 Shishkin often went to the island of Valaam, where the pupils of the Academy had practical summer courses. The severe, majestic scenery there reminded the young artist of the natural beauty of the Urals area, where he had spent his childhood.

In 1860, for two of his Valaam landscapes, Shishkin received a first-class gold medal and

1. I. N. Kramskoi. Portrait of I. I. Shishkin

FIFTY
RUSSIAN
ARTISTS
122

I. I. SHISHKIN

NINETEENTH
CENTURY

the right to go abroad. He was in no hurry to leave, however, and in the spring of 1861 went to Yelabuga, where he did a good deal of painting in the countryside—'which can only be of considerable benefit to the landscape-painter'.

He finally went abroad in 1862. Berlin and Dresden left him cold; all he felt was homesickness ('why am I not in Russia, that I love so?'). Shishkin came to life, however, in Prague, where he 'met many Czechs; the people are wonderful and are glad to speak Russian'. He was impressed by the drawings of 'Slavonic types' by the great Czech realist of the 1860s, Joseph Manes. In 1863 in Zurich Shishkin visited the studio of the painter and engraver Sir Robert Collier, where he learned about the technique of etching.

The mountain scenes of Switzerland were new ground for the artist, and he produced dozens of sketches, from which he later painted three pictures, in St. Petersburg. Presently, with his colleagues from the Academy, L. L. Kamenev and Ye. E. Dyukker, he began working in the Teutoburg Forest near Dusseldorf. His pen-drawings attracted the attention of many art-lovers. Shishkin himself recalled: 'Everywhere I went people pointed—"there goes that Russian"—and even in shops they would ask whether I was that Russian, Shishkin, who did such marvellous drawings.'

In 1865 Shishkin returned to Russia and received the title of academician for the picture *View in the Environs of Dusseldorf* (1865, RM). He quickly slipped into the capital's artistic circles and attended the Thursday meetings of the Artists' Artel. 'Loudest of all,' recalled Repin, 'was the voice of the mighty Ivan Shishkin. Like an enormous green forest he infected everyone with his health, jollity, good appetite and sincere Russian talk. He produced a fair amount of marvellous pen-drawings at these evenings. The audience behind his back used to gasp when he started erasing his wonderful drawing with his huge drayman's hands and coarse hard-worked fingers, but by some miracle or magic the drawing would emerge from this rough treatment even more elegant and brilliant.'

Shishkin's paintings *Tree-Felling* (1867, TG), *At Sunset* (1869, RM) and *Midday in the Outskirts of Moscow* (1869, TG), which reveal the distinctive beauty of the Russian landscape, foreshadowed the direction later developed by the Society of *Peredvizhniki* In 1870 Shishkin was one of the founding members of the Society, together with Kramskoi, Perov, Myasoyedov, Savrasov, Ghe and others. Ivan Kramskoi, who rated Shishkin's art very highly and helped him—to the extent of giving him the use of his studio for his work on the competition painting *Forest of Mast Timber in Vyatka Region* (1872, in TG under the title *Pine Forest)*—wrote the following about Shishkin's merits: 'He simply amazes us with his knowledge . . . And when he has the landscape before him it's as if he is in his element; immediately he is bold and agile and does not need to think about how, what or why . . . I think he is the only one among us who knows nature in a scholarly way. . . Shishkin is a milepost in the development of Russian landscape-painting he is a whole school in one man.'

At the Second Exhibition of *Peredvizhniki* Shishkin presented the painting *In the Backwoods* (RM), for which in 1873 he received the title of professor. The composition leads the eye from the shaded foreground to the weak patch of sunlight between the stunted trees in the depths of the wood, and the artist allows one to sense the humid air, the dampness of the mosses and fallen branches, and to soak in this atmosphere, as though one were alone in the oppressive wilderness. Quite different is the famous picture *Rye* (1878, TG), which is spacious and full of sunlight and air; it is an epic piece, a synthesis of the national characteristics of the Russian countryside, of the beloved, important traits which Shishkin saw in it—'expansiveness; space; fields of rye; God's paradise; Russian riches . . .'

NINETEENTH
CENTURY

I. I. SHISHKIN

FIFTY
RUSSIAN
ARTISTS
123

2

The canvas *Among the Even Valley* (1883, State Museum of Russian Art, Kiev)—which took its title from a poem by A. F. Merzlyakov, known as a folk song—is suffused with a mixture of majesty and heartfelt lyricism. But the picture is not an illustration of the poetry. The imagery of the canvas results from a sense of the expansiveness of the Russian landscape. There is something joyful, yet pensive too, in the broad, flung-open steppe (it is precisely this sensation that is evoked by the picture's free, unrestrained composition), in the alternation of illuminated and darkened patches, in the dried stalks strewn, so to speak, beneath the wayfarer's feet, and in the majestic oak which commands the scene.

Despite Shishkin's successes in landscape-painting, his close friends strongly advised him to pay attention to expressive devices, particularly in conveying qualities of light and air. One had only to think of the fine colouring in the works of Repin and Surikov which were well-

known by that time to appreciate the good sense of this advice. As a result, the appealing thing in Shishkin's pictures *Misty Morning* (1885, Gorky State Art Museum) and *Pine-Trees in Sunlight* (1886, TG) is not so much the composition as the harmony of chiaroscuro and colour. The same goes for other landscapes, such as *Oaks* (1887, RM), *Golden Autumn* (1888, Perm State Art Gallery) and others.

Forest life is well conveyed in *Morning in a Pine Forest* (1889, TG), which Shishkin painted with K. A. Savitsky, and in *Rain in an Oak Forest* (1891, TG).

Apart from painting, Shishkin was also a master of drawing and engraving. His drawing went through the same evolution as his painting. Those of the eighties, which were executed in charcoal and chalk, are much more expressive than the pen-drawings of the sixties. In 1891 more than 600 études and etchings were exhibited at the Academy. The exhibition gave a good idea of the scope of this artist who was deeply

FIFTY
RUSSIAN
ARTISTS
124

I. I. SHISHKIN

NINETEENTH
CENTURY

aware of and sought to express the beauty and heroic power of the Russian countryside.

Shishkin's career culminated in the grand composition *Grove of Ship Timber* (1898, RM), in which the artist's experience and mastery expressed the indelible impressions of his childhood. The painting, completed not long before the artist's death, depicts the Afonasov grove of ship-building timber near Yelabuga. It displays that familiar combination of great and small, of mighty and fragile, which Shishkin saw so clearly in the scenery of his homeland, and which he loved and glorified so sincerely in his art.

Shishkin died suddenly, on 8 March 1898, while working on the painting *Forest Kingdom*.

2. Rye
3. Grasses

NINETEENTH
CENTURY

FIFTY
RUSSIAN
ARTISTS
125

Alexei Kondratievich SAVRASOV

(1830-1897)

Alexei Savrasov was the son of a Moscow merchant. In his early youth he displayed an uncommon talent for painting. Despite the wishes of his father, who hoped to attract his son into the world of commerce, Savrasov entered the Moscow School of Painting and Sculpture. That was in 1844, and four years later the report of the Council of the Moscow Art Society mentioned his name as the best pupil in the perspective and landscape class taken by the artist K. I. Rabus.

Supported financially by I. V. Likhachov, an art patron and member of the Council of the Moscow Art Society, Savrasov was one of a number of students who travelled in the summer of 1849 to the south of Russia, where he painted views of Odessa and the Ukraine. For his class works of that year he was awarded a merit certificate, and on 25 September 1850 he received a civil rank for *View of the Moscow Kremlin by Moonlight* and *Stone at a Small Stream,* but he remained registered as a pupil.

Savrasov's first landscapes followed directly in the traditions of the academic school. Academic landscape-painting in the forties and fifties was predominantly romantic in direction, and Savrasov's teacher also favoured this style. The artist's youthful works—*View of Moscow from Vorobyovy Hills* (1848, TG) and *View of the Kremlin in Inclement Weather* (1851, TG) —therefore betray the influence of Romanticism, but they are distinguished by real observation and sincerity of feeling.

In the summer of 1854 the artist worked near St. Petersburg on the Gulf of Finland. Two of his paintings which drew attention at an autumn exhibition at the Academy of Arts (6 October 1854)—*View in the Environs of Oranienbaum* and *Coastline in the Environs of Oranienbaum* —brought Savrasov the title of academician.

Both of these paintings differ substantially from his earlier works. Having selected a traditional romantic motif, the artist sought poetry not in superficial effects but in lyrical reproduction of nature. With great affection he

FIFTY
RUSSIAN
ARTISTS
126

A. K. SAVRASOV

NINETEENTH
CENTURY

describes the charm of a summer evening at the sea, the moistness of the sea air in the shade of ancient rocks, and the twilight under the spreading branches of trees.

In Moscow Savrasov again took part in exhibitions at the School of Painting and Sculpture, and after his teacher's death in 1857 he took over the landscape class. His teaching went well and he soon found himself surrounded by affectionate friends and pupils.

Also in 1857 he married Sofia Herz, the sister of a well-known archeologist and art historian. Their house became a meeting-place for artists and art-patrons (including Pavel Tretyakov), new works of literature were read, and there were lively discussions of the issues current in Russian society of the day. One of Savrasov's closest friends was Vasily Perov, the initiator of the *Peredvizhniki* Society.

One of the landmarks in Savrasov's development as an artist was the painting *Landscape with River and Fisherman* (1859, State Art Museum of Latvia). Here there is neither the struggle of the elements nor striking contrasts in lighting. The line of the bank is calm, the silhouette of the group of trees is smooth, and the sunlight gently illuminates the suburban Moscow valley.

In Russian art, the 1860s were marked by the affirmation of the national characteristics of the Russian landscape. More and more often landscape-artists turned to the primarily rural area of central Russia, seeking to give an authentic impression of the beauty of their native land.

Savrasov did a lot of work in the environs of Moscow: cf. *View of the Village of Kuntsevo* (1855, TG), *Evening Landscape* (1861, State Art Museum of Latvia), *Rural View* (1867, TG).

In the spring of 1862 the Society of Art Lovers offered Savrasov a trip abroad, and he visited the World Art Exhibition in London, went to Copenhagen, Berlin, Dresden, Leipzig, Paris, Munich, and spent two months in the mountains of Switzerland. He expressed admiration of the Eng-

lish and German masters' 'aspiration for truth and independence'.

Savrasov's most important work of the sixties was *Elk Island* (1869, TG), which won first prize at a competition organised by the Moscow Society of Art Lovers. One of his contemporaries commented on his 'ability to transfer to the canvas a piece of the nature we all know so well, from the vicinity of Moscow'. A solemn and majestic pine forest stands like a guardian over the spreading fields: it is a clear summer day; a herd grazes peacefully in the meadows. The landscape is complete down to the last detail—the bushes, the trees, the grass in the forest clearing. The artist pinpoints here what is significant in the commonplace in nature. *Elk Island* marked the beginning of the artist's prime, and the following years saw the creation of his finest works.

In December 1870 Savrasov and his wife travelled to the Volga and stayed in Yaroslavl, near Kostroma, in Nizhny Novgorod and in Yuryevets.

The painting *Pechersky Monastery near Nizhny Novgorod* (1871, Gorky State Art Museum) is one of Savrasov's largest works and the first of his well-known Volga landscapes. He was utterly won over by the solemn grandeur and expansiveness of the Volga countryside, and by its organic unity with the life of the Russian people. Village houses and gardens, green meadows, blue lagoons and sand banks are all woven quite naturally into the broad panorama, and above it all rises a white-stone monastery. Man and nature in the picture are one.

'The quiet life at Yaroslavl allows me to concentrate on art,' wrote the artist to Pavel Tretyakov. New paintings followed on each other's heels—*The Volga by Yuryevets* (1871, whereabouts unknown), *The Volga in Spate by Yaroslavl* (1871, RM), and finally *The Rooks Have Come* (1871, TG) which appeared at the First *Peredvizhniki* Exhibition and was given a rapturous reception.

'The landscape *The Rooks Have Come* is the best,' wrote Kramskoi to F. A. Vasiliev. 'And it

NINETEENTH
CENTURY

A. K. SAVRASOV

FIFTY
RUSSIAN
ARTISTS
127

FIFTY
RUSSIAN
ARTISTS
128

A. K. SAVRASOV

NINETEENTH
CENTURY

is indeed beautiful, although Bogolyubov and Baron Klodt and I. I. (i.e. Shishkin—*O. P.*) are all here. They all have trees, water, and even air, but only *The Rooks* has a soul.'

The actual painting of the picture was preceded by sketches from nature, which the artist did in Yaroslavl and in the village of Molvitinovo near Kostroma. The subdued, delicate colouring, comprising gentle shades of grey, brown, white and blue, conveys the iridescent softness of colours in spring. In the north the awakening of nature after the long winter is slow. The snow lies long in the fields, the trees stand frozen in the wind, and suddenly it all fills with a light tremor of life, with the joyful sound of birds. The white-barked birch-trees stretch their slender branches to the clouds and pale sky, buds grow pink and swell in the warm caressing wind, and noisy rooks build their nests. The air is light, clear and springlike, a tall stone church with a pointed bell-tower can clearly be seen, and in the distance a river winds in the broad expanses.

'What simplicity!' wrote Isaak Levitan. 'But behind this simplicity one can feel the good and gentle soul of an artist who holds all this very close to his heart.' No one had ever expressed the beauty and lyricism of the Russian landscape so profoundly and poetically. *The Rooks Have Come* was one of the reasons for the success of the First *Peredvizhniki* Exhibition, and from then on Savrasov firmly linked his work to that of the Society.

Many of the artist's works which appeared at the *peredvizhniki* exhibitions were painted in the Volga area. Savrasov worked near Nizhny Novgorod and near Kazan, but his favourite spots were between Yaroslavl and Kostroma. His pictures are varied both in terms of the states of nature conveyed and in terms of the spectrum of emotions evoked. The landscape *The Volga in Spate by Yaroslavl* (1871, RM) expresses the tranquil might of Russian nature, in which 'rivers flood and turn into seas'.

In some works nature appears renewed and rejoicing—*Country Road* (1873, TG), *Rainbow* (1875, RM)—while in others it is agitated and poetically elevated—*Evening; Migration of Birds* (1874, Odessa Picture Gallery).

In the seventies Savrasov's works began to express more sadness, anxiety, or even acute grief—*A Moonlit Night. A Marsh* (1870, TG), *Sunset Over the Marsh* (1871, RM).

Under the impression of a personal tragedy, the death of his daughter in 1871, Savrasov created one of his most dramatic works—*Graves Above the Volga* (1874, private collection).

At the end of the seventies the artist fell seriously ill, and his work showed signs of decline. But even in his late period he produced some genuinely poetic works, including *Rye* (1881, TG), *Winter Landscape* (private collection), *A Northern Village* and *Spring. Kitchen-Gardens* (1883, Perm State Art Gallery).

The last decades were not easy ones for the artist. It is known that Savrasov asked for loans of money and for a flat from the state. He spent his last years in destitution and died on 26 September 1897 in Moscow.

His pupil Isaak Levitan wrote: 'One of the most profound Russian landscape-artists has passed away. With him, lyricism came to landscape-painting, and boundless love for one's native land. Yes, Savrasov was the father of Russian landscape-painting, and this undisputed merit of his will never be forgotten in the field of Russian art.'

1. V. G. Perov. Portrait of A. K. Savrasov
2. Winter. A Yard
3. The Rooks Have Come

NINETEENTH
CENTURY

FIFTY
RUSSIAN
ARTISTS
129

Fyodor Alexandrovich VASILIEV

(1850-1873)

I. N. Kramskoi. Portrait of F. A. Vasiliev

Fyodor Vasiliev was born at Gatchina, into the family of a low-rank post-office official. When he was twelve the family moved to St. Petersburg and settled on the Vasilievsky Island. Fyodor's childhood was joyless, with his family in constant material difficulties. For a time the future artist worked as a postman and then joined the drawing school run by the Society for the Furtherance of the Arts. Two small, freshly-coloured landscapes—*In the Church Grounds* (1867, RM) and *A Village Yard* (1867, RM)—and several drawings, the best of which were done on the island of Valaam, all date from this period.

The young artist was exhilarated by the beauty of the wild, untouched scenery of Valaam, which he visited with Ivan Shishkin in 1867. Shishkin gave him advice, teaching him to observe nature closely and to depict it in minute detail. Shishkin's influence can partly be seen in Vasiliev's early landscape *A Village* (1868, TG), although it is even closer to some Russian landscapes of the early nineteenth century. The motif is commonplace. The landscape is narrative. With small brush-strokes, the artist gives a detailed description of run-down cottages, a winding road and pools of water reflecting the clouds. The composition suffers from being rather fragmented, however, and the colour harmony is not quite right.

Having finished the drawing school in 1868, Vasiliev was drawn towards the St. Petersburg Artists' Artel. Witty and charming, he soon became everybody's favourite, but he was particularly friendly with Ivan Kramskoi. Kramskoi never ceased to admire the young man's extraordinary giftedness, likening him to 'a rich man in a fairy tale, who at the same time is fabulously generous and flings his riches in handfuls in all directions, without counting them or even appreciating their value'.

Vasiliev spent the summer of 1869 first at Znamenskoye, Stroganov's Tambov estate, then at Khoten in the Ukraine. The fruit of this trip was the painting *After the Rain* (1869, TG) in

FIFTY
RUSSIAN
ARTISTS
130

F. A. VASILIEV

NINETEENTH
CENTURY

which the artist strove not only to give a concrete representation of the motif, but to convey the state of nature: the earth moist from recent rain, the freshness of the foliage, the puddles sparkling in the rays of sunlight breaking through the storm-clouds. In this landscape one can already hear the lyrical notes that would sound in all of Vasiliev's subsequent works.

An important phase in the painter's artistic development was the trip on the Volga which he undertook in 1870 with Ilya Repin and Ye. Makarov. Vasiliev's enormous capacity for work, his powers of observation and the high artistic qualities of his brief travel sketches astonished his companions. In his book *Far and Near* Repin recalled: 'He impressed us at every even faintly interesting stop. For ten minutes, while the steamer was still, his finely sharpened pencil would dash with the speed of a sewing-machine needle over the small page of his pocket album, faithfully and impressively marking out a whole picture of the steep bank, with crooked little cottages above the slope, fences, stunted trees and pointed church bell-towers in the distance. . . The steamer would move off and the wizard would shut the book and stuff it into his side-pocket. The first few times we simply gaped in wonder.'

Vasiliev was interested in everything: the distinctive Volga landscapes, the life of the local people, the labour of the barge-haulers; but he was particularly fascinated by the boundless expanses of the huge river. From this time onwards the Volga was a recurrent theme in his work.

The character of the river is best conveyed in the painting *View of the Volga* (1870, RM). Here Vasiliev depicts the distant sandy bank, with moored long-boats and barge-haulers near them. Woolly clouds scud low over the land, not hiding the sun. The peaceful blue of the sky and the golden glance of the banks are reflected in rainbow colours in the smooth mirror of the water. There is harmony in nature. Painted in an untrammelled style, the landscape demonstrates the artist's ability to single out the essence of the scene; the lighting is natural and the colours are pure and rich.

It was *The Thaw* (1871, RM) that brought fame to the artist. It is early spring; the melting snow has flooded a narrow country road; gusts of wind incline the bare branches on the trees; a weak ray of sun barely penetrates the heavy clouds; nature is in the throes of waking from its deep winter sleep. The picture's composition emphasises the desolation and vastness of the scene, and the combination of doleful brownish-grey and yellow shades helps to express the melancholy mood. Other details—the little cottage at the side of the road, the figures of a peasant and a little girl wandering out in the dismal weather—add more weight to the impression of homelessness. The sad lyricism of the painting evokes thoughts of the poverty and unsettled nature of Russian life, and there is a hint of the social motif characteristic of the art of the time. This idea is expressed emotionally, however, not obtrusively or didactically. *The Thaw* gave a new direction to Russian landscape-painting; its author, according to Kramskoi, 'was destined to introduce into the Russian landscape what it had always lacked—poetry as well as naturalness of execution'. The work was awarded a prize at a competition of the Society for the Furtherance of the Arts, and in 1872 it was sent to an exhibition in London, where it also met with success. The *Morning Post* published a review expressing confidence that no one was better qualified than the author of this work to paint the streets of London during the thaw and Vasiliev was invited to London; but the artist was no longer in St. Petersburg when this news arrived.

In the winter of 1871 Vasiliev had contracted tuberculosis and in July he went to Yalta at the expense of the Society for the Furtherarre of the Arts.

In Yalta Vasiliev continued to paint—from sketches, studies and memories. In 1872 he produced his masterpiece—*A Wet Meadow*

NINETEENTH
CENTURY

F. A. VASILIEV

FIFTY
RUSSIAN
ARTISTS
131

2

(TG)—a generalised evocation of Russian nature. The fine balance of the composition, the complex colour relations and the picture's smooth rhythm convey an impression of grandeur and significance. *A Wet Meadow* is one of the finest examples of Russian landscape-painting.

Vasiliev's life in the Crimea was not happy. Far from the centre of Russia, he was deprived of the chance to see the works of other artists; moreover, he was perpetually in financial straits and was even forced to accept a commission by Grand Prince Vladimir Alexandrovich for Crimean landscapes. Carrying out this commission was a torture for the artist, who was uninspired by the Crimea, and he produced only one painting: *Eriklik* (1872, RM), a view of the Yalta bay from the mountains. The painting turned out cold and rather unsuccessful.

With time, however, Vasiliev grew accustomed to the Crimean scenery and found spots that

harmonised with his mental state—principally the unpopulated, wild, mountainous areas. *In the Crimean Mountains* (1873, TG), is a romantic elevated image of the Crimea. The solemn rhythm of the composition and the severe, almost monochromatic colouring evoke a tragic mood of abandonment. Ivan Kramskoi wrote: '. . . there is something misty, almost mystical, bewitching, as though it were not a picture but a symphony, reaching our ears from above, and below, on Earth where objects should be real . . . a sick and suffering man. Never before had I imagined that a landscape could evoke such strong sensations . . .'

In the last year of his life Vasiliev was again seized by a feeling of loneliness and homesickness, and he painted the Russian landscapes *Derelict Windmill* (1872-73, TG) and *Marsh in the Forest. Autumn* (1872-73, RM). The emotion and sorrow with which the artist worked at that time may be judged from his letter to Kramskoi:

FIFTY
RUSSIAN
ARTISTS
132

F. A. VASILIEV

NINETEENTH
CENTURY

3

2. A Wet Meadow
3. Marsh in the Forest. Autumn

'In this instance I want to depict morning over a marshland. Don't think, by the way, that this is a real marsh. No, the real one lies ahead, and this is only a preparation. Oh that marsh! If only you knew how my heart aches with dark foreboding. Shall I really never again breathe this freedom, this life-giving power of the morning awaking over the misty water? For everything, everything will be taken from me if this is taken. As an artist I shall lose more than half the world.'

The picture was painted during a sweltering Crimean summer, but what appeared on the canvas was a Russian autumn. There is a dense forest, and a marsh grown with unusual grasses and ferns; it is an eerie, ugly swamp, eternally wrapped in a sinister desolate silence; the shadow of a dark cloud which hangs above the woods lies motionless over the water, and the last ray of sun lights up the foliage in a fantastic flame; everything is still, holding its breath. The motif is very simple, and the viewer is affected above all by the painting itself—the colour and texture. The artist succeeded in subtly conveying the wealth of autumn colours, isolating what is most important in the juxtaposition of the blue sky and reddish leaves. The colour contrasts and dynamic brushwork express the tension in nature before a storm and the tragedy of the artist's sufferings. With this work Vasiliev set the course of Russian landscape-painting for a long time to come.

Marsh in the Forest. Autumn was the artist's farewell to his homeland. Vasiliev died on 24 September 1873 and was buried in the Old Massandra Cemetery in Yalta.

NINETEENTH
CENTURY

FIFTY
RUSSIAN
ARTISTS
133

Arkhip Ivanovich KUINJI

(1842-1910)

It is no accident that Arkhip Kuinji is sometimes known as the bard of the Ukrainian night. And although he also painted the severe scenery of the island of Valaam, Ukrainian highways awash with rain, and the flowering steppe, it is for his inimitable evocations of the beauty and mysterious charm of Ukrainian moonlit nights that he will always be remembered.

The son of a poor cobbler of Greek descent, Kuinji was born on the outskirts of Mariupole (now Zhdanov). His surname came from his grandfather's nickname and means 'goldsmith' in Tatar. Orphaned at an early age, the boy lived with relatives and took on various jobs—with a corn-merchant, a contractor, and as a retoucher with a photographer.

Kuinji received the rudiments of education from a Greek friend of the family who was a teacher, and then went to the local school. In his childhood he used to draw whenever there was an opportunity—on fences, walls and scraps of paper. His passion for drawing drew him to Feodosia, to see Ivan Aivazovsky. After spending several months with the famous artist he went to St. Petersburg with the dream of entering the Academy of Arts. But he did not succeed in this at once: he was, as yet, poorly trained. Twice he took examinations, both times without success, but this did not deter the persistent young man. In 1868 he had a picture—*Tatar House*—exhibited at the Academy, and later that year he was accepted as an external student. Kuinji immersed himself in the artistic atmosphere. He made friends with Ilya Repin and Viktor Vasnetsov, and was an acquaintance of Ivan Kramskoi, the ideologist of the progressive Russian artists. Now the young painter's eyes were opened up to the lyrical landscapes of Savrasov, to the poetic perception of nature in Vasiliev's pictures and to Shishkin's epic canvases.

Kuinji set about defining his own style in art. In its realism, his painting *Bad Roads in Autumn* (1872, RM) was akin to the works of the *peredvizhniki* Artists. He did not merely paint a cold autumn day and a slushy road with murky pud-

1. I. Ye. Repin. Portrait of A. I. Kuinji

FIFTY
RUSSIAN
ARTISTS
134

A. I. KUINJI

NINETEENTH
CENTURY

dles: into this landscape he introduced the lonely figures of a woman and child, picking their way through the mud. The autumn landscape, with its dampness and gloom, became the sad story of the Russian common people and their weary, joyless lives.

The summer of 1872 was spent on the island of Valaam in Lake Ladoga, and as a result Kuinji painted the pictures *Lake Ladoga* (1872, RM) and *On the Island of Valaam* (1873, TG). The latter is a calm, unhurried narrative about the scenery of the island, with its granite banks and its dark, dense woods and fallen trees. It is like a folk epic, descriptive legend of the mighty North. The painting's silvery-bluish tone lends it great emotionality. After the exhibition in 1873 at which the painting was put on display, Kuinji's great talent and originality began to be discussed in the press.

In 1874 Kuinji painted *A Forgotten Village* (TG) which, with the sharp social message in its strikingly truthful depiction of Russian village life, echoed the pictures of the Travelling Artists. The following year he exhibited three more paintings: *Highway at Mariupole* (TG), *The Steppe in Blossom* and *The Steppe in the Evening* (whereabouts unknown). In the first of these three works, the artist depicted an unending stream of carts slowly moving across the steppe on an overcast autumn day. The sense of coldness and dampness is heightened by the aptly chosen range of colours.

In the other two—*The Steppe in Blossom* and *The Steppe in the Evening*—the artist affirmed the beauty of nature, rejoicing in the life-giving power of the warmth of the sun. In essence, these works marked the beginning of a new stage in the work of a mature artist. Hoping to broaden his knowledge Kuinji undertook a journey abroad. His stays in Britain, France, Belgium and Germany, and his acquaintance with the art of these countries, invigorated him with new impressions and also bolstered his confidence in his own strengths and in the rightness of his chosen path. In 1876 Kuinji put the painting *Ukrainian Night* (TG) on display at the Fifth *Peredvizhniki* Exhibition.

With tremendous poetic power the painting reveals the remarkable beauty of a Ukrainian night ... Typical Ukrainian cottages, clear in the moonlight, stand along the bank of a small river; poplars stretch upwards; nature is bathed in silence and calm; stars blink in the deep-blue, velvety sky. In order to convey the moonlight and the twinkling of the stars so naturally and expressively, the artist was required to solve extremely complex artistic problems. Everything in the picture is built on his masterly treatment of tonal relationships, on the accentuated generalisation of forms and on the intensity and precision of the colour combinations. The originality of Kuinji's manner of painting attracted the attention of both Russian and foreign critics. In 1878 *Ukrainian Night* was shown at a World Exhibition in Paris. 'Kuinji,' wrote a French critic, 'is indubitably the most interesting of the young Russian painters. His nationality shows through even more strongly than with the others.'

In 1879 Kuinji painted three landscapes: *The North, After a Thunderstorm,* and *Birch Grove* (all in TG). Though their motifs are different, they are united by their poetry. *The North* continued the series of northern landscapes started with *Lake Ladoga*. This time Kuinji did not depict any particular spot: it is a generalised poetic representation of the North, the result of the artist's recollections and imagination. The painting completed the trilogy conceived back in 1872. After this Kuinji devoted many years to extolling the scenery of southern and central Russia. *After a Thunderstorm* is full of life, movement and a sense of the freshness of nature after a downpour. But the painting which enjoyed most success when these three were exhibited was *Birch Grove*. Crowds of people stood for hours in front of it; it was as though the sun itself had burst into the exhibition hall, illuminating the grassy glade and playing on the white bark and green leaves of the birches. During his work

NINETEENTH
CENTURY

A. I. KUINJI

FIFTY
RUSSIAN
ARTISTS
135

2

on the picture, Kuinji's chief concern was to find the most expressive composition. From sketch to sketch he gradually arrived at the perfect positioning of the trees and dimensions of the glade; in the final version there is nothing fortuitous, nothing merely 'copied' from nature. The foreground is in shadow, and this accentuates the richness and brilliance of the green glade. Avoiding theatrical effects, the artist succeeded in creating a decorative picture in the best sense of the word. It is an inspired glorification of the beauty and poetry of nature, of the blinding power of sunshine.

In 1880 an unusual exhibition was mounted on Bolshaya Morskaya (now Herzen) Street in St. Petersburg: one painting was on display —Kuinji's *Moonlit Night on the Dnieper* (RM).

It caused a storm of approval: a long queue formed at the entrance to the exhibition.

Kuinji became the talk of the town, his name was on everybody's lips. The poet Yakov Polonsky wrote: 'I positively cannot think of any other painting in front of which people stood for so long, and from which, having gazed and gazed, they took away with them such an extraordinary impression.'

The picture shackled the onlookers' attention. Illuminated from both sides by special lamps, it seemed like a window opening onto a bewitching Ukrainian night.

. . . The Dnieper is calm, unruffled, in the pale moonlight. A little Ukrainian village lies asleep on the bank, only a few white-walled cottages gleam in the darkness . . . The moonlight is mag-

FIFTY
RUSSIAN
ARTISTS
136

A. I. KUINJI

NINETEENTH
CENTURY

nificent—strong in the centre, comprising all shades of green, it gradually fades towards the sides of the painting, merging into the blackness of the water and clouds. Many people could not believe that the artist had painted all this by normal artistic methods.

Kuinji's brilliant technique of reproducing moonlight was the result of long arduous searching. His studio was a research laboratory, where he experimented and studied the laws of colours, searching for the correct shade, checking it against the colour relations in nature itself. It was only by such persistence that Kuinji achieved the skill in manipulating colour and the compositional simplicity which mark his best works.

In 1881 Kuinji painted the picture *The Dnieper in the Morning* (TG). This time there was no play of light or vivid decorativeness; the painting expressed the tranquil grandeur and inner might of nature. The delightful sight of early morning over the steppe, with blooming herbs and a boundless panorama, is put across in a delicate fabric of pure golden-pink, lilac, silvery and greenish-grey shades.

The exhibition in 1882 was Kuinji's last. It was followed by many years of silence, which even the artist's friends could not understand. Kuinji himself explained it thus: 'An artist should display his works at exhibitions for as long—like a singer—as he has a voice. But as soon as his voice begins to falter he should retire, and not show himself, to avoid derision. I made a name for myself, everybody had heard of me, and all was well; but then I saw that I could not keep it up, that my voice, as it were, was beginning to falter. And people would say: there used to be an artist called Kuinji. But I would rather remain Kuinji for ever.'

In his last thirty years he produced relatively little, compared to the decade when he took an active part in exhibitions. According to the reminiscences of his friends, Kuinji invited them to his studio at the beginning of this century and showed them the paintings *Evening in the Ukraine, Christ in the Garden at Gethsemane,*

The Dnieper and *Birch Grove*, by which they were enraptured. But Kuinji was dissatisfied with them and would not exhibit them publicly.

Horses Grazing at Night, one of Kuinji's last works, reminds one of the artist in his prime. Here, too, one feels his poetic attitude to nature, his attempt to extol its stately beauty.

Several other pictures, interesting in intention and new in content, remained unfinished. In *A Cloud, Crimea* and *Fog on the Sea* (1900-05, RM), for example, the artist was seeking a more philosophical, more profound treatment of nature.

In his later years Kuinji travelled widely. He was attracted to the Crimean and Caucasian mountains, snow-capped and lit up by the sun or moon (cf. the études *Elbrus, Moonlit Night, Kazbek in the Evening, Patches of Moonlight,* etc.).

Kuinji's artistic method involved a great deal of preparatory painted études and studies. In his studies he sought compositional expressiveness and harmonious colouring for the future painting. His études, on the other hand, which were painted both from nature and from impressions, were for him only one of the stages in the work, preliminary paintings which could later be reworked in the final process of creating a picture.

Kuinji passed on much of his skill and experience to his pupils. In 1894 he was offered a post at the Academy as professor of landscape-painting. He gave long consideration to his teaching methods, wishing to instill in his pupils not only professional skills but also an active attitude towards creation. In his pupils' études he wished to see the result of a close study of nature, and in their paintings—freedom in using the material of the études and in generalising their observations. Among those who benefited by his methods were such talented artists as A. A. Rylov, N. K. Roerich, K. F. Bogayevsky, A. A. Borisov, V.G. Purvit and others.

In 1897 Kuinji was put under house arrest for two days and stripped of his professorship for

NINETEENTH
CENTURY

A. I. KUINJI

FIFTY
RUSSIAN
ARTISTS
137

3

taking part in a student strike. But he continued to give private lessons and helped students prepare works for competitions. In 1898, at his own expense, he organised a trip abroad for young artists and made a donation of 100,000 roubles to the Academy for this purpose. When his pupils decided to set up a Kuinji Society, the artist presented it with all the paintings and money in his possession, plus the land he owned in the Crimea.

On 11 July 1910, Arkhip Kuinji died. With his sincere and inspired art he had brought glory to Russian art and made an invaluable contribution to its treasure-store.

2. Moonlit Night on the Dnieper
3. Birch Grove

Viktor Mikhailovich VASNETSOV

(1848-1926)

1

Viktor Vasnetsov was born into the large patriarchal family of the local priest in the remote village of Lopyal, near Vyatka. Shortly thereafter the family moved to the village of Ryabovo where the artist's childhood passed. He began drawing at an early age, but tradition had it that sons should follow in their fathers' footsteps and in 1858 he was sent to an ecclesiastical school, and in a short time to the Vyatka theological seminary.

Vyatka Gubernia was famous at that time for its folk arts and crafts. The craftsmen and women produced all sorts of things—embroidery, wood-carving (from shaft-bows and household articles to shutters for peasant houses), painted spoons and furniture, decorated clay toys and the famous Vyatka gingerbread cakes —and all these artefacts must have been familiar to the inquisitive young boy.

The countryside of that area, with its hilly copses and dense forest, its meandering streams and broad valleys, has a special charm of its own: it would be impossible not to fall in love with it. From his earliest years Vasnetsov heard folk legends and epic tales about the Russian heroes, or 'bogatyrs', and sad, drawling songs sung by the womenfolk on evenings lit by burning splinters. All this, of course, influenced the future artist's outlook: it was here, in Vyatka, that his passionate affection for art and for the folk epic was born.

At the seminary, Vasnetsov used every spare minute to draw, and soon this passion developed from a pleasurable pastime into the main point of his life. He did not become a priest, as his father desired. In his final year at the seminary Vasnetsov resolved to leave Vyatka for St. Petersburg and enter the Academy of Arts.

By raffling two of his genre paintings—*The Milkmaid* and *The Reaper* (1867)—he made enough money to get to St. Petersburg and start studying at the school run by the Society for the Furtherance of the Arts. In 1868 he became a pupil at the Academy. Forced to pay his own

1. Self-Portrait

NINETEENTH
CENTURY

V. M. VASNETSOV

FIFTY
RUSSIAN
ARTISTS
139

way in life, Vasnetsov gave private lessons and illustrated various publications.

At the Academy he made friends with Repin, Antokolsky, Kramskoi and Stasov. His favourite teacher was Pavel Chistyakov who immediately realised his remarkable talent and worked with him, encouraging him when things went badly and rejoicing in his triumphs. 'My conversations with Pavel Chistyakov brought much warmth and light into my life,' he recalled. Vasnetsov studied at the Academy from 1868 to 1875.

His first paintings—*Beggars, Tea-Drinking, Workman with Wheelbarrow, Old Woman Feeding Hens* and *Children Destroying Nests* —were displayed in 1872-74 at exhibitions of the Society for the Furtherance of the Arts. They revealed what were to be two of Vasnetsov's most characteristic qualities—keen observation and a close interest in the life of the people. His next two works—*The Little Book-Shop* (1876, TG) and *From House to House* (1876, TG)—clinched his reputation as a genre artist who knew life and who knew how to reproduce it vividly and expressively.

Stasov justly remarked that Vasnetsov loved the people 'not like a Populist or a nobleman, with a condescending, artificial love, but simply, as his friends and acquaintances'. Especially successful was the picture *From House to House,* which Vasnetsov began in 1875. The fate of poor, lonely old people, thrown onto the street on a cold and frosty day, looking for refuge, disturbed the artist. This is an alarmingly sad painting, which tells the tragedy of people unwanted and homeless in their old age. 'I think we have all come across such people,' wrote Stasov. 'What poverty! How sad is human nature! A wonderful painting!'

In 1876, on the persistent advice of his friends, Vasnetsov went abroad and settled in the outskirts of Paris, where he did a lot of work from nature. His album from this period was full of drawings of people from the 'lower estates', workers and peasants, and the principal result of his observations was the painting *Showbooths in the Outskirts of Paris* (1877, RM).

In 1878, back in Russia, Vasnetsov moved with his family to Moscow. 'When I arrived in Moscow,' he wrote, 'I felt I had arrived home and need travel no further; the Kremlin and Saint Basil's brought tears to my eyes, so dear to my soul, so unforgettable were they.' Here he turned to new subjects—the Russian folk epic, the fairy-tale, and Russian history. This change from genre-painting to historical was not entirely unexpected: even while at the Academy Vasnetsov had done a series of sketches on epic themes and also a study entitled *The Icon-Painting Workshop.*

'There was never a conflict within me between genre and history,' he wrote, 'and therefore there was no turning-point or transitional struggle... I have always been convinced that both genre and historical pictures, and fairy-tales, songs, folk epics and dramas, all reflect the whole inner and outer make-up of a nation, with its past and present, and perhaps even its future... It is a poor nation that does not remember, value and love its history.'

His first historical painting, *After the Battle of Igor Svyatoslavich with the Polovtsi* (1880, TG), was shown at the Eighth *Peredvizhniki* Exhibition. The old Russian legend related in *The Lay of Igor's Host* appealed to Vasnetsov because of its great epic power. Having decided to use a motif from the immortal poem, he studied history, visited the Armoury and made a great many preparatory études, searching for the best way to treat the subject. Gradually he progressed from sketches showing the fury and intensity of the battle to a solemn evocation of the tragedy of it. Striving to convey both the deep purport and the heroic tenor of the poem, the artist depicted the fallen warriors, lying as though asleep in the never-ending southern steppe, in the light of the ascending moon. The work marked a change in the artist's creative manner: from small, detailed pictures he turned now to a large, sweeping monumental canvas.

FIFTY
RUSSIAN
ARTISTS
140

V. M. VASNETSOV

NINETEENTH
CENTURY

The dark grey-brown colouring of his earlier works is replaced by rich, though restrained yellows, blues, reds and greyish-greens. The painting did not win general recognition. Some, like Pavel Chistyakov, acclaimed it as an 'unusual, remarkable, new and deeply poetical work' while others, not understanding Vasnetsov's innovatoriness, were more than indifferent towards it.

In Moscow Vasnetsov got to know the family of a famous art patron, the rich industrialist Savva Mamontov, who had grouped around himself the flower of the Russian intelligentsia. Many artists would spend the summer at Abramtsevo, Mamontov's estate near Moscow, where theatrical productions were staged and artists had ample opportunities for fruitful work. In 1881 at Abramtsevo Vasnetsov painted one of his best works, *Alenushka* (TG), on the Russian fairy-tale subject. The gentleness and poetry of the fairy-tale touched the artist's sensitive, responsive heart. The painting, however, does not literally reproduce the story of the fairy-tale, but gets to the bottom of its emotional structure. The little girl's posture, her head bent, her chestnut hair bouncing on her shoulders, her gaze full of sadness—everything speaks of Alenushka's sorrow. Nature, too, is in consonance with the girl's mood, mourning, as it were, in sympathy. The slender birches and young firs around Alenushka seem to be guarding her from the evil world. *Alenushka* was one of the first pictures in Russian art in which the poetry of folk-tales was inseparably fused with the lyricism of the Russian countryside.

At Abramtsevo Vasnetsov helped to produce sets for an amateur production in 1881 of a play based on the fairy-tale *The Snow Maiden*. The actors were the members of Mamontov's circle, and Vasnetsov played the part of Frost. Vasnetsov's stage-decorations did much to convey the charm of the lyrical tale: 'Never before,' wrote Stasov, 'had the imagination gone so far and so deep in recreating the fabulous,

legendary, epic architectural forms and ornaments of Ancient Rus.' Stasov managed to have the decorations transferred to the large professional stage of Mamontov's private opera house. Vasnetsov also did some work as an architect at Abramtsevo: he designed a small church-cum-burial-vault which can still be seen in the grounds. In the early 1900s the main façade of the Tretyakov Gallery, and several private houses, were built according to Vasnetsov's designs.

One very interesting piece of work was Vasnetsov's frieze—*The Stone Age*—which he made for the Moscow Historical Museum. At first Vasnetsov categorically rejected the suggestion of the historian A. S. Uvarov to produce a mural depicting the people of the stone age. Presently, however, he agreed to take the commission and immediately set about the work. He studied historical documents and held discussions with archeologists to gain insight into stone age life. His work on the 25-metre-long frieze took about two years—both in Moscow and Abramtsevo—and was not completed until 10 April 1885.

'The impression made by *The Stone Age* on the artist's contemporaries,' wrote the artist and art historian Igor Grabar, 'can probably be compared only to that once made by Karl Bryullov's *Pompeii*.'

Vasnetsov's talent as a monumental artist was so manifest that he was invited the same year to help decorate the recently built St. Vladimir's Cathedral in Kiev. The murals, as conceived by Vasnetsov, were to be a monument to ancient Rus, for which reason they are largely devoted to portrayals of princes—Vladimir, Andrei Bogolyubsky, Alexander Nevsky, Dmitri Donskoi and others. Vasnetsov covered the walls of the Cathedral with ornamental decorations in which fantastic flowers and strange animals were interwoven in whimsical, colourful patterns. The work entailed certain difficulties: the church's rulers demanded murals in the official, traditional style, but the artist could not re-

NINETEENTH
CENTURY

V. M. VASNETSOV

FIFTY
RUSSIAN
ARTISTS
141

2

nounce his perception of the world, nor his realist aspirations. It is not, therefore, the stylised faces of saints that look down from the walls of St. Vladimir's Cathedral, but convincingly portrayed Russian people, brave, powerful champions of freedom and justice.

Vasnetsov's intense work on the Cathedral did not prevent him from realising other artistic plans. In 1889 he painted the picture *Tsarevich Ivan on a Grey Wolf* (TG) and displayed it at a *Peredvizhniki* Exhibition, and did illustrations for Lermontov's *The Lay of Tsar Ivan Vassilyevich, His Young Oprichnik and the Stouthearted Merchant Kalashnikov* (1891).

In 1891 Vasnetsov and his family returned from Kiev to Moscow and settled near Abramtsevo. With the help of Tretyakov, who bought his pictures and études, and Mamontov, Vasnetsov realised a long-cherished dream

of his—to design and build his own studio. Here he began work on the painting *Bogatyrs,* a study for which he had done many years before.

The picture *Ivan the Terrible* (TG) appeared at the Tenth *Peredvizhniki* Exhibition in 1897. At his first personal exhibition in 1898 Vasnetsov presented *Bogatyrs,* on which he had worked, all in all, for about twenty years.

In this large monumental-decorative work, the artist recreated the images of the three favourite heroes of the Russian folk epic: Ilya Muromets, Dobrynya Nikitich and Alyosha Popovich. Each of them has his own individual characteristics.

To intensify the monumental effect, Vasnetsov raises the line of the horizon somewhat, and the viewer seems to look up from below

FIFTY
RUSSIAN
ARTISTS
142

V. M. VASNETSOV

NINETEENTH
CENTURY

3

is suppressed and trampled on, while in the latter it is triumphant, calm and important, unafraid and accomplishing by its own will whatever it regards as necessary for all the people.'

Maxim Gorky wrote enthusiastically about the artist: 'I love and respect this great bard more and more . . And how many more living, beautiful, mighty subjects there are for him to treat! I wish him immortality.'

At the beginning of the new century Vasnetsov executed numerous compositions on religious subjects and worked simultaneously on several pictures—*The Bard* (1910, RM), *The Sleeping Princess, The Frog Princess* (1918), *Kashchei the Deathless* (1917-26), *The Princess Who Would Not Laugh* (1914-26)—and on other large compositions (all in the Vasnetsov House Museum in Moscow).

The artist's creative imagination seemed inexhaustible, but many of his plans were fated never to be realised. On 23 July 1926 Vasnetsov died in his studio in Moscow, while working on a portrait of the artist Mikhail Nesterov.

at the horsemen, who are clearly silhouetted against the bright clouds. The canvas is all the more decorative because of the delicate, noble combination of bright, rich colours —green, brown, red, white and blue. The broad landscape, with its sloping hills and meadows overgrown with wild grass, is united with the figures of the epic heroes by the picture's smooth, calm rhythms.

In 1898 *Bogatyrs* was given a place of honour in the Tretyakov Gallery. 'I consider Vasnetsov's *Bogatyrs* to be one of the foremost works in the history of Russian painting,' wrote Vladimir Stasov. Comparing Repin's *Barge-Haulers* with Vasnetsov's picture, the critic went on: 'Both express all the power and might of the Russian people. Only, in the former that power

2. Bogatyrs
3. Alenushka

NINETEENTH
CENTURY

FIFTY
RUSSIAN
ARTISTS
143

Vasily Vasilyevich VERESHCHAGIN

(1842-1904)

The great Russian battle-painter Vasily Vereshchagin, the son of a landowner, was born in Cherepovets. When he was eight he was sent to the Junior Cadet Corps, and in 1853 he was transferred to the St. Petersburg Naval School. It was here that he developed an interest in drawing and began to devote more and more time to it. In 1858 Vereshchagin began to attend drawing classes at the St. Petersburg Society for the Furtherance of the Arts. His teachers gave good reports about his progress, and he himself now dreamt of becoming an artist.

In 1860, having graduated from Naval School with flying colours, Vereshchagin sent in his papers against his parents' wishes and entered the Academy of Arts. Outraged by this action, his father cut off all material assistance and Vereshchagin was left to fend for himself. He applied himself wholeheartedly to painting, but the Academy system of teaching, with its standards and traditions, weighed heavy on the artist. As an act of protest he destroyed one of his paintings—*Ulysses' Slaughter of the Young Men of Penelopa*. In 1863 he left the Academy and went to the Caucasus 'to learn from interesting objects of Nature'. His first independent works were numerous drawings of popular types, genre scenes and Caucasian landscapes.

In 1866, living in the village of Lyubets on the River Sheksna, Vereshchagin observed the backbreaking work of the barge-haulers. He planned a large painting which would show the desperate fate of poor folk in tsarist Russia, but, though he did several studies on this theme, the work was never completed.

In 1867 he went to Turkestan, which was then the scene of military confrontations. 'I went to find out what war, about which I had read and heard so much, was really like . . .' Not only did he witness the war; he took part in it. In 1868 he joined the Russian garrison defending the Samarkand fortress against the troops of the Emir of Bukhara and was given the George Cross for bravery and courage. In 1869-70 Vereshchagin undertook another trip to Turkestan; he learnt

FIFTY
RUSSIAN
ARTISTS
144

V. V. VERESHCHAGIN

NINETEENTH
CENTURY

about the country, studied the customs and mores of the feudal East and as a result created a large series of pictures about Central Asia.

The exotic character of the sunny East and the people's colourful dress did not blind the great artist and humanist to their poverty and lack of civil rights: cf. *Beggars in Samarkand* (1870, TG), *Opium Smokers* (Uzbek State Museum of Arts), *Sale of a Slave Child* (1872, TG), *Samarkand Dungeon* (Uzbek State Museum of Arts), *Uzbek Woman in Tashkent* (1873, TG) and many others. Having complete control over his brush, the artist uses rich colours to convey the scorching southern sky, the vernal green steppe, the cool of mountain tops covered with snow, and the complicated ornamentation of the buildings in Samarkand . . .

Central to this series were Vereshchagin's battle-pieces, and it was they that enjoyed greatest success both in Russia and abroad, and helped determine the basic orientation of the artist's work. From his earliest works Vereshchagin spoke out in protest against aggressive wars, throwing the blame at the feet of those who were responsible for the deaths of human beings. This antimilitarist stance was the result of the artist's personal observations and deliberations on the matter. He introduced to battle-painting a bare-faced truthfulness which Russian art had never known before. His heroes were soldiers, the simple Russian people— 'only wearing uniforms and carrying rifles', as Stasov wrote.

In the picture *At the Fortress Wall. Let Them In* (1871, TG) Russian soldiers anxiously await battle. Their faces are stern, their poses resolute. The picture *They Entered* showed the same place in the fortress, but after the battle. In a series of battle-pieces Vereshchagin develops his thoughts about the cruelty of feudal lords, about the barbarity of battle orders and about the heroism and courage of Russian soldiers: *Looking Out* (1873, TG), *Surprise Attack* (1871, TG), *Display of Trophies* (1872, TG), *They Are Triumphant* (1872, TG) and *Apotheosis of War* (1871-72, TG).

Apotheosis of War shows a pyramid of human skulls against the background of a town destroyed by war and charred trees. The original idea for the picture was linked with the name of the Central Asian conqueror of the late fourteenth and early fifteenth centuries, Tamerlane, whose troops used to leave such pyramids behind them. But the meaning of the painting extends beyond its historical context. Ruins, skulls and wasteland have always been seen as symbols of death and devastation, and Vereshchagin inscribed the frame with the words: 'Dedicated to all great conquerors, past, present and future.' *Apotheosis of War* is a crushing condemnation of all wars that bring destruction and unhappiness.

'I do not know if there is any artist equal to him at the present time, either here or abroad,' wrote Ivan Kramskoi. Vereshchagin's bold accusatory paintings drew a hostile attitude from reactionary circles in Russia who accused him of slandering the Russian army. The artist took these unjust accusations badly and burned three paintings: *The Forgotten Soldier, They Have Encircled and Pursue* and *They Entered*. A ban was placed on exhibitions of Vereshchagin's works and on reproductions of them in books and periodicals. For thirty years the tsarist government did not acquire a single picture by the already world-famous artist. Pavel Tretyakov bought most of his Turkestan works.

In 1874-76 and 1882-83 Vereshchagin made two trips to India to study the scenery and way of life of the country. On this journey he had to contend with all sorts of difficulties: he almost froze to death in the snowy heights of the Himalayas, and in the fatiguing tropical heat he fell ill with a fever. It was a productive period, however, and he painted more than 150 études depicting the grandeur of Indian white-stone architecture, the blue of the tropical sky and the Indians' gay national costumes. Among his best études were *Buddhist Temple at Darjeeling* (1874-75, TG), *Glacier on the Road from Kashmir to Ladakh* (1875, TG) and *The Taj Mahal* (1874-76, TG).

INETEENTH
CENTURY

V. V. VERESHCHAGIN

FIFTY
RUSSIAN
ARTISTS
145

Wait, Let Them Come Nearer
Tamerlane's Guards
Photograph of V. V. Vereshchagin
Mortally Wounded

4

Vereshchagin decided to devote a series of ictures to the British takeover of India. His lan was to create a large pictorial poem about he historical fate of India, about its transforma-on from a powerful independent country into a British colony. His plan was only partly realised, owever, one of the best paintings being *The Procession of the British and Native Authorities 1 Jeypore* (1875-79, Victoria Memorial Museum, Calcutta).

The Russo-Turkish war which broke out in 877-78 again brought Vereshchagin to the ront. Wholeheartedly supporting the liberation truggle of the Slavs, he took part in many bat-tles. In one of them he was seriously wounded and almost died.

'It would be impossible,' wrote Vereshchagin, 'to achieve the aim I have set myself, to give society a picture of war as it really is, by observing battles through binoculars from a comfortable distance: I have to feel and go through it all myself, I have to participate in the attacks, storms, victories and defeats, experience cold, disease and wounds. I must not be afraid to sacrifice my flesh and my blood, otherwise my pictures will mean nothing.'

Once again war appeared in Vereshchagin's paintings as a dramatic event, severe and coura-

FIFTY
RUSSIAN
ARTISTS
146

V. V. VERESHCHAGIN

NINETEENT
CENTURY

geous. The artist painfully and bitterly regretted the enormous toll of human lives in this bloody war in the Balkans.

The pictures of the Balkans series reproduce scenes from the war with unexampled realism—the Russian army's difficult marches in the mountains, field hospitals, and Turkish atrocities. The reverse side of war is also shown: the artist demonstrates the careerism and the criminal nature of the tsarist commanders who doomed Russian soldiers to a senseless death. The central group of pictures treats the heroic defence of the Shipka Pass: *Dug-outs on the Shipka* (State Museum of Russian Art, Kiev), *Batteries on the Shipka* (State Museum of Russian Art, Kiev), *All Quiet on the Shipka* (1878-79, whereabouts unknown), *Shipka-Sheinovo* (1878-79, TG).

Several of Vereshchagin's paintings dealt with the storm of Plevna: *Attack* (1881, Central Artillery Historical Museum), *After the Attack* (1881, TG). The pictures entitled *The Victors* (1878-79, State Museum of Russian Art, Kiev) and *The Vanquished. Requiem for the Dead* (1878-79, TG) are concerned with the Battle of Telish, at which the high command was responsible for the annihilation of almost a whole regiment of chasseurs. *The Victors* depicts a grotesque masquerade: the Turks on the field of battle have changed into the uniforms of the dead Russian soldiers; the other—*The Vanquished*—shows an enormous field littered with soldiers' corpses. The paintings of the Balkans series are marked by simplicity and restraint in their colouring, in which either gloomy autumnal or overcast wintry shades prevail. The series was exhibited in St. Petersburg in 1880 and 1883 and its success surpassed all expectations: in forty days it was visited by more than 200,000 people.

The 1880s were marked by great activity, with the artist on the search for new themes. He went to India for the second time (1882-83) and then to Syria and Palestine (1883-84). His 'Palestine series' consisted mainly of études and

pictures of a documental, ethnographical type. Particularly important was his 'trilogy of executions'—*Crucifixion at the Time of the Roma Empire, The Execution of Conspirators in Rus sia* (1884-85, State Museum of the Revolution and *The Suppression of an Indian Uprising b the British* (c. 1884, whereabouts unknown The second picture of the trilogy was inspire by the punishment meted out by the Russia autocracy to members of the revolutionary *N rodnaya Volya* (People's Will) organisation o 3 April 1881.

The fruit of Vereshchagin's travels in th North in the eighties and nineties was a series o drawings and études of ancient woode architectures, the scenery of northern Russi and the common folk. From 1887 to 1901 th artist worked on a series of paintings—mor than twenty—about the Patriotic War of 181. His aim was 'to show in pictures of the 181 War the great national spirit of the Russian peo ple, their selflessness and heroism in fighting a enemy'. Vereshchagin managed to express th emancipatory, popular character of the war an to dethrone Napoleon, setting him down fro the 'hero's pedestal on which he had bee placed'.

The 1812 series begins with the Battle of B rodino, to which Vereshchagin devoted two pi tures—*Napoleon on the Borodino Heigh* (1897) and *The End of the Battle of Borodin* (1899–1900, State Historical Museum). Th stay of Napoleon's army in Moscow is reflecte in fourteen paintings, including *In the Assump tion Cathedral* (1887–95), *The Fire* (1896–97 *Through the Fire* (1899–1900) and *Execution i the Kremlin* (1897–98; all in State Historic: Museum). Several canvases depict the retre: and defeat of the French army—*At Grodno: Strike Back or Retreat?, Halting Place: Ba News From France* (1887–95), *On the Hig Road: Retreat and Flight* (1887–95), *The Gran Army Halts for the Night* (1896–97, State Hi torical Museum). The theme of the popular part san war against the invaders is important in th

NINETEENTH
CENTURY

V. V. VERESHCHAGIN

FIFTY
RUSSIAN
ARTISTS
147

series, and it should be noted that the artist did not portray the celebrated partisan commanders such as D. Davydov and A. Figner but stressed the feat of the ordinary peasants who took part in the popular liberation movement.

. . .The pine-trees are capped with fluffy white snow. The peasants lie in wait of the enemy. Up front, peering into the thick of the forest, stands a tall old man with an axe in his hand. The enemy approaches. The guerillas' faces show trepidation and impatience, but their old, experienced, wise leader restrains them. 'Wait, let them come nearer,' he seems to be saying—and this is the title of the painting (1887-95, State Historical Museum). Here Vereshchagin treats nature in a broad, rather decorative manner, seeking to create a generalised, epic image of the Russian landscape.

The picture *With Gun in Hands—Fire!* (1887–95, State Historical Museum) records the reprisals taken against partisans who fell into the hands of the French. *The Grand Army Halts for the Night,* one of the last works in the series, represents the invaders' ignominious end, the rout of a once invincible army.

Because of its strong patriotic ideas, the depth and acuteness of the subjects, the vivid images of popular types and the interesting compositional structures, this last major series of the artist's made a great contribution to the genre of historical painting of the late nineteenth century.

Vereshchagin continued to travel right up to the end of his life. After his trip to Syria and Palestine at the end of the eighties and beginning of the nineties he twice went to America, in 1901–02 he was in the Philippines and Cuba, and in 1903 he visited Japan. His impressions of Japan found an outlet in a series of études which give some idea of the unusual ancient architecture and national customs of the country.

At the outbreak of the Russo-Japanese War Vereshchagin was busy on several paintings, all of which he dropped and rushed off to the Far East intending to take part in the battles and tell about them in his works. 'Some people,' he wrote, 'spread the idea of peace with powerful words, others defend it by various arguments, religious, economic and others, and I preach the same thing by means of colours.'

On 31 March 1904 Vereshchagin perished, together with Admiral Makarov, on the battleship *Petropavlovsk* which was blown up by an enemy mine near Port Arthur.

FIFTY
RUSSIAN
ARTISTS
148

NINETEENTH
CENTURY

Mark Matveyevich
ANTOKOLSKY

(1843–1902)

1

2

The greatest Russian sculptor of the second half of the nineteenth century, Mark Antokolsky, was born into a large Jewish family of modest means. At nights, instead of resting after his exhausting work in the tavern where he helped his father out, he would give himself up to his favourite occupation—moulding or cutting out little figures. The rest of his family found this hobby of his rather unusual, but still he was later sent to work as an apprentice with a wood-cutter. In 1862 he became an external student at the St. Petersburg Academy of Arts. In the capital Antokolsky mixed with the leading representatives of Russian culture—Shishkin, Vasnetsov, Kramskoi, Stasov, Serov, Mussorgsky—and became a friend of Repin's. He studied in N. S. Pimenov's class, and after his death under the engraver and sculptor I. I. Reimers. His first high reliefs—*Jewish Tailor* (1864, RM) and *Jewish Miser* (1865, RM)—which were awarded with second-class and first–class silver medals respectively, already displayed the artist's tendency towards realism. The critic Stasov wrote: 'None of our sculptors has ever tried to do this kind of thing before; they had no time for such trifles as life and truth, they had to soar somewhere above the clouds, in allegories . . . But now it would be a great fortune for our sculpture if Mr Antokolsky's example did not fall on stony ground.' *

The psychological qualities of these first genre works were not lost when Antokolsky turned to a historical subject in the high relief *The Assault of the Spanish Inquisition on Jews Secretly Celebrating the Passover* (1869, TG).

The first major landmark in Antokolsky's work was the statue *Ivan the Terrible* (1871, bronze, RM; marble, TG; plaster, Kensington Museum, London), which was shown at the First *Peredvizhniki* Exhibition. This image of a

* That reflects the critic's negative attitude to Russian classicism which, as we can see, has produced some brilliant works of plastic art; in the heart of polemics Stasov, while rightly advocating closeness to reality, is too sharp in opposing Antokolsky to previous Russian sculptors. — *Ed.*

NINETEENTH
CENTURY

M. M. ANTOKOLSKY

FIFTY
RUSSIAN
ARTISTS
149

'tormentor and martyr', as Antokolsky called Ivan the Terrible, was clearly influenced by the progressive trends in Russian art and literature. The work had a tremendous impact. The Academy awarded the sculptor the title of academician, and he was spoken of as a master whose spectacular arrival in the sphere of Russian art was 'a consequence not of great talent alone, but of a large heart and an original mind'. Devoid of conventional rhetoric, the statue of Ivan the Terrible is a dramatic, realistic expression of 'a mighty spirit before which the whole Russian land trembled'. The sculptor put his heart into this work—'every cut, every stroke I did with trepidation'—and this shows in the finished work, in the tsar's attitude, gesture and appearance. Nonetheless, the actual form, which the sculptor wanted to 'speak in a terse and powerful language', looks a little dry and diffuse both in marble and in bronze—a fact which naturally impairs the wholeness of the image itself. The success of the work was understandable, however, both because of its evident merits and the tastes of the period, and, it seems, because it was precisely this conception of the 'terrible' tsar that prevailed in the public of the time.

Antokolsky's triumph was quite exceptional. Crowds of people besieged the Academy, where the statue was on display. Ivan Turgenev and Vladimir Stasov wrote enthusiastically in praise of the sculptor.

In 1871, after graduating from the Academy, Antokolsky's ill health forced him to go abroad, to Rome and Paris, and from then on he only occasionally returned home. But his thoughts and affections were always with Russia. 'My whole soul belongs to the country in which I was born and to which I am accustomed,' he wrote to Stasov. 'In the North my heart beats harder. I breathe deeper there and am more sensitive to all that goes on there. That is why whatever I do will always be the result of those heartfelt impressions that Mother Russia imbued me with.'

On his arrival in Rome Antokolsky began work on a statue of Peter the Great which he had planned while still in Russia. It is an integrated, energetic work, embodying both the character of the great reformer and the age of progress in Russia which 'came of age with the genius of Peter'. The statue served as a model for monuments in Taganrog and Arkhangelsk; a smaller version is kept at Peterhof; and it is represented by bronze copies in the Tretyakov Gallery and the Russian Museum. A comparison of these almost contemporaneous works— *Ivan the Terrible* and *Peter the Great*— clearly illustrates the sculptor's ability to find different artistic means to embody personalities representative of two critical periods in Russian history.

At the same time as working on the statue of Peter the Great, Antokolsky produced studies for equestrian statues of Yaroslav the Wise, Dmitri Donskoi and Ivan III, which were to be erected on the Alexandrovsky Bridge over the Neva and would have formed a kind of 'sculptural gallery' of major Russian historical figures.The plan was never realised, however, as the architectural draft was not approved. This work marked the end of what may be regarded as the first period in the sculptor's development. Now Antokolsky was drawn to new characters and heroes. 'From now on,' wrote Stasov, 'dramatic power, effervescence, emotion and enthusiasm were absent from his works. The former stormy activity of his heroes disappeared and was replaced by benign passivity—though full of poetry, humanity, peace of mind and indignation at evil and falsity.'

The first of these new heroes was *Christ Judged by the People* (1874, bronze, RM; marble, TG). In the sculptor's own words, his Christ conformed to 'the image we have of him in the nineteenth century'. It is no coincidence that other artists such as Kramskoi, Ghe and Polenov also treated the image of Christ. In Antokolsky's interpretation (about which he often spoke in his letters to Vladimir Stasov, excerpts from which are cited below) the image of

FIFTY
RUSSIAN
ARTISTS
150

M. M. ANTOKOLSKY

NINETEENTH
CENTURY

Christ is linked not so much with the accepted religious legend as with the moral problems of past history and contemporary life. The underlying idea—that of self-sacrifice—was permeating the sculptor's work more and more. But in contrast to the active images of Repin and Yaroshenko—images of 'active resistance', as it were (e.g. Repin's *Refusal to Confess* and *The Arrest of a Propagandist,* Yaroshenko's *Lithuanian Castle* and *The Prisoner)*—the leading idea in Antokolsky's work is one of a martyr's estrangement and doom. Christ's appearance contains both silent reproach and the conviction of a preacher. At the same time, he is outwardly calm, and this is the true power of elevated feeling that penetrates the inmost recesses of the human soul. It was such 'difficult simplicity' that Antokolsky was aspiring to in this image: 'In the statue I wanted to create quietness and profundity, outer simplicity and inner depth . . .'

For all their differences in character, most of Antokolsky's heroes share a common striving for truth, sometimes at the cost of their own lives. Such, for example, are *Socrates' Death* (1875, marble, RM) and *Spinoza* (1882, marble, RM). As an antithesis to this, as early as 1874 the sculptor conceived the idea for a statue of Mephistopheles. His *Mephistopheles,* earlier called *The Nineteenth Century* (1883, marble, RM; smaller copy in marlbe, TG) is not so much the embodiment of all evil as the personification of tormenting doubt and scepticism; the sharp, angular forms and sarcastic face lend the image great expressiveness.

In the seventies Antokolsky also worked in the genre of memorial sculpture. One of his most moving works was a gravestone for M. A. Obolenskaya at the Monte Testaccio Cemetery in Rome (1874; plaster model in Scientific-Research Museum of the Academy of Arts). The sculptor was shaken by the death of a girl whose intelligence and virtue he valued highly, and the memorial expresses his strong, sincere emotions.

Antokolsky attached great importance to portraiture. In June 1873 he wrote to Stasov from Rome: '. . . I should like to make busts of all the outstanding people there are in Russia . . . I am sure that such busts could be of much more value to posterity than all those monuments that are put up in squares: they are all false and mannered . . .' Among those whose portraits he did were Vladimir Stasov (1873, marble, in the Saltykov-Shchedrin Public Library, Leningrad), Ivan Turgenev (1880, tinted plaster, RM), Mikhail Saltykov-Shchedrin, A. Polovtsev, Sergei Botkin and Savva Mamontov.

In the eighties Antokolsky returned to historical subjects. Inspired by the image of Pushkin's Pimen, he produced the statue *Nestor the Chronicler* (1889, marble, RM). In 1891 he did two more pieces—*Yaroslav the Wise* (majolica, RM) and the bronze statue *Yermak* (RM). Both characters are seen as people who determined the future of Russia. While Yaroslav, though outwardly calm, is full of intense, searching thoughts, Yermak is in all respects a dynamic figure: weighed down by his heavy armour, a pole-axe in his strong hand, the legendary subjugator of Siberia steps out decisively. 'I wanted him to be a lively, powerful expression of Russian daring and bravery,' the sculptor wrote to Stasov.

In 1893 the St. Petersburg Academy of Arts mounted a wide-ranging personal exhibition of Antokolsky's works. But many of them remained misunderstood and he was subjected to blatant attacks by ill-disposed critics in the press. Despite Stasov's support, the sculptor took it badly and left St. Petersburg in a state of depression.

In Paris Antokolsky sculptured various small pieces, such as *Sleep, Dream, Mermaid* and *Sleeping Beauty.*

The sculptor died in June 1902 while in Germany. He was buried in St. Petersburg, in the Preobrazhensky Cemetery.

NINETEENTH
CENTURY

M. M. ANTOKOLSKY

FIFTY
RUSSIAN
ARTISTS
151

1. I. N. Kramskoi. Portrait of M. M. Antokolsky
2. Nestor the Chronicler
3. Christ Judged by the People
4. Ivan the Terrible

Nikolai Alexandrovich YAROSHENKO

(1846–1898)

1

Nikolai Yaroshenko was born in Poltava. His father, a highly educated man, was a military officer who had advanced to the rank of major-general, his mother was the daughter of a retired lieutenant. The boy's propensity for drawing was clear at an early age, but in keeping with the family tradition his father wished him to have a military career and sent him at the age of nine to the Poltava cadet corps.

Drawings that have been preserved give reason to believe that the young artist studied diligently and not without success under his teacher I. K. Zaitsev. After finishing the cadet corps, in 1863, Yaroshenko moved to St. Petersburg and entered the Pavlovsk military school, whence he was transferred to the Mikhailovsky artillery school. His interest in art did not weaken, however: he studied privately under A. M. Volkov, an artist popular in the sixties, and also attended evening classes at the drawing school of the Society for the Furtherance of the Arts, at which Ivan Kramskoi taught. In 1867 Yaroshenko entered the Mikhailovsky artillery academy and at the same time became an external student at the Academy of Arts. Two years later he graduated from the military academy 'with distinction in the sciences', while continuing to make progress in art.

Yaroshenko's world-outlook was directly influenced by the ideas of the Russian revolutionary democrats. His friend, the artist I. S. Ostroukhov, recalled that 'Chernyshevsky and Dobrolyubov became his leaders, and the progressive journals his favourite reading-matter'. At the Academy he mixed with the *peredvizhniki* and the writers grouped around the progressive journal *Otechestvennye Zapiski* (Fatherland Notes). All this left its mark on the social orientation of Yaroshenko's art. In 1875 several portrait études and his first picture, *Nevsky Prospekt at Night* (which perished during the Second World War), were displayed at the Fourth *Peredvizhniki* Exhibition. The latter showed St. Petersburg's main street on a rainy night, empty apart from two women whom

1. The Stoker

NINETEENTH
CENTURY

N. A. YAROSHENKO

FIFTY
RUSSIAN
ARTISTS
153

poverty had driven out to walk the streets. 'The picture's meaning lies in the colours,' wrote Yaroshenko, 'which show the dampness and the cold drizzle outside—in a word, weather which no decent master would put his dog out in.'

On 7 March 1876, on the strength of this picture, Yaroshenko was unanimously elected member of the Society of *Peredvizhniki,* and soon he was made a member of the board. For over ten years he and Ivan Kramskoi headed the Society, and after Kramskoi's death Yaroshenko acted as his ideological successor, preserving the best traditions of the Society. Mikhail Nesterov wrote of Yaroshenko: 'After Kramskoi's death he was one of the most active leaders of the Society . . . His voice could be heard at the meetings and he was listened to as closely as Kramskoi used to be. Yaroshenko was modest, exacting towards himself, reserved yet firm. Gentle in appearance, he was rock-hard in spirit.' His contemporaries called him 'the artists' conscience'.

Following the leading trends of the age, Yaroshenko affirmed the positive hero in his work. Two pictures shown at the Sixth *Peredvizhniki* Exhibition in 1878—*The Stoker* and *The Prisoner*—evoked a broad public response.

The Stoker (TG) is the first vivid realistic image of a working man in Russian painting. The picture made a huge impression on the writer Vsevolod Garshin, who managed to convey this in his story *Artists*: here the idea is of the responsibility of society for the monstrous exploitation of the working people. But the stoker depicted by Yaroshenko is not only a victim: he is also the force engendered by capitalism and opposing it.

In *The Prisoner* (TG) the artist expressed sympathy with the fighters for freedom and exposed the autocracy. The étude for the work was painted from Yaroshenko's close friend, the writer Gleb Uspensky. Both of these works represented a step forward in the development of democratic realism in the seventies, and if

The Stoker was the first image of a worker in Russian art, *The Prisoner* was one of the first works of that period dedicated to the revolutionaries.

In his work of the early eighties Yaroshenko developed the theme of the revolutionary struggle of the Russian intelligentsia in the light of the new upsurge of social concern in Russia. The subject of *The Lithuanian Castle* (1881, not preserved) was linked with Vera Zasulich's attempt on the life of the mayor of St. Petersburg. This event was conceived as a protest against the frightful conditions under which political prisoners were kept in the Lithuanian Castle. The police banned the painting from being shown at the *Peredvizhniki* Exhibition, which opened on the day Alexander II was assassinated. The artist himself was held under house arrest for a week and received a 'visit' from the Minister of Internal Affairs, Loris-Melikov.

At the same time as *The Lithuanian Castle,* another painting—*The Old and the Young* (1881, RM)—was exhibited. It reflected the conflict between 'fathers' and 'sons' which was on everyone's mind at the time—the clash of two ideologies, one conservative, one rebellious.

Yaroshenko was married to a former student, M. Navrotina, and their 'Saturday nights' were attended by writers, artists, scholars and younger members of the intelligentsia. This helped the artist keep in touch with the burning issues of the time and reflect them in sharp psychological works which became a landmark in the development of Russian democratic painting.

An important place in Yaroshenko's work belonged to portraiture. Considering it his social duty to paint leading representatives of contemporary society, he did more than a hundred portraits, mainly of intellectuals—progressive writers, artists, actors and so on. As a pupil of Kramskoi's, he saw the portraitist's task above all in cognising the subject's psychology. In the words of his wife, 'he could not paint people who were of no spiritual interest'.

FIFTY
RUSSIAN
ARTISTS
154

N. A. YAROSHENKO

NINETEENTH
CENTURY

NINETEENTH
CENTURY

N. A. YAROSHENKO

FIFTY
RUSSIAN
ARTISTS

155

It is interesting that Vladimir Stasov considered Yaroshenko 'principally a portraitist of the younger generation, whose nature, life and character he deeply understood and knew how to convey'.

The best known of the artist's paintings of young people are *A Student* (1881, TG) and *A Girl-Student* (1883, State Museum of Russian Art, Kiev; another version in Kaluga Regional Art Museum). These are basically picture-portraits, whose prototypes were, respectively, F. A. Chirok, a pupil at the Academy of Arts, and A. K. Chertkova, who attended the Bestuzhev university courses for women.

Yaroshenko also painted psychologically penetrating portraits of Ivan Kramskoi (1876, RM), Gleb Uspensky (1884, Sverdlovsk Picture Gallery), Dmitri Mendeleyev (1885, The Mendeleyev Museum at Leningrad University), Nikolai Ghe (1890, RM) and Vladimir Korolenko (1898, not preserved), to name but a few. One of the best is that of Polina Strepetova (1884, TG), an actress who created striking scenic images of the downtrodden Russian woman. The artist brilliantly brings out the spiritual beauty and strength of a woman who was endowed with a great civic conscience and who yearned for a free life. Kramskoi rated this portrait among the finest of the time and saw it as a universalised expression of the artist's own ideas, 'occasioned' by Strepetova.

At the end of the 1880s one of Yaroshenko's most popular works appeared—*Life Goes On* (1888, TG): the people languishing behind the barred window of the convict wagon are not, the artist seems to be saying, criminals but unfortunate victims of social reality.

Yaroshenko's next works included several genre paintings—*On a Swing* (1888, RM), *A Peasant Girl* (1891, Gorky State Art Museum), *In a Carriage* (late 1880s, private collection) and others.

In his last years, despite a grave illness, Yaroshenko travelled widely in Russia and abroad: he went to the Volga, lived a long time in the Caucasus, and visited Italy, Syria, Palestine and Egypt. Not long before his death he was working in the mining area of the Urals on études for a planned large painting depicting the life of the miners.

In 1892 Yaroshenko was promoted for excellent service to the rank of major-general. That year he was forced by ill health to move to Kislovodsk. The following year he retired from military service but continued his public activities and still displayed his works at *Peredvizhniki* Exhibitions. He was full of artistic plans, but they were cut short by his untimely death, caused by heart failure, on 25 June 1898.

Vladimir Lenin called Yaroshenko 'a marvellous artist and wonderful psychologist of real life.'

Ilya Yefimovich REPIN

(1844–1930)

1. Self-Portrait
2. Nevsky Prospekt
3. A Religious Procession in Kursk Gubernia

Ilya Repin, the son of an officer, was born in the town of Chuguyev, Kharkov Gubernia. In his childhood and youth the future artist suffered privations and painted icons and portraits to earn money. He had his first lessons in drawing at the school of topography.

The first teachers who directed his talent were the Chuguyev artists I. M. Bunakov and L. I. Persanov. In 1863 Repin decided to take the risk and go to St. Petersburg. At the Stock-Exchange Drawing School he met Ivan Kramskoi, who immediately noticed his outstanding talent and became his friend and mentor for many years. In 1864 Repin entered the Academy of Arts and in 1871 he graduated brilliantly with the painting *The Raising of Jairus's Daughter* (1871, RM). The merit of this work lay in Repin's ability to reinterpret traditional academic laws.

Repin's other 'academy' in those years was Kramskoi's famous Artel, which was started up in St. Petersburg in 1865 and played an important role in the artist's development. Repin's *Barge-Haulers on the Volga* (RM) caused a stir when it was exhibited in 1873. 'Never before has the bitter fate of these human pack-animals been expressed on canvas in such a terrifying, penetrating chord. 'It is a human mosaic from all corners of Russia,' wrote Stasov. Contemporaries saw the power of the human spirit in the picture, and many articles appeared about it in the press. Repin's name was quickly famous. He becomes generally acknowledged as an artist of truly immense range.

In the sixties the artist turned to another genre and painted portraits of his brother V.Ye. Repin (1867, RM), the architect F. D. Khloboshchin (1868, RM) and his fiancée V. A. Shevtsova (1869, RM).

The award of a gold medal brought with it the right to travel to France. In May 1873 he set off on a journey round Austria and Italy. In letters to Stasov, Kramskoi and Tretyakov he shared his thoughts about art, wrote of his admiration for Michelangelo and the colour perfection in

NINETEENTH
CENTURY

I. YE. REPIN

FIFTY
RUSSIAN
ARTISTS
157

the works of Veronese, Titian and Tintoretto, and enthused about portraits by Velazquez and Rembrandt.

In Paris Repin painted études, the pictures *A Paris Café* (1875, private collection, Stockholm) and *A Negress* (1875, RM) and also *Sadko* (1876, RM), based on the Russian epic subject.

Repin really got into his stride once he returned to Russia in 1876. He joined the Society of *Peredvizhniki* and in the eighties became its leading artist, the author of historical and genre compositions and a brilliant portraitist.

Many aspects of contemporary life and a wealth of popular types and characters found their reflection in Repin's work, embodied in a kind of artistic chronicle of the age. These types range from the irate, long-suffering peasant of *The Peasant with the Evil Eye* (1877, TG) to the

Archdeacon (1877, TG)—'the concentrated essence of our deacons who have not an ounce of spirit in them, but are all flesh and blood, lobster-eyed, slothful and wrathful'; from the reckless gay dances of Ukrainian peasants in the picture *Folk Parties* (1881, TG) to the array of people shown in *A Religious Procession in Kursk Gubernia* (1880-83, TG)—'as though "reformed Russia" had burst out onto the road, with all its social contrasts and deep contradictions'.

Ilya Repin was the first artist to portray the revolutionary Populists. They can be seen in such works as *Under Escort* (1876, TG), *Arrest of a Propagandist* (1880-89, TG), *Refusal to Confess* (1879-85, TG) and *Unexpected Return* (1884, TG). These works clearly betray the artist's warm sympathy with the revolutionary struggle, almost a call for radical changes in life.

FIFTY
RUSSIAN
ARTISTS
158

I. YE. REPIN

NINETEENTH
CENTURY

4

5

Even when Repin looks at the past it is to understand more deeply the present, the roots of the national character, the causes of historical conflicts, the depth of psychological sufferings.

His first work on a subject from Russian history was *The Tsar's Daughter Sofia Alexeyevna at Novodevichy Nunnery in 1698* (1879, TG). In the years of reaction that quelled the Populist movement there appeared the painting *Ivan the Terrible and his Son Ivan on 16 November 1581* (1885, TG). The idea for the picture came about in response to the sanguinary events of the period, as an angry protest against despotism. Repin recalled: 'The bloody event of March 1 upset everyone. A kind of bloody streak went through this year . . . I worked like a madman. At times I was terrified'. The procurator of the Synod, Pobedonostsev, reported angrily to the tsar about the painting: 'Remarkable art we have these days: without the slightest ideals—just bare realism, with a tendency to criticise and expose.' The appearance of Ivan the Terrible synthesises certain features of the artist Myasoyedov and the composer Blaramberg, while his son Ivan includes traits of the writer Garshin and the artist Menk.

Repin worked for about twelve years on the painting *The Zaporozhian Cossacks Write a Letter to the Turkish Sultan* (1880–91, RM), the original idea for the work having arisen in 1878. In it he wanted to show the broad, freedom-loving characters of the Zaporozhians—'daredevils . . . the most gifted people of their time', as he called them.

The determining factor in Repin's work was his acute sense of contemporary life. By the nineties he had painted about 300 portraits, and he is rightly considered the leading Russian portraitist of this period.

The range of Repin's portraits is extremely wide. They include many of his close friends, relations and children—e.g. *Nadya* (1881, Radishchev Art Museum, Saratov), *Dragon-Fly* (1884, TG) and *Autumn Bouquet* (1892, TG),

NINETEENTH
CENTURY

I. YE. REPIN

FIFTY
RUSSIAN
ARTISTS
159

6

the last two both being of the artist's daughter Vera. His best portraits are those of prominent figures in Russian society—writers, musicians, artists, scholars. The artist not only approves the new progressive personality but also discloses his vital power. For this reason most of his portraits underline the energy and will of the mod-

els: cf. those of Stasov (1883, RM), Tolstoy (1887, TG) and Rubinstein (1881, TG).

Repin liked to capture movement, but not for its own sake: every facial expression, gesture and attitude is tied up with the person's state of mind. The dynamism of his portraits is therefore very important. 'Here he uses unheard-of de-

FIFTY
RUSSIAN
ARTISTS
160

I. YE. REPIN

NINETEENTH
CENTURY

7

troukhov all exhibit skilful and beautiful drawing.

By the end of the century Repin had gained wide public recognition. A personal exhibition of his works was opened, and after the reform of the Academy of Arts he was made a professor. Many talented youngsters learned in his studio, among them I. S. Kulikov, F. A. Malyavin, A. P. Ostroumova-Lebedeva and B. M. Kustodiev.

In 1901 the artist received a government commission—to paint the celebratory session of the State Council on the day of its hundredth anniversary. The grand picture (35 m^2) *Ceremonial Session of the State Council, 7 May 1901* (1901–03, RM), on which Boris Kustodiyev and I. S. Kulikov collaborated, took two years to complete. This multiple portrait depicts more than eighty dignitaries of the State Council, headed by the tsar and members of the royal family. Repin did more than fifty études and sketches for the work. His flowing, easy brushwork and power of typification make these portrait-études the peak of Repin's achievements.

The artist spent the last thirty years of his life in Kuokkala where he had a refurbished house with a studio, called Penates. In August 1930, at the age of eighty-six, Ilya Repin died.

vices, which no one has ever tried out before,' wrote Kramskoi about Repin's portrait of the composer Mussorgsky (1881, TG). Each of the subjects is portrayed in a vivid individual manner, with the stress on those unique features that most fully disclose the essence of his character. Thus, the penetrating, inquisitive gaze of the surgeon N. I. Pirogov (1881, TG) expresses his restless, searching, wilful character. And the inspiration and excitability of the actress P. A. Strepetova are clearly shown in the intense look of her shaded eyes and in her gesture.

Repin achieved great mastery in the field of graphic portraiture. His portraits of the actress Eleonora Duse (1891, TG), the artist V. A. Serov (1901, TG), Princess M. Tenisheva (1898, TG) who contributed to the revival of Russian folk crafts and the painter and founder of the Moscow Museum of Icon-Painting I. S. Os-

4. Portrait of M. P. Mussorgsky
5. Portrait of P. A. Strepetova
6. Unexpected Return
7. Portrait of L. N. Tolstoy

NINETEENTH
CENTURY

FIFTY
RUSSIAN
ARTISTS
161

Vasily Ivanovich SURIKOV

(1848–1916)

1. Self-Portrait
2. Portrait of an Unknown Woman

The epic works of Vasily Surikov are a magnificent manifestation of the creative genius of the Russian people. In breadth and power of imagery, his canvases are a match for the musical images of Glinka and Mussorgsky.

Surikov came of Cossack stock and was born in the Siberian town of Krasnoyarsk. His father's family came to Siberia from the Don area, with Yermak; his mother came from the old Cossack family Torgoshin, and it was from these roots that the artist inherited his proud, freedom-loving character. Pyotr and Ilya Surikov and Vasily Torgoshin are mentioned among those who took part in the Krasnoyarsk uprising of 1695–98. Surikov was proud of his origins and wrote: 'I am a Cossack through and through, with a pedigree going back over two hundred years.' His parents were also artistically gifted, in a broad sense. His father, a passionate lover of music, played guitar excellently and was considered the best amateur singer in Krasnoyarsk; his mother, a wonderful embroideress, had inborn artistic taste. The source of Surikov's conception of beauty was Siberia, with all its severity, with its sometimes cruel customs, its courageous people, the 'old Russian' beauty of its girls, its majestic scenery and its living history. 'Siberia,' he recalled, 'brought me up from childhood with the ideals of historical types.' His first attempts at drawing also took place in his early childhood: 'I was six, I remember—I drew Peter the Great from an engraving. The colours I did myself: blue for the uniform and crimson for the lapels.'

The first person to notice the boy's abilities was ·N. V. Grebnev, the teacher of drawing at Krasnoyarsk district school, which Surikov finished in 1861 with a certificate of merit. Grebnev set him the task of copying etchings from the old masters. Surikov later spoke with gratitude of his first tutor: 'Grebnev nearly wept over me, teaching me to draw.'

In order to support the family after his father's death Surikov had to work as an office clerk. Sometimes, as he recalled later, he even

FIFTY
RUSSIAN
ARTISTS
162

V. I. SURIKOV

NINETEENTH
CENTURY

3

had to 'paint Easter eggs for three roubles per hundred' and once he took a commission to paint an icon entitled *The Holy Virgin's Feasts*.

Surikov's drawings attracted the attention of the governor of Krasnoyarsk, P. N. Zamyatin, who put in a word for him at the Council of the Academy of Arts. From St. Petersburg came a positive response, but with the reservation that he would not be provided with a scholarship. The rich gold-mine owner P. I. Kuznetsov, an art lover and collector, came to Surikov's aid and offered to pay for his studies and upkeep. In the middle of December 1868 the young artist set off on a two-month journey to the capital with a string of carts transporting Kuznetsov's merchandise. Surikov proved to be insufficiently prepared for the Academy examinations. He entered M. V. Dyakonov's class at the school of the Society for the Furtherance of the Arts and in the three summer months mastered a three-year course. On 28 August 1869 he passed the Academy's entrance ex-

aminations and was accepted as an external student. By the following autumn he was already at work on his first independent work: *View of the Monument to Peter the Great on Senate Square in St. Petersburg* (1870, RM).

Surikov made great progress at the Academy, extracting the maximum benefit from the lessons. His achievements were particularly spectacular in composition—so much so that his colleagues called him 'the composer'.

The development of his natural gifts owed much to Pavel Chistyakov, who trained many masters of Russian art. At the Academy Surikov successfully executed a series of compositions on classical themes, and also a picture from early Russian history—*A Prince's Judgment* (1874, TG).

In April 1875 the artist embarked on a programme work for a gold medal—*The Apostle Paul Expounding the Dogmata of Christianity to Herod, Agrippa, His Sister Bernice and the Roman Proconsul Festus* (TG). Compositionally,

NINETEENTH
CENTURY

V. I. SURIKOV

FIFTY
RUSSIAN
ARTISTS
163

the picture does not venture beyond academic canons, but it does already show the artist's interest in his characters' psychologies. In Chistyakov's words 'the antediluvian dunderheads failed the best pupil in the whole Academy, Surikov, because he didn't manage to finish a few details of the picture', and the gold medal, which also gave the right to a trip abroad, went to someone else. When six months later, 'by way of an exception', he was given a chance to travel abroad he asked instead of this to be allowed to carry out a commission to decorate the Church of Christ the Saviour in Moscow. Surikov did

the preparatory work for this in St. Petersburg and only added the final touches in Moscow. From June 1877 the artist lived permanently in Moscow, having spent two years doing frescoes depicting the four oecumenical councils. Thereafter Surikov took on no more commissions for work.

In 1878 Surikov married Elizaveta Sharé, grand-daughter of the Decembrist P. Svistunov. The artist's happy family life and relative material security allowed him to 'do his own thing', and that was to paint scenes from Russian history. 'Arriving in Moscow, I found myself in the

FIFTY
RUSSIAN
ARTISTS
164

V. I. SURIKOV

NINETEENT:
CENTURY

centre of the life of the Russian people and immediately found my bearings,' he recalled subsequently.

It seems the very walls of the ancient city spoke to him. Figures from the past rose up in his imagination, followed by the plan of a picture which was for him 'staggering'. *The Morning of the Streltsi's Execution* (1878–81, TG) is truly staggering. Not because of the horrors of death, but because of the power of the characters and the tragic nature of one of the crucial periods in Russian history. The subject of the picture comes from the Petrine age and reflects one of the episodes in the struggle for the throne between Peter the Great and his sister Sophia, the upshot of which was the defeat of Sophia and the *streltsi* who supported her. 'It was not the execution I wanted to convey, but the solemnity of the last minutes,' wrote Surikov about this painting. The *streltsi* are full of dignity as they go to meet their deaths; they have lost the fight and ask for no mercy. In the crowd, 'which is agitated like "the noise of much water" ', Surikov singles out interesting characters. Particularly expressive is the ginger-bearded *strelets* whose wrathful gaze—almost the axis of the whole composition—meets Peter's eyes.

The architectural landscape, with St. Basil's Cathedral which seemed 'blood-stained' to Surikov, is more than a historical background: it is compositionally tied in with the motion of the masses. The artist conveys the 'solemnity of the last minutes' not only in the proud beauty of the Russian people, but in the picture's colour-scheme, which captures the shades of the dawn sky, the colours of the clothes and the cathedral, the patterns on the shaft-bows and even the sparkling rims of the cartwheels. This picture already manifested the great merits of Surikov as a colourist. 'When I thought up the picture,' he wrote, 'all the faces emerged at once, and the colouring along with the composition. Everything springs from the canvas itself'.

The painting was bought by Pavel Tretyakov as soon as it was exhibited, and the artist immediately set about other themes that ap pealed to him: 'I thought of *Boyarynya Morozo va* even earlier than *Menshikov,* straight afte the *Streltsi;* but then I started *Menshikov,* to giv myself a break.'

While *Streltsi* showed the tragedy of the mas ses, made up of the fates of individual people, i *Menshikov in Beryozovo** (1883, TG) Suriko concentrated his attention on one strong char acter whose personal drama echoed the trage dy of Russia. However localised the episod may have been which suggested to Surikov th subject of his future picture, the image he wen on to create assumed historical importance . . We see the interior of a low wooden cottag dimly lit by a candle, with a tiny window covere in whimsical frosty patterns. Menshikov's hug figure seems cramped in this enclosed space, un der low ceilings: this strong and imperious ma is accustomed to a different scale of life. Wit him are his three children, who were to hav been the perpetrators of his ambitious designs Were to have been . . . The situation is dra matic. And Surikov brilliantly catches in it th beauty and subtlety of human feelings, convey ing them in the appearance of the character and in the colouring. 'Of all Surikov's dramas *Menshikov* is the most "Shakespearean" in it treatment of man's eternal, inexplicable fates, wrote Mikhail Nesterov.

The first study for *Boyarynya Morozova* ap peared in 1881; Surikov began work on the pic ture itself three years later, having meanwhil painted *Menshikov in Beryozovo* and made trip abroad. Here the artist chooses as his heroi ne Feodosiya Morozova, a fanatical follower o archpriest Avvakum, an active adherent of th Old-believer movement in the Russian church Once again, the tragic fate of a strong, passionat figure is, for the artist, indivisible from the fat

---

* Menshikov, a Russian military leader and state man, was one of Peter the Great's closest allies. 1 the struggle for power after Peter's death, he wa exiled, together with his family, to Beryozovo. Su rikov's painting epitomises the end of the Petrir age.—*Ed.*

NINETEENTH
CENTURY

V. I. SURIKOV

FIFTY
RUSSIAN
ARTISTS
165

5

of the people, who opposed the church re-
forms introduced by Patriarch Nicon, seeing
in them an encroachment on the customary run
of their lives, on their rites and—in the final
analysis—on their spiritual freedom.

In this picture Surikov wished to show a person who was not only herself capable of strong
feelings but could also arouse such feelings in
others. The artist wrote: 'I cannot understand
the actions of individual historical figures without the people, without the crowd. I have to
drag them onto the street.' The 'crowd', however, is not faceless, but is made up of vivid
individuals.

All the components of the picture—form, colours, linear composition—have a tremendous
emotional effect. The work is national not only
in subject (based on events of the seventeenth
century) but in its national types, its architecture, its winter landscape, and its treatment of
colour, whose rich, limpid strength is akin to the
Russian people's sunny perception of the world.
In *Boyarynya Morozova* (1887, TG) Surikov
succeeded in expressing the inner firmness,
selflessness, courage and beauty of Russian man.

The painting was first shown at the Fifteenth
Peredvizhniki Exhibition and was showered
with the highest praise. Vladimir Stasov wrote:
'Surikov has now produced a painting which in
my opinion is foremost among all our pictures
on subjects from Russian history. Nothing in
that sphere of our art which sets itself the task of
illustrating Russian history has gone as far or as
high as this picture.'

In early 1888 the artist suffered a grave
shock: his wife died. Consumed by grief, he almost abandoned art. A testimony to Surikov's
state at that time was the painting *The Healing
of a Man Blind From Birth,* which was first seen
at a *Peredvizhniki* Exhibition in 1893.

Heeding the advice of his relatives, Surikov
and his daughters went to Siberia, to Krasnoyarsk. 'I moved on from dramas to the great joy
of living,' wrote the artist in retrospect. 'I have
always had leaps like that into cheerfulness.
I painted the genre picture of the game village at
that time. I returned to my childhood memories . . .' Noticeable in the picture *The Taking of
a Snow-Built Fortress* (1891, RM), which appeared after three historical canvases, were the

FIFTY
RUSSIAN
ARTISTS
166

V. I. SURIKOV

NINETEENTH
CENTURY

roots of the artist's great love of living, which helped him overcome grief and adversity. The heroes of his works are also endowed with this love of living.

In 1891 Surikov returned to Moscow, bringing with him, in his own words, 'an incredible strength of spirit'. Now he began work on a new canvas—*Yermak's Subjugation of Siberia* (1895, RM). 'Two elements encounter one another'—these words of Surikov's stick in one's mind when one sees the grand battle scene depicted here. The people appear in all the grandeur of their exploit. The army is led by the legendary Yermak, whose figure is at once singled out and indivisible from the Cossacks. The distinguishing feature of the Cossack force is its unity, its oneness. In contrast, the army of Kuchum, seized by panic, appears disconnected. While glorifying the courage of the Russians, Surikov also sees deserving features in the enemy and stresses the distinctive beauty of the 'aliens'. Modelling them from living Khakass and Ostyak people, Surikov remarked: 'They may have snub-noses and high cheek-bones, but everything is harmonious.'

The epic character of the picture derives not only from the import of the subject (the clash of two historic forces) and not only from the concise expression of the movement of an enormous mass of people, but also from the manner of painting. In Nesterov's assessment, Surikov's painting was 'firm, thick and rich, seized out of the essence of the action, flowing by necessity'.

Suvorov Crossing the Alps (1899, RM) developed the theme of the military heroism of the Russian people, which was started in *Yermak's Subjugation of Siberia.* The appearance of the painting at the Twenty-seventh *Peredvizhniki* Exhibition coincided with the centenary of the event which it depicted. Surikov had begun work on it in 1895, and in 1898, at the site of the historic crossing in Switzerland, he made études for it.

'The main thing in the picture is the move-

ment,' wrote the artist, 'and the whole-hearted bravery of the men, obedient to the command of their general.' The landscape—mountain-peaks disappearing in a shroud of clouds, some dark, some shining with a pale cold blue—allows the spectator to sense the difficulty of the crossing and to feel the significance of the feat achieved by Suvorov's men.

Surikov spent several years working on his last large-scale work, *Stepan Razin* (1907-10, RM). This painting caused him some trouble, and he returned to it even after it had been shown in public. In 1909 the artist wrote in a letter: 'As far as *Razin* is concerned, I am still working on it, emphasising the characterisation of Razin. I went back home to Siberia and there I found the realisation of my dream of him.'

The picture impresses one by its sense of freedom and space. Its beauty lies in the rippling mother-of-pearl colours, in the air suffused with sunlight and in the overall poetic quality. The beauty of nature helps to bring out the deep pensiveness of the ataman, isolating him in a way from the tipsy merriment of the Cossacks. Evidently Surikov's aim was to convey the inner state of this strong, rebellious character, and this fact is borne out by his words to the artist Ya. D. Minchenkov: 'Today I painted Stepan's forehead: he's got much more pensiveness about him now, hasn't he?'

The last historical figure to be painted by Surikov was Pugachov. A study dating from 1911 shows the leader of the eighteenth-century peasant uprising locked up in a cage . . .

An exhibition mounted in 1912 by the Union of Russian Artists included Surikov's *The Tsarevna Visits a Nunnery* (TG). The fusion of historical and genre art in this picture sets it alongside similar works by Andrei Ryabushkin and Sergei Ivanov.

Surikov's work as a portraitist is of considerable importance, especially his wonderful études for his historical canvases and for *The Taking of a Snow-Built Fortress.* The characterisation in *Portrait of Doctor Yezersky* (1911, pri-

NINETEENTH
CENTURY

V. I. SURIKOV

FIFTY
RUSSIAN
ARTISTS
167

6

vate collection), *Portrait of a Man with a Sore Arm* (1913, RM) and his self-portraits of the 1913 (TG) and 1915 (RM) is powerful, and his female portraits are extremely beautiful.

Surikov died on 6 March 1916 and was buried beside his wife in the Vagankovskoye Cemetery in Moscow.

3. The Morning of the Streltsi's Execution
4. Menshikov in Beryozovo
5. Boyarynya Morozova
6. Stepan Razin

Isaak Ilyich
LEVITAN

(1860-1900)

1

1. V. A. Serov. Portrait of I. I. Levitan
2. Autumn Day at Sokolniki
3. Golden Autumn

2

Isaak Levitan lived and worked at a period when Russian culture in all spheres was flourishing. His contemporaries were Repin and Surikov, Nesterov and Serov, Chekhov and Gorky, Chaliapin and Yermolova. In his short creative life Levitan produced about a thousand paintings, pastels and drawings.

He was born in the small Lithuanian town of Kibarty. His father worked as cashier at the railway station; the family was large and poor. In the hope of improving matters, the father took his family to Moscow, but his wife died suddenly and shortly thereafter he himself passed away.

When he was thirteen Levitan entered the Moscow School of Painting, Sculpture and Architecture. Though constantly hungry and penniless, often without even a roof over his head, he studied diligently. In September 1876 he found himself in Savrasov's landscape class and later he became a pupil of Vasily Polenov.

Despite his success, the Council of the School declined to award him a silver medal, and the diploma he received merely entitled him to be a teacher of drawing. Levitan left the Moscow School. Later he would return there, a famous artist, and would run the landscape studio.

Among the earliest surviving works by Levitan are two small landscapes which were shown at student exhibitions—*Evening* (1877, TG) and *Sunny Day. Spring* (1877, private collection). And although they are not devoid of faults —a certain naiveté, and an overabundance of details—these works are full of a bright youthful love of nature. At a student exhibition of 1880 Pavel Tretyakov acquired the nineteen-year-old artist's painting *Autumn Day at Sokolniki* (TG). This was the first recognition of his talent. The work attempts to recreate the mood people have on a dismal wet autumn day. Yet the attempt to work in a new manner, sweeping and generalised, was still in many ways studentish: the young artist still had to study nature more and master new painting devices.

In the summer months from 1880 to 1884 Levitan lived in Ostankino and painted a lot from

LATE
NINETEENTH
-EARLY
TWENTIETH
CENTURIES

I. I. LEVITAN

FIFTY
RUSSIAN
ARTISTS
169

3

nature, producing, among others, *Oak Grove in Autumn* (1880, Gorky State Art Museum), *Oak-Tree* (1880, TG) and *Pines* (1880, private collection). At Savvinskaya Settlement near Zvenigorod he painted the landscapes *Last Snow. Savvinskaya Settlement* (1884, TG) and *A Bridge at Savvinskaya Settlement* (1884, TG).

In 1885, at the Kiselev estate in Babkino, Levitan met the writer Anton Chekhov, with whom he remained friends for the rest of his life.

It was not until the mid-eighties that the painter's material circumstances improved. But his hungry childhood, hardships and intense work had already done damage to his health: his heart condition worsened considerably and he went to the Crimea to regain his strength. On his return he mounted an exhibition of sixty of his landscapes.

In 1887 Levitan at last realised his dream of visiting the Volga. The 'Volga period' in his work continued until 1890.

Levitan is one of the greatest poets of the Volga. The scenery of the Volga region, with its boundless expanses and its alternating forests, valleys, fields, large towns and tiny villages, inspired him with new artistic material. His Volga landscapes are quite varied . . . In *Evening on the Volga* (1888, TG) and *Evening, Golden Pool* (1889, TG), there is a sense of solemn silence and majestic tranquility. The picture *After Rain; Plyos* (1889, TG), on the other hand, has an altogether different emotional timbre. Here there is no peace: the wind chases the clouds and the water is disturbed . . . The bluish-silvery colours, with innumerable intermediate shades, give an impression of moving light and quivering air. Particularly noteworthy are the pictures *Golden Autumn in the Village* (1889, RM) and *Birch Grove* (1889, TG) in which Levitan con-

FIFTY
RUSSIAN
ARTISTS
170

I. I. LEVITAN

LATE
NINETEENTH
-EARLY
TWENTIETH
CENTURIES

4

veys with great immediacy his perception of various states of nature. The artist's infatuation with nature is evident in all these works.

'I cannot be even vaguely happy, or at ease, I cannot understand myself, without painting. Never before have I loved nature as I do now, or been so sensitive to it,' he wrote at this time to Chekhov.

In March 1891 Levitan became a member of the Society of *Peredvizhniki*. S. T. Morozov, a lover and patron of art, provided him with a studio.

Levitan's work from 1890 to 1895 shows a desire to depict nature in an epic way: cf. *A Pond* (1892, TG), *Vladimirsky Highroad* (1892, TG), *Eternal Peace* (1894, TG). In *Vladimirsky*

Highroad, one of Levitan's best works, he depicted a well-known highway which was taken by exiles heading for Siberia. The highway stretches into the distant violet horizon; at a crossroads, where there is a rise in the soft undulating land, stands a wayside shelter in which the exiles could rest. The darkened copses are silent, and the sweeping sky, the low horizon and the boundless plain create an impression of infinite space. In this painting we have an example of the enormous social message which a landscape-painter can invest in his works. Levitan gave the painting to the Tretyakov Gallery as a gift.

The artist's constant search for new artistic forms found its expression in his picture *Eternal Peace.*

LATE
NINETEENTH
-EARLY
TWENTIETH
CENTURIES

I. I. LEVITIAN

FIFTY
RUSSIAN
ARTISTS
171

The vast Russian scenery forever attracted Levitan, which is seen both in his early paintings and in the majestic panoramas of his Volga cycle.

The year 1895 was a difficult one for Levitan. His heart-disease was sapping his strength, and was accompanied by attacks of pain and asthma. These physical disorders and his state of melancholy sometimes brought Levitan to the brink of despair and attempts to commit suicide. But the life-giving force of his love of nature and art was strong enough to overcome his illness and even to lead him to new creative discoveries.

Levitan's move in March 1894 to Tver Gubernia—to Ostrovno, and later to Gorki—ushered in the last period in his art.

In the sunny days of March nature comes to life (*March,* 1895, TG), streams rush and sing (*Spring. Last Snow,* 1895, RM) and apple-trees blossom fragrantly (*Apple-Trees in Blossom,* 1896, private collection); in the crystal clearness of autumn, leaves flash like gold, the rivers are blue and the groves empty (*Golden Autumn,* 1895, TG), and 'nature's splendid fading' begins (*Autumn,* 1895, private collection; *A Highway. A Sunny Day in Autumn,* 1897, private collection). The lyrical beauty of nature is presented as a glorious hymn to the artist's homeland.

The cycle of lyrical landscapes painted in 1895-96 is completed by the picture *Flooding in Spring* (1896-97, TG).

Levitan's last landscapes are remarkably delicate and profound, reflecting the artist's desire to perfect his art so that one could 'hear the grass growing' in it. More and more he tried to catch nature's most elusive moments and sought to achieve extreme succinctness: cf . *The Last Rays of the Sun,* (1899, TG), *The Moon. Twilight* (1899, RM), and the artist's acknowledged masterpieces *Dusk* (1900, TG) and *Haystacks at Dusk* (1899, TG).

Several marvellous water-colours and pastels also date from this time—for example *Mist in Autumn* (1899, RM) and *Meadow at the Edge of a Forest* (1898, RM).

In 1898 Levitan was awarded the title of academician of landscape painting. He taught at the Moscow School of Painting, Sculpture and Architecture, and his landscapes were exhibited at All-Russia exhibitions, and in Munich and Paris. But, just as he gained universal recognition and fame, his health took a sharp turn for the worse and his heart-disease steadily progressed. A course of treatment abroad helped for a short while.

'Levitan is dying, it seems,' wrote Chekhov. . . Still his 'terrible thirst for life' fought against his illness.

The Lake (1899–1900, RM) was the last picture he painted. Levitan considered calling the work *Russia*; it was to be a kind of synthesis of all his searchings. *The Lake* is a generalised image of the beautiful Russian countryside. Russia, the Motherland—such were the artist's last thoughts and feelings. He did not complete the picture as he wanted to. On 22 July 1900, Levitan passed away.

4. Eternal Peace

Valentin Alexandrovich SEROV

(1865–1911)

1. The Abduction of Europa

Valentin Serov was born in St. Petersburg, the son of the well-known composer Alexander Serov. In his childhood the future artist was steeped in an artistic atmosphere: not only musicians, but also artists such as Mark Antokolsky and Ilya Repin were visitors to the house, and Alexander Serov himself was an ardent amateur artist. His son's powers of observation and talent for drawing became apparent from an early age and the conditions in which he grew up were conducive to their development. At first he studied under the German etcher A. Kemping, and then he was taught by Repin, whom his mother had shown his drawings, on the advice of Antokolsky.

Repin gave the young Serov his first lessons in Paris and continued them in Moscow and Abramtsevo. After a trip with his talented pupil to Zaporozhye, Repin sent him in 1880 to the celebrated Pavel Chistyakov at the Academy of Arts.

Here the young artist's talent won admiration and respect all round. Chistyakov remarked that he had never come across anyone endowed with so much versatile artistic talent: 'Drawing, colouring, chiaroscuro, characterisation, a sense of the wholeness of his task, composition—Serov could cope with all these things, and cope with them to the highest degree.'

The artist's friends valued his human qualities too, especially his straightforwardness and honesty.

The formation of Serov's artistic outlook was greatly affected by his life at Abramtsevo and Domotkanovo, not far from Moscow. He came to love the central-Russian countryside with its groves, glades, ravines, coppices and villages. And the estate of the famous art-patron Mamontov at Abramtsevo, where Korovin and Vrubel worked on stage decorations, where there was a majolica workshop, and a successful private opera house, inspired the young artist to great creative heights. At the age of twenty-two or twenty-three Serov produced works which have become classics of Russian art.

At Abramtsevo he painted his famous portrait of the twelve-year-old Vera Mamontova (*Girl with Peaches*, 1887, TG), in which he wished to achieve, in his own words, 'perfection without sacrificing freshness of painting—as in the old masters'. At Domotkanovo he painted his cousin, Maria Simonovich: *A Girl in the Sun* (1888, TG). Recalling this period his cousin wrote: 'We worked avidly, both equally carried away—he by the success of his painting, I by the importance of my task. He was searching for a new means of expressing in fresh colours the infinitely varied play of light and shade. Yes, I spent three months sitting for him, almost without a break, except when the sitting had to be cancelled because of bad weather. On those unfortunate days he painted the pond.' (*An Overgrown Pond at Domotkanovo*, 1888, TG). Both these portraits were executed not only with a fascination for a new technique of painting, but also with great inspiration and lyricism, and it was this that immediately singled out the young artist and made him famous. Serov received an award from the Moscow Society of Art Lovers, and the second portrait was immediately bought by Pavel Tretyakov.

Other works completed at Domotkanovo included *October* (1895, TG), *Yearlings at a Watering-Place* (1904, TG), *A Woman with a Horse* (1898, TG) and many illustrations to Krylov's fables.

In 1887 Serov married Olga Trubnikova, and their family was large and happy. Serov loved children and enjoyed painting them. The picture-portrait *Children* (1899, RM), which shows his sons Yura and Sasha, the drawing *The Botkin Sisters* (1900, TG) and the portrait of Micky Morozov (1901, TG) are all noteworthy for their lyrical qualities and sensitive understanding of the children's characters.

Serov reported to his friend Mamontov in 1890: 'I have painted two portraits at Kostroma. I'm becoming quite a portraitist!' Serov's psychological perceptiveness, his ability to see and show the spirit of the person sitting in front of him, soon made him the leading portraitist in Russia. His portraits show his contemporaries: the temperamental singer Francesco Tamagno (1893, TG), who had—as the artist put it—a 'golden throat'; the artist's cheerful friend, the landscape-painter Konstantin Korovin (1891, TG); an inspired image of Isaak Levitan; a nervous-looking Nikolai Leskov, the writer (1894, TG).

Reminiscing about her father, Serov's elder daughter described the creative fervour with which he used to work on his portraits: 'And his eyes—his eyes would steal a quick glance, with such intensity and such a desire to take in everything he needed, that this glance would seem like a flash of lightning, and like lightning it would momentarily light up everything, right down to the finest details.'

In the middle of the nineties Serov was inundated with commissions to paint high-ranking persons. After the portrait of Maria Morozova (1897, RM), the mother of multimillionaire Savva Morozov and the picture-portrait of S. Botkina (1899, RM), which was shown at a World Exhibition in Paris, a new line began to develop in the artist's work. Serov's contemporaries said that people were often afraid of him, afraid of his perspicacity and frankness, and even reproved him for caricaturing his models. 'I have never caricatured,' he replied. 'What can I do if the caricature is there in the model himself, how am I to blame? I merely picked it out.'

This approach is evident in the portraits of the Yusupov princes (1901-03, RM), which Serov began in St. Petersburg in 1901 and completed at their estate in Arkhangelskoye near Moscow; and in the portrait of the millionaire and assistant professor at Moscow University, M. Morozov (1902, TG). One of the best-known portraits is that of the banker V. Girshman (1911, TG) who, according to Serov's daughter, 'begged him to remove his hand, which looked as though it were groping for gold coins in his pocket'.

FIFTY
RUSSIAN
ARTISTS
174

V. A. SEROV

LATE
NINETEENTH
-EARLY
TWENTIETH
CENTURIES

2

LATE
NINETEENTH
-EARLY
TWENTIETH
CENTURIES

V. A. SEROV

FIFTY
RUSSIAN
ARTISTS
175

Serov did not intend to expose faults, he merely sharpened those features which were sometimes deeply hidden and not immediately apparent to everyone. If he liked a person, even though it was an official commission, the master's brush would produce an attractive image: for example, Z. Yusupova (1902, RM) is charmingly feminine and gentle, and G. Girshman (1907, TG) is a pleasing image of aristocratic refinement.

Serov's painting and drawing skills are quite outstanding. The great emotional effectiveness of his works can be explained by his ability to find precisely the right means of representation and to embody a many-faceted picture of life in a perfect form. Take any of Serov's portraits: it is not just a talented reproduction of some individual's features, but an image of the world in which that person lives.

The revolution of 1905 left noticeable traces in the artist's life and work. It was precisely in this period that Serov developed as a 'citizen', acutely aware of social injustices. In St. Petersburg Serov witnessed the shooting-down of workers on the Vasilievsky Island, and was profoundly shaken by the event. 'He heard the shots and saw the victims. From then on his character changed sharply—he became morose, brusque, irascible and intolerant; everyone was particularly surprised by his extreme political convictions,' wrote Repin. As a sign of protest he rescinded his membership of the Academy of Arts. The day political prisoners were released Serov was among those outside the Taganka prison, he watched barricades being erected at the University, and he attended the funeral of the revolutionary Bauman. The artist's album began to include drawings of the Cossacks' charges on the defenceless crowd; and then pictures too, for example. *Soldiers, Brave Fellows, Where Is Your Glory?* (tempera, 1905, RM) and *Barricades; the Funeral of N. E. Bauman* (1905, USSR Museum of the Revolution), and biting political caricatures exposing Nicholas II as the hangman of the revolution: *1905. After the Suppression* and *1905. Views of the 1906 Harvest* (1905, TG).

These years also saw Serov achieve perfection as a graphic-artist. His portrait-drawings of the singer Fyodor Chaliapin, the actor and stage-director Konstantin Stanislavsky, the actors Ivan Moskvin and Vasily Kachalov, the composer Nikolai Rimsky-Korsakov, the artist Mikhail Vrubel and the writer Leonid Andreyev are the pride of Russian art.

Around the turn of the century the artist treated themes from earlier Russian history, producing a cycle of pencil drawings, guaches, water-colours and pictures in tempera and oils. These small compositions are extremely vibrant, as though done from nature (cf. *Peter the Second and Yelizaveta Petrovna Set Out on the Hunt*, 1900, RM).

The heroic Petrine age, severe and unprecedented, took possession of the artist's imagination. One of the best works was *Peter the Great* (1907, TG), in tempera. 'Spindle-shanked', threatening and impulsive, Peter is moving against a strong wind. His preposterous carnival-like retinue, their clothes flapping in the wind, struggles with difficulty behind him. In everything—in Peter's determined striding towards a new building, in the turbulent water, in the thin masts of the ships, and in the racing clouds—one feels the dynamism of transformations which were only possible thanks to the will, energy and efforts of courageous people.

In May 1907 Serov went to Greece, which made a deep impression on him. He was delighted by the decorative qualities and balance of classical architecture. In an effort to express what he saw, and to convey the essence and beauty of ancient Greek mythology, he painted a picture based on the legend *The Abduction of Europa* (1910, TG) and several versions of *Odysseus and Nausika* (1910, TG, RM).

Serov's work in the theatre was also interesting: his curtain for the ballet *Scheherazade* was greatly admired in Paris and London.

FIFTY
RUSSIAN
ARTISTS
176

V. A. SEROV

LATE
NINETEENTH
-EARLY
TWENTIETH
CENTURIES

3

LATE
NINETEENTH
-EARLY
TWENTIETH
CENTURIES

V. A. SEROV

FIFTY
RUSSIAN
ARTISTS
177

His interest in monumental-decorative art led to the highly original portrait of the dancer Ida Rubinstein (1910, RM). The artist found reminders of the Orient in the dancer's appearance, and compared her with the figures of classical bas-reliefs.

In his last works Serov strove towards increased expressiveness of form. This is very evident in his portraits of O. Orlova (1911, RM), V. Girshman (1911, TG), and especially G. Girshman (1911, TG) and in the unfinished portrait of P. Shcherbatova.

Early on the morning of 22 November 1911 Valentin Serov was hurrying to the Shcherbatovs for a portrait sitting when he fell and suffered an attack of stenocardia. He died at the peak of his talent, at the age of forty-six.

His death shocked his contemporaries. The poet Valery Bryussov, an ardent admirer of the artist, wrote: 'Serov was a realist in the best sense of the word. He unerringly saw the secret truth of life, and the things he painted revealed the very essence of phenomena, which other eyes cannot even see.'

5

2. Maxim Gorky
3. Portrait of M. N. Yermolova
4. Self-Portrait
5. Portrait of Anna Pavlova

Konstantin Alexeyevich KOROVIN

(1861-1939)

1

Konstantin Korovin was born into a well-to-do merchant family. At fourteen he entered the architecture department of the Moscow School of Painting, Sculpture and Architecture, where his elder brother Sergei—later a well-known realist painter—was already a student. By this time the family had run into hard times: 'I was extremely hard-up,' wrote Korovin, recalling his student years, 'and at the age of fifteen I was giving drawing lessons and earning my bread.'

After two years of study, having submitted landscapes painted during the holidays for assessment, Korovin transferred to the painting department. His teacher there was Alexei Savrasov, who laid great stress on painting from nature and helped his pupils appreciate the beauty of the Russian countryside. Later, Korovin remembered Savrasov's exhortations: 'When you set about painting, paint études, study, and most importantly—feel!'

Under Savrasov's influence, Korovin was soon strongly drawn towards landscape-painting. Even as a student, trying to preserve the freshness of the impression, he used to put the finishing touches to his works at the actual sites of the landscapes he was painting. In paintings such as *The Village* (1878, Kharkov State Museum of Fine Arts), *Early Spring* (1870s, TG) and *A Little Bridge* (1880s, TG) close observation of nature is combined with direct perception of it.

To complete his education, Korovin went to St. Petersburg and entered the Academy of Arts, but within three months he left, disappointed by the outdated teaching methods, and returned to Moscow. In his last years at the School he studied under Vasily Polenov, who attached particular importance to artistic form.

Fame came to the young artist with his *Portrait of a Chorister* (1883, TG), with its impression of *plein-air*. The woman's face, dress and hat are flooded by gentle, dispersed light marbled by the reflection of green trees. With its unconstrained brushwork and shining colours the portrait is a fine achievement, and it

1. V. A. Serov. Portrait of K. A. Korovin

LATE
NINETEENTH
-EARLY
TWENTIETH
CENTURIES

K. A. KOROVIN

FIFTY
RUSSIAN
ARTISTS
179

should be remembered that it was painted five years earlier than Serov's *Girl with Peaches* and *A Girl in the Sun*.

Polenov introduced Korovin to Mamontov's Abramtsevo circle, which included the Vasnetsov brothers, Ilya Repin, Vasily and Yelena Polenov, Mark Antokolsky, Ilya Ostroukhov and others. The Abramtsevo circle's fascination for Russian themes is reflected in Korovin's picture *A Northern Idyll* (1886, TG): the folklore element and smooth rhythmical composition of this picture call to mind the works of Viktor Vasnetsov, whom Korovin admired.

In 1885 Mamontov set up his private opera house and Konstantin Korovin designed the stage décor for Verdi's *Aida*, and the next season for Delibes' *Lakmé* and Bizet's *Carmen*. Mamontov wrote about the production of *Aida*: 'Korovin's sets were marvellous, especially the "moonlit night on the bank of the Nile" and the "doorway of the temple" in which the trial of Radames took place.'

Korovin used the money he earned at the theatre to go to France and Spain. His impressions of Spain found expression in the best of his early genre paintings *The Spanish Girls Leonora and Ampara on a Balcony* (1889, TG), in which the national motif is interpreted with good taste and a feel for the local colour.

In the best of Korovin's portraits, man and nature merge together, the beauty of each complementing the other. The excellent portrait of Tatiana Lyubatovich (c. 1886, RM) brings out the poetic nature of the well-known singer. The artist coped admirably with a complex task here: the woman is seated with her back to a window, with a lush green background, wearing a white dress and holding a book in her hands; her bearing is simple and natural; the creeping violet and rose-coloured patches of sunlight on her dress lend her figure a light, delicate quality.

The artist's subsequent work was strongly influenced by his trips to the North. During his travels of 1888 he was captivated by the panoramas of the stern northern coastlines, as seen in

The Coast of Norway and *The Northern Sea* (private collection, Leningrad).

His second trip to the North, with Valentin Serov in 1894, was occasioned by the construction of the Northern Railway. Korovin captured the beauty of these parts in a large number of landscapes: *Norwegian Port, Saint Trifon's Brook in Pechenega, Hammerfest: Aurora Borealis, The Coast at Murmansk* (all in TG) and others. The colouring of the landscapes is especially fine, many of them being built on a delicate web of shades of grey. The 'étude style' of these works was characteristic of Korovin's art of the 1890s.

Using material from this trip, Korovin designed the Northern Railway pavilion at the All-Russia Exhibition of 1896 at Nizhny Novgorod. On huge panels he created broad, generalised images of the life and scenery of the North.

The decoration of the pavilion was so successful that Korovin was designated head artistic designer of the Russian pavilions at the World Exhibition in Paris in 1900. The immensity of this task drew out the best of his talent, and he painted several large decoratively coloured panels. For this work Korovin received a gold medal at the Exhibition. He now enjoyed worldwide renown and his works were exhibited in many European cities.

From the start of the twentieth century Korovin focussed his attention more and more on the theatre. His move from Mamontov's private opera to the public Mariinsky Theatre in St. Petersburg allowed him to work on a larger scale. His designs revolutionised the art of theatrical decoration. Departing from the traditional type of décor, which merely indicated the place of action, Korovin produced 'mood décor', which conveyed the general emotional tenor of the performance.

Korovin designed sets for some of Stanislavsky's drama productions, but his scenery for operas and ballets enjoyed the greatest success. His colourful costumes and scenery for such productions as *Faust* (1899), *The Little Hump-backed Horse* (1901) and *Sadko* (1906)

FIFTY
RUSSIAN
ARTISTS
180

K. A. KOROVIN

LATE
NINETEENTH
-EARLY
TWENTIETH
CENTURIES

greatly increased the artistic expressiveness of the productions.

A colourist by nature, Korovin made colour the principal means of expression both in his theatrical work and in his easel painting. 'Colours and form combine to give harmony of beauty,' he wrote. 'Colours can be a celebration for the eyes, and your eyes speak to your soul of joy and delight. . . Colours, chords of colours and forms—that is what I was trying to achieve in my stage-sets for the ballet and opera.'

One of the artist's favourite themes was Paris. In the town landscapes *A Paris Café* (1890s, TG), *Café de la Paix* (1905,TG), *La Place de la Bastille* (1906, private collection, Moscow) one notices the seemingly fortuitous composition, and the artist's free manner of painting and striving towards richness of colours.

In the first decade of this century Konstantin Korovin showed great interest in painting Paris by night and by evening, with the bright lights of advertisements and dashing carriages: cf. *Paris at Night; Le Boulevard Italien* (1908, TG), *Night Carnival* (1901, Latvian State Art Museum, Riga), *Paris in the Evening* (1907, private collection) and others.

Korovin knew western painting well and admired the achievements of the Impressionists. This influenced his own work—especially the Paris series, in which he brilliantly records impressions of the city's bright, colourful, changeable life. In the evening twilight or in the morning haze, his colours lose their concreteness and form a system of vibrating patches, and objects become less clearly defined. Yet in Korovin's best works, as well as conveying an emotional state, he also gives objects an almost tangible material quality.

Korovin's love of theatrical work left its mark on his painting too. From about 1910 his canvases became more colourful and displayed a broader, freer manner of painting. He was now at his peak as an artist, as can be seen in such pictures as *The Jetty at Gurzuf* (1914, RM) and *A Bazaar* (1916, RM). At the same time he painted many still-lifes. *Roses and Violets* (1912, TG) is executed in a lush, buoyant gamut of colours. In *Fish* (1916, RM), the objects, rather than 'dissolving' in the masterly manner of painting, are remarkably concrete and tangible.

Konstantin Korovin's pupil B. Johanson wrote the following about his teacher: 'Unusually emotional and impatient to act, he quickly burned with enthusiasm about everything that fell under his painter's eye—snow thawing on the banks of the Istra, a girl in a white dress beside a lilac bush, roses in the sun against the blue sea, a remote corner of a provincial town, Venice or Tashkent, Arkhangelsk . . . or the night lights of Paris . . . In everything he found the poetry of truth . . . His greatest joy was the fascinating process of battling with nature, at the end of which a new, second life, enriched by the artist's poetic feeling, would emerge on the canvas.'

Throughout his career Korovin displayed his works at exhibitions of the *peredvizhniki,* the 'World of Art' * society and the Union of Russian Artists. * From 1901 Konstantin Korovin taught at the Moscow School of Painting, Sculpture and Architecture; many Soviet artists studied under him.

During the First World War Korovin worked as a camouflage consultant at the headquarters of one of the Russian armies. Despite his poor state of health (an old nervous illness and heart-disease) he was often at the front line.

After the Revolution he led an active artistic life; apart from being involved with the task of preserving art treasures and organising auctions and exhibitions for the benefit of released political prisoners, he continued to work in the theatre, designing productions of Wagner's *Die Walküre* and *Siegfried* and Tchaikovsky's *Nutcracker* ballet (1918-20).

Apart from being incurably ill himself Korovin had an invalid son who could be treated only

---

* For more details about this society see p. 195

* This society, which has leanings towards Impressionism, was founded in Moscow in 1903 and Korovin played a leading role in it.

LATE
NINETEENTH
-EARLY
TWENTIETH
CENTURIES

K. A. KOROVIN

FIFTY
RUSSIAN
ARTISTS
181

FIFTY
RUSSIAN
ARTISTS
182

K. A. KOROVIN

LATE
NINETEENTH
-EARLY
TWENTIETH
CENTURIES

in Paris, and on the advice of the People's Commissar for Education Lunacharsky, he moved to the French capital. Here an exhibition of his works was to have taken place, but his pictures were stolen and the artist was left penniless. He was forced to agree to any kind of work. Under these circumstances Korovin signed various shackling agreements and in a short period, for a negligible fee, painted forty pictures of a 'souvenir' type—countless 'Russian winters' and 'boulevards of Paris'. The rich colours and sweeping style that had marked much of his earlier work now became almost excessive. Indicative of his continuing interest in Russian music and culture was his scenery for a production by the Turin Opera House of Rimsky-Korsakov's *The Golden Cockerel*. In the last years of his life he worked fruitfully in many of the major theatres of Europe, America, Asia and Australia.

Konstantin Korovin died in 1939.

The artist Konstantin Yuon had this to say about his work: 'Korovin's painting is the embodiment in imagery of the artist's happiness and joy of living. All the colours of the world beckoned to him and smiled at him.'

2. A Paris Café
3. Portrait of a Chorister

LATE
NINETEENTH
-EARLY
TWENTIETH
CENTURIES

FIFTY
RUSSIAN
ARTISTS
183

Mikhail Alexandrovich VRUBEL

(1856-1910)

1. Self-Portrait

On 12 April 1918 Vladimir Lenin signed a decree which became known as the Plan for Monumental Propaganda, which included a list of the world's leading cultural figures, the memory of whom was to be perpetuated in revolutionary Russia. Among these names was Mikhail Vrubel.

Vrubel was a man of extremely versatile talent. He was renowned as a master of monumental murals, easel paintings and theatrical scenery, as a graphic artist, a sculptor and even as an architect. And in every sphere he produced first-class works. 'Vrubel expressed his thoughts perfectly,' wrote Alexander Golovin. 'There was an unerring quality about everything he did.'

Even among the brilliant artists of the turn of the century Vrubel stands out because of the originality, uniqueness even, of his art. His originality of thought and novelty of form often prevented his work from being properly understood, and the sensitive artist was sorely wounded by the unjust criticism of some of his contemporaries. 'What a long-suffering life he had,' recalled Ilya Repin, 'and yet, what pearls his genius produced.'

Vrubel was the son of a military lawyer in Omsk. His father had a benevolent attitude towards his enthusiasm for painting. During a short stay in St. Petersburg Vrubel attended the Drawing School and was a frequent visitor to the Hermitage. After leaving the grammar school in Odessa, where he had studied literature, history, German, French and Latin, Vrubel passed the entrance examinations for St. Petersburg University, and in 1879 he graduated from the Law Faculty.

By this time the future artist had firmly decided to devote his life to art, and in 1880 he entered the Academy of Arts where he studied under Pavel Chistyakov. He was a keen, hardworking student. 'You cannot imagine,' he wrote to his sister, 'how completely immersed I am in art: I just can't take in any ideas that are unconnected with art.'

FIFTY
RUSSIAN
ARTISTS
184

M. A. VRUBEL

LATE
NINETEENTH
-EARLY
TWENTIETH
CENTURIES

One of the best of Vrubel's student works was the water-colour *Mary's Betrothal to Joseph* (1881, RM). The composition recalls Raphael's picture on the same subject, and one can also perceive the influence of Alexander Ivanov's Biblical études, though both the compositional structure and movement of the figures is more dynamic.

In the autumn of 1883 Vrubel rented a studio for independent work. Here he painted the water-colour *Girl in Renaissance Surroundings* (State Museum of Russian Art, Kiev) which demonstrated his ability to convey a wide variety of material forms and shades of colour.

While still at the Academy of Arts, Vrubel began to take an interest in universal, philosophical subjects, and he was attracted to strong, rebellious, often tragic individuals. Symptomatically, his first oil-painting was based on Shakespeare: *Hamlet and Ophelia* (1884, RM).

In April 1884 Vrubel left the Academy and took up the offer of the well-known art critic A. Prakhov to go to Kiev and help restore the ancient murals of St. Cyril's Church. Vrubel restored 150 fragments of frescos and produced four new compositions where the originals were lost. Apart from the frescos he also painted four icons. On these he worked in Venice, where he went to study early Renaissance art. The best of the icons—*The Mother of God* (1885, State Museum of Russian Art, Kiev)—is a tender but sad, womanly image of a mother who has a presentiment of her son's tragic fate.

The finest achievement of Vrubel's Kiev period, however, was his water-colour studies for murals in St. Vladimir's Cathedral (1887, State Museum of Russian Art, Kiev). By working in St. Cyril's Church and studying the frescos of St. Sophia's Cathedral, the artist came to understand the essence of the great monumental art of ancient Rus, and the Vladimir studies clearly show the link between Vrubel's work and the ancient heritage, which suited both his talent and his frame of mind. They include the noble *Resurrection*, the radiant *Angel with Censer and Candle* and, finally, the shattering, tragic *Mourning*. In this last work, Mary stands with wide, tearful eyes, overwhelmed by suffering, over her son's grave. The extent of her sorrow is brought out by the solemn rhythm of the folds in her clothes, by the severe lines, the simplicity of the colour relations and the laconic composition. In *Mourning*—an altogether unique work in world art—Vrubel successfully brought together the harmony and monumental stature of early art, and an expression of the feelings of contemporary man.

Vrubel did not manage to turn these studies into actual murals; his part in the decoration of the Cathedral was limited to producing some fanciful ornaments, but this too he did with great enthusiasm and imagination. In the words of the artist Nesterov, Vrubel was 'innocently absent from our planet, wrapped up in his visions; and these visions, when they visited him, were not his guests for long, but gave place to new dreams and new images, hitherto unheard-of, unexpected and unconjectured—the wonderful fantasies of a marvellous artist from another world'.

In 1889 Vrubel left Kiev for Moscow, and this was the start of his most fruitful period. He received several commissions for decorative panels, one of which—*Venice* (1893, RM)—embodied his impressions of a trip to Italy in 1891-92. The Renaissance city is shown in all the magnificence of a splendid carnival procession.

The subject of the picture entitled *Spain* (1894, TG) may be connected with the opera *Carmen*, which Vrubel loved and considered an epoch-making piece of music. The agitation of the characters, the intensity of the colours and the flood of scorching sunlight arouse a sense of conflict and drama; we see a country which is full of life, where emotions bubble and both love and hate are strong. In a somewhat similar vein is *The Fortune-Teller* (1895, TG), a deeply psychological work. Vrubel brilliantly highlights the face, against the lilac and rose-coloured sheen of the carpet and silks. The fortune-tell-

LATE
NINETEENTH
-EARLY
TWENTIETH
CENTURIES

M. A. VRUBEL

FIFTY
RUSSIAN
ARTISTS
185

2

er's eyes stare fixedly, as though she has divined some terrible secret of the future.

In this period Vrubel painted many portraits, constantly employing new devices. In his portrait of the writer K. Artsybushev (1897, TG) there is a sense of calm and balance; the contrasts of compositional rhythms, details and colour in his portrait of Savva Mamontov (1897, TG) make for a poignant image in which the titanic borders on the helpless.

Vrubel's love of music led him to Mamontov's private opera house, where he met Rimsky-Korsakov and designed productions of his operas *The Tsar's Bride* and *The Tale of the Tsar Saltan*. Of the architectural projects in which he was then engaged, only one was realised—an annexe to Mamontov's house in Moscow. At Abramtsevo Vrubel ran the ceramics workshop and produced a series of unusual majolica sculptures on fairy-tale subjects.

Abramtsevo stimulated many of Vrubel's artistic searchings. Here he developed an interest in national traditions and folk art. In a letter to his sister, he says: 'I am at Abramtsevo at the moment and again I can feel, or rather, hear that intimate national note which I would so love to capture on canvas or in an ornament. It is the music of an integrated man, not fractured by the abstractions of the regulated, differentiated, pale West.'

Vrubel found the 'music of an integrated man' in Russian folklore, which he treated again and again in his work of the nineties. It was not a case of illustrating particular epic tales and fairy stories, however; the artist strove to understand the conception which his forefathers had of man and nature, to look at the world through their eyes.

Vrubel's *Bogatyr* (1898, RM) is born of surrounding nature, which gives the Herculean figure grandeur and might.

In the picture *Pan* (1899, TG) the Greek god is transformed into a Russian wood-demon. Old and wrinkled, with fathomless blue eyes and gnarled fingers, he almost seems to grow out of the moss-grown tree-stump. Fantastic, bewitch-

FIFTY
RUSSIAN
ARTISTS
186

M. A. VRUBEL

LATE
NINETEENTH
-EARLY
TWENTIETH
CENTURIES

ing shades are used for the typical Russian land-scape—expansive wet meadows, a meandering stream, slender birches caught in the silence of the falling twilight and tinged by the glow of the horned moon. A harmonious combination of the fantastic and the real can also be seen in *The Swan Princess* (1900, TG). The composition is so constructed as to give the impression of glancing into a fairy-tale world where a magic swan-maiden has just appeared and is about to disappear again, floating away towards a distant mysterious shore. The last beams of sunshine play on her snowy white feathers, producing a rainbow of colours. The maiden is turning, her delicate face looks sad, and there is a mysterious mixture of melancholy and loneliness in her eyes. The Swan Princess is one of Vrubel's most enticing and heartfelt feminine images.

The artist's fervent love of nature helped him to convey its beauty. The luxuriant clusters of lilac in the painting *Lilac* (1900, TG) are alive and fragrant in the starlit night. One of Vrubel's contemporaries wrote that nature blinded him (the artist did indeed go blind near the end of his life) because he looked too closely at its secrets.

Throughout the nineties Vrubel worked on the image of the Demon. In a letter to his father the artist expressed his conception of the Demon: 'The Demon is not so much an evil spirit as a suffering, sorrowful one, and at the same time an imperious, majestic one.' His first attempt to treat the subject was in 1885, but the artist destroyed this work.

In the picture *Seated Demon* (1890, TG) the young Titan is depicted on a clifftop in the sunset. His fine, powerful body, seems almost too big for the picture; he wrings his hands; his face is touchingly handsome; and his eyes express inhuman sorrow. Vrubel's Demon is a union of opposites: beauty, majesty, strength, and constraint, helplessness and yearning. He is surrounded by a fabulous, beautiful, yet petrified and cold world. The picture's colouring is also full of contrasts: a cold lilac is in 'combat' with a warm golden-orange. The rocks, the flowers

and the figure are painted in a peculiar Vrube-lesque manner: the artist seems to hew the shapes from a block, creating an impression of a world composed of precious stones. There is a sense of primordiality about the picture.

While thinking in fantastic imagery, Vrubel was firmly rooted in reality, and his Demon was profoundly modern, reflecting not only the artist's personal emotional states but also the age itself with its contrasts and contradictions. As the poet Alexander Blok wrote, 'Vrubel's Demon is a symbol of our times, neither night nor day, neither dark nor light.'

In 1891 Vrubel did the illustrations for a jubilee edition of Mikhail Lermontov's works, edited by Konchalovsky. Of thirty illustrations half refer to Lermontov's *Demon*. In fact, these are all works of art in their own right, important in the history of Russian book illustrations, and demonstrate Vrubel's profound comprehension of Lermontov's poetry. Particularly noteworthy is the monumental water-colour *Head of the Demon*. Against a background of stony, snow-covered mountain-tops is a close-up head, with black hair and a pale face: the lips are parched, the eyes burning and penetrating; this gaze is full of unbearable torment, it expresses a thirst for knowledge and freedom, the rebellious spirit of doubt.

Some years later Vrubel painted *Flying Demon* (1899, RM)—a sombre picture, full of a foreboding of ruin and doom.

Finally, in 1901-02, appeared the last picture, *The Demon Prostrated,* on wich Vrubel worked intensively and painstakingly. Alexander Benois recalled that the painting already appeared at the 'World of Art' exhibition of 1902, but Vrubel continued to work on the face of the Demon, altering the colouring.

The broken, deformed body of the Demon, his wings fractured, is flung out in a gorge, and his eyes burn with fury. It is dusk and the last sunray flashes on the Demon's crown and on the mountain-tops. The spirit of rebellion is overthrown, but not crushed.

LATE
NINETEENTH
-EARLY
TWENTIETH
CENTURIES

M. A. VRUBEL

FIFTY
RUSSIAN
ARTISTS
187

FIFTY
RUSSIAN
ARTISTS
188

M. A. VRUBEL

LATE
NINETEENTH
-EARLY
TWENTIETH
CENTURIES

4

2. Seated Demon
3. Portrait of C. I. Mamontov
4. Lilacs
5. Mourning
6. Pearl

At the time people saw the element of protest, a symbol of beautiful, unsubdued man in this image. Remember the words of Alexander Blok:

> *What of moments of powerlessness!*
> *Time is a gossamer haze!*
> *We shall unfurl our wings once more,*
> *And again we shall take to the skies!* . . .

And Chaliapin said, somewhat later: 'What Demons he painted!—strong, terrible, dreadful and irresistible. . . My Demon comes from Vrubel.'

Shortly after finishing his *Demon Prostrated*, Mikhail Vrubel fell seriously ill and was admitted to hospital. His illness lasted almost continuously until 1904, when he made a short-lived recovery.

In 1904 he went to St. Petersburg. Now the last period in his work began.

That year Vrubel painted *Six-Winged Seraph*, which is linked thematically with Pushkin's poem *The Prophet*. To some extent, the mighty angel with his shining opalescent plumage continues the theme of the Demon, but this image is integrated and harmonious.

In 1904 Vrubel painted one of his most tender, fragile images—*Portrait of N. Zabela with Birch-Trees* (RM). It was also at this time that his interesting self-portraits were painted.

From 1905 onwards the artist was confined to hospital, but he carried on working, proving to be a marvellous graphic-artist. He drew various hospital scenes, portraits of doctors and landscapes. His drawings show a variety of styles, and are keenly perceptive and full of emotional power. Doctor Usoltsev, who was treating Vrubel, wrote: 'He was a creative artist through, in every recess of his psyche. He created constantly, and creation was for him as easy and as necessary as breathing. So long as a man lives, he breathes; so long as Vrubel breathed, he created.'

A few years before his death Vrubel began painting a portrait of the poet Valery Bryusov (1906, RM). Bryusov later wrote that he tried all his life to resemble that portrait. But Vrubel never completed the work; in 1906 he went blind. It was a tragic blow, and in the heavy hos-

LATE
NINETEENTH
-EARLY
TWENTIETH
CENTURIES

M. A. VRUBEL

FIFTY
RUSSIAN
ARTISTS
189

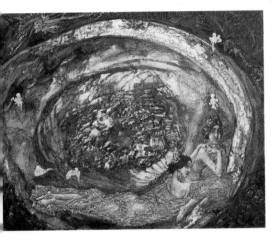

pital atmosphere the artist dreamt of the blue of the sky over dark fields and of the colours of spring. His love of music was his only consolation. Vrubel died on 1 April 1910.

The work of this artist was a heartfelt protest against evil. Even his tragic images contain a bright, noble element. The struggle of light and darkness—such is the content of most of Vrubel's works. Alexander Blok spoke of this eloquently at the artist's grave: 'Vrubel came to us as a messenger to tell us that the violet night is sprinkled with the gold of a clear evening. He left us his Demons to exorcise the violet evil and the night. What Vrubel and those like him reveal to mankind once a century, make me tremble with awe.'

LATE
NINETEENTH
-EARLY
TWENTIETH
CENTURIES

Viktor Elpidiforovich
BORISOV - MUSATOV
(1870-1905)

1

Viktor Borisov-Musatov, who became known as the creator of what one might call elegies in painting, was the son of a railway official and was born in Saratov. When he was three he fell and damaged his spinal cord, and this childhood injury had a certain effect on the future artist's character: even at an early age he tended to be dreamy and reserved and liked to be alone.

In 1884 Borisov-Musatov entered the Saratov college, where he was taught drawing by F. Vasiliev, and later by V. Konovalov, who arrived from St. Petersburg. Both teachers noticed his unusual abilities, and soon Borisov-Musatov left the college to apply himself seriously to painting. From Konovalov he received his first technical skills and his first aesthetic values. At this period he drew a great deal (most often, domestic scenes) and painted the picture *A Window* (1886, TG), which gives a detailed, but almost illusory impression of a corner of the garden as seen from a window of his house.

In August 1890 the young artist went to Moscow and joined the School of Painting, Sculpture and Architecture. Dissatisfied with his studies there, he left after a year for St. Petersburg, where he attended the Academy as an external student and also the private studio of the well-known teacher Pavel Chistyakov.

In the spring of 1893, after an operation, the artist had to leave St. Petersburg because of its climate and returned to Moscow and the School there.

Borisov-Musatov usually spent the summers in Saratov, where he painted a large number of études, principally landscapes. His success in painting from nature is evident in the picture *May Flowers* (1894, RM). In this sunny landscape one can feel the immediate, fresh perception of life which was so characteristic of Borisov-Musatov's work of this period.

In the autumn of 1895 the artist went to Paris. In order to complete his artistic training he studied under the historical painter and teacher Fernand Cormon, did a lot of drawing, and visited the Louvre—where he particularly admired

LATE
NINETEENTH
-EARLY
TWENTIETH
CENTURIES

V. E. BORISOV-MUSATOV

FIFTY
RUSSIAN
ARTISTS
191

2

the Botticellis. Of the French artists he met, he was closest to Pierre Puvis de Chavannes.

On his return to Russia three years later he settled once more in Saratov. From now on his works began to show his own distinctive hand, his own vision of the world.

Borisov-Musatov's career in art came on the threshold of a new century—a complex period, rich in great creative personalities. And like Vrubel, Nesterov, Serov and Levitan, he developed a distinctive, highly original approach to art.

The real beginning of his career can be considered his *Self-Portrait with Sister* (1898, RM), for which there is no analogy in Russian art. The picture's composition is unusual—in the centre

is a pensive young girl in an old-fashioned white dress, while the figure of the artist is partly lopped off by the edge of the canvas. This introduces an element of fortuitousness, recalling the pictures of the Impressionists. The style of painting is new: colour and form are generalised—especially in the background landscape, which resembles theatrical scenery. In this picture we see for the first time an expression of Borisov-Musatov's dream of a perfect, harmonious world; we see his attempt to escape from the disorder of reality into an ideal world of his imagination. This mood, which affected many members of the Russian intelligentsia at the turn of the century, became the leitmotif of Borisov-Musatov's art. His works do not reflect

FIFTY
RUSSIAN
ARTISTS
192

V. E. BORISOV-MUSATOV

LATE
NINETEENTH
-EARLY
TWENTIETH
CENTURIES

any concrete historical period: 'it is just a beautiful age', as the artist himself said.

The self-portrait was followed by a cycle of lyrical pictures—*An Autumn Motif* (1899, Radishchev Art Museum, Saratov), *Untitled Motif* (1900, TG), *Harmony* (1900, in collection of A. V. Gordon, Moscow). Here Borisov-Musatov conveys the atmosphere of autumn's fading beauty and the quietness of old country-estates; there is an aroma of past life, and the sad poetry of a love long departed. The content of these works was to some degree inspired by his summer trips to the estate of Sleptsovka, where he visited his godfather, who was steward there; here, for the first time, he deeply felt the charm of times gone by.

Borisov-Musatov reached the peak of his talent at the beginning of the twentieth century, when he produced such works as *Spring* (1898-1901, RM), *Tapestry* (1901, TG), *The Pool* (1902, TG) and *Emerald Necklace* (1903-1904, TG).

This new creative period was opened by the picture *Spring*, which, though completed only in 1901, had been planned some time before. In this work the artist completely got rid of all elements of action or narrative. The emotive imagery is the result of the musical lines and the soft, full colours. Everything is in delicate harmony: the white cherry blossom, the down of dandelions in the fresh spring grass, the pink glow of the sky and the light figure of a girl in a lilac dress and red shawl.

In the summer of 1901 the artist visited Zubrilovka, an estate owned by the Prozorovsky-Golitsyn princes. From that time on the landscape of the Zubrilovka park was a constant source of inspiration and was incorporated —poeticised by the artist's rich imagination—in many of his works. Impressions of this trip found their way into the picture *Tapestry*. Amid the decoratively reproduced vegetation of the park are two women, caught in a light, elegant movement, entirely at one with the landscape. The title of the picture is significant: both the

landscape and the figures are painted in a very generalised, flat manner, the colouring consists of large patches of soft, muted shades, and all this creates a shadowy, mirage-like impression. At the same time the decorativeness and delicacy of the colouring evoke associations with the noble colours of an antique tapestry. The success of the painting at an exhibition of the Moscow Fellowship of Artists, which Borisov-Musatov joined in 1899, helped greatly to bring about a change in people's attitudes to his works, which were not at first understood or appreciated.

The artist's real masterpiece was *The Pool*, in which his poetic visions were expressed in a perfect, complete form. The picture was painted at a happy time in the artist's life, when the girl he had long loved agreed to marry him. In the summer of 1902 he stayed at Zubrilovka with his sister Lena and his fiancée V. Alexandrova, and both girls posed for études and sketches for the picture. In *The Pool,* everything is balanced and conforms to a distinct, complex musical rhythm of lines and shapes. The colouring too, is strictly rhythmical, based on the repetition of blues, soft lilacs and greens in various combinations. The painting is both monumental and lyrical; the most intimate workings of the artist's soul find expression in an arrested wonderful moment, in a bewitching, magical world of beauty.

In 1903-04 Borisov-Musatov painted the unusual panel entitled *Emerald Necklace*, in which the female figures moving against a background of variegated green are almost woven into the pattern of grasses and leaves. Nature and man are so fused together that an impression arises of the naturalness and primitiveness of being.

In 1903 Borisov-Musatov painted two more canvases: *A Walk at Sunset* (TG), which is serene and calm in mood, and *Ghosts* (TG), a sombre work, full of melancholy and inner tension. Zubrilovka park with women's shadows now turns into a hazy, mystical apparition: the fading colours seem to vibrate and blur outlines.

LATE
NINETEENTH
-EARLY
TWENTIETH
CENTURIES

V. E. BORISOV-MUSATOV

FIFTY
RUSSIAN
ARTISTS
193

In the spring of 1903 the artist married, and in December he moved with his wife to Podolsk, nearer to Moscow and St. Petersburg. Early in 1903 Borisov-Musatov had joined the Union of Russian Artists, which was organised in Moscow by a group of artists who left the 'World of Art' society. His works were now gaining fame not only in Russia but also abroad: in Germany and France, for example, there were successful exhibitions of his works.

More and more Borisov-Musatov was acquiring a taste for monumental painting, and in 1904-05 he did studies for decorative murals. The first group of studies was done for a competition run by the Moscow Electric Traction Board and was unsuccessful, but the second cycle—commissioned for a private house—roused great interest. It consisted of four studies around the theme of the seasons—*Spring Tale, Summer Melody, Autumn Evening* and *The Deity's Dream* (TG). All are allegorical, and in their emotionality they recall Borisov-Musatov's earlier works. The studies were not destined to be turned into murals, however. In the

FIFTY
RUSSIAN
ARTISTS
194

V. E. BORISOV-MUSATOV

LATE
NINETEENT
-EARLY
TWENTIETH
CENTURIE<

spring of 1905 the artist left with his wife and daughter for Tarusa on the Oka, where the last months of his life and work passed. At Tarusa he painted his best landscapes: *On the Balcony; Tarusa* (1905, TG), *A Nut-Tree* (1905, TG) and *Autumn Song* (1905, TG), all of which are executed in gentle, melting colours and have great power of generalisation. Their basic theme—the fading of nature in autumn—was close to the artist's state of mind.

At Tarusa Borisov-Musatov produced his final work—a large water-colour entitled *Requiem* (1905, TG), dedicated to the memory of his friend P. Yu. Stanyukovich, the wife of the well-known writer, after her early death. *Requiem* is a sad, solemn work, symbolically conveying the joys and sorrows of human life.

The work was fated to be the painter's own requiem too. On the night of 25-26 October 1905 Borisov-Musatov passed away. He wa buried in Tarusa, on a high bank over the Rive Oka.

LATE
INETEENTH
-EARLY
TWENTIETH
CENTURIES

FIFTY
RUSSIAN
ARTISTS
195

Alexander Nikolayevich BENOIS

(1870-1960)

Alexander Benois was extremely versatile: he was a painter, a graphic, an art-critic, a leading figure of the 'World of Art' society, a prolific writer on the work of Russian and foreign masters, and an outstanding scene-painter who worked in the theatres of Moscow, St. Petersburg and in many cities in Europe and America. His life was one of hard work and extensive searches, marked both by failures and by glorious successes. As a talented artist, a populariser of art and organiser of many exhibitions, as a museum worker and an active figure in the world of theatre and cinema, Benois made an enormous contribution to the history of twentieth-century Russian art.

He was born in St. Petersburg in an artistic family: his father, Nikolai Benois, was an academician in the field of architecture. The artist spent his childhood and much of his life in St. Petersburg.

The atmosphere at home contributed to his artistic development. From an early age he loved 'old St. Petersburg' and the suburbs of the capital. He soon developed a love for the stage, too, which he retained all his life. He was endowed both with musical talent and with a rare visual memory. His artistic 'memoirs', which he drew much later, in old age, demonstrate the amazing power and permanence of his perception of life.

Benois began drawing at a private kindergarten, and all his life he remained totally absorbed by art. At the grammar-school, which he attended from 1885 to 1890, he made friends with V. Nuvel, D. Filosofov and K. Somov. Later, with Sergei Diaghilev, they would become the organisers of the 'World of Art' group and of the journal of the same title, whose main aim was to propagandise foreign and, especially, Russian art. The 'World of Art' uncovered a good many forgotten or unnoticed names, drew people's attention to applied art, architecture and folk crafts, and raised the standing of graphic art, designing and book-illustration. Alexander Benois was the heart of the 'World of Art' and a regular contributor to the journal. He never

FIFTY
RUSSIAN
ARTISTS
196

A. N. BENOIS

LATE
NINETEENTH
-EARLY
TWENTIETH
CENTURIES

2

graduated from the Academy of Arts because he considered the only way to become an artist was by constant work. With his exceptional capacity for work, he was able to complete a whole album of drawings, do some work in his studio on a painting, and visit the studios of a theatre —going into the details of scenery and costumes, discussing the production and even going through the parts with the actors—all in a single day. On top of all that, he might prepare an article for a journal or newspaper, and write several letters—which invariably contained interesting reflections about art.

He still had time for his family, too. His son Nikolai, his daughters Yelena and Anna, his nephews and their little friends found 'Uncle Shura' both good fun and instructive, and they never sensed either irritability or tiredness in this busy but indefatigable man.

At the end of 1896, with some friends, Alexander Benois arrived in Paris for the first time and fell in love with it; here he painted his celebrated 'Versailles series' which depicted the beautiful parks and walks of the 'sun king' (Louis XIV). While perfectly understanding events of the past, Benois was able to see things with the eyes of a man of the twentieth century. An example of this is the picture *A Parade Under Paul I,* which betrays not only a good knowledge of the history, costumes, architecture and life of the period, but also a touch of humour— almost satire. 'However much nonsense contemporary artistic pen-pushers might talk about me and my "aestheticism", my sympathies have always lain—and still do lie—with the simplest and truest depictions of reality,' wrote Benois.

Benois valued the grandeur of the art of the past. This was extremely important in Russia a

LATE
NINETEENTH
-EARLY
TWENTIETH
CENTURIES

A. N. BENOIS

FIFTY
RUSSIAN
ARTISTS
197

FIFTY
RUSSIAN
ARTISTS
198

A. N. BENOIS

LATE
NINETEENTH
-EARLY
TWENTIETH
CENTURIES

the beginning of this century, when factory chimneys and ugly but lucrative housing were beginning to threaten the classical skyline of the city. Benois was an outspoken advocate of preserving antique art treasures.

Among Benois' best works are his illustrations for works of literature, especially those for Pushkin's poem *The Bronze Horseman,* on which he spent over twenty years. Unique in their artistic merits, passion and power, these alone would be enough to earn Benois the reputation of the greatest artist of the early twentieth century.

Alexander Benois was also well-known for his work in the theatre. At first he worked with Konstantin Stanislavsky, and after the 1917 Revolution he collaborated with Maxim Gorky in organising the Leningrad Bolshoi Drama

Theatre, at which he designed sets for several productions. His scenery for *The Marriage of Figaro,* staged in 1926, was Benois' last work in the Soviet Union.

The artist spent the rest of his life in Paris, and also worked at the famous La Scala Opera House in Milan. But the memory of his motherland—where he had participated in the realisation of the Soviet government's first plans for the organisation of museums, where he had an important position in the Hermitage and the Russian Museum and had done much to preserve ancient monuments—this memory remained precious to him for the rest of his days.

Even before the Revolution, as one of the most active organisers (together with Sergei Diaghilev) of guest performances of the Russian ballet in Paris, Benois was concerned above all that these performances should bring world-wide renown to the Russian arts. All his later works were developments and variations of the 'Russsian series' begun back in 1907-10. Again and again he returned to the images he loved from Pushkin's poetry: cf. *Where Lonely Waters, Struggling, Sought to Reach the Sea, The Flood in St. Petersburg, 1824.* He treated the same subjects again at the end of his life, this time in painting. In his cinema work, too, Benois turned to Dostoyevsky and other Russian themes. His favourite composers were Tchaikovsky, Borodin and Rimsky-Korsakov.

Alexander Benois died on 9 February 1960.

4

LATE
NINETEENTH
-EARLY
TWENTIETH
CENTURIES

FIFTY
RUSSIAN
ARTISTS
199

Konstantin Andreyevich SOMOV

(1869–1939)

1. Self-Portrait

Konstantin Somov was born in St. Petersburg. His father, Andrei Somov, was curator of the Hermitage, editor of *The Fine Arts Herald* and a connoisseur of painting and etching.

Ever since he was a child Konstantin Somov dreamed of becoming a painter. After receiving a general education in K. I. Mai's private grammar-school, he entered the Academy of Arts, where from 1894 till 1897 he studied under Ilya Repin. In February 1897, not having graduated from the Academy, Somov left for Paris, but in the autumn of 1899 he returned and settled in St. Petersburg for a long time.

While still at grammar-school, Somov had been friendly with Alexander Benois, V. Nuvel and D. Filosofov, and later with Sergei Diaghilev—the founders of the 'World of Art' society.

The 'World of Art' was a heterogeneous organisation with contradictory ideological principles, like many other artistic groups which sprang up at the turn of the century. For Somov the most important and precious thing in painting was the 'cult of beauty', which was associated with a contemplative attitude to the world, and especially to the world of things. He observed life from a kind of artificially created 'realm of beauty'. He merely 'admired' life, as a fine connoisseur of antiquity and a man of highly developed taste.

As Repin's pupil he revealed various sides of his talent. He was keen on portraiture, rejoiced in elegant lines and was sensitive to the beauty of nature. He painted charming harlequins and eighteenth-century ladies amid bosquets, and in these small, elegant works there emerged a curious world of the past.

'I vividly remember my feeling of astonishment, and then delight,' wrote Anna Ostroumova-Lebedeva, 'when he showed me a study he had done on a subject set by Repin—"Beside a Pond".' A lady in eighteenth-century coiffure and dress was standing with her back to the viewer in front of an open-work railing, feeding swans. There was an impression of tremendous refinement in the combination of the colours, an

FIFTY
RUSSIAN
ARTISTS
200

K. A. SOMOV

LATE
NINETEENTH
-EARLY
TWENTIETH
CENTURIES

2. Portrait of the Composer S. V. Rakhmaninov
3. Kisses and Jeers
4. Lady in Blue
5. Winter. Skating

impression of great freshness, delicacy and sick-liness.'

The early work *In August* (1898, where-abouts unknown) portrays lovers sitting at a pond. Their figures are quite still. The scenery around them is cold and inhospitable. A strong wind is bending the branches and foliage of the trees and one feels that the next blast will carry the whole lot off into the distance. The land-scape and figures are shown in such an unusual aspect that an impression of unreality emerges, of a phantasmal dream, of whimsical fantasy. The picture gives rise to a feeling of alarm and plaintiveness. There is a clear kinship here with the poetry of the Symbolists.

Perhaps without realising it completely him-self, Somov looked at the things around him with bitter irony, and there was a cruel truth in this irony. In contemporary life he felt the spirit of Philistinism. As S. Yaremich points out: '. . .Somov is by nature a powerful realist, akin to Jan Vermeer or Pieter de Hooch, and the drama of his position lies in the dichotomy that affects every great Russian painter. On the one hand he is attracted by life, as the most valuable and delightful thing, and on the other hand the discrepancy between life in general and the artist's own life draws him away from the pre-sent into other, more distant spheres, where the artist is left to his own devices.'

The artist creates his own 'Somovian' world. His small canvases show ladies in rosy and silvery silks and crinolines, tired and lost in dreams. Lovers talk in whispers, pass secret notes and steal kisses. Somov feasts his eyes on this life and at the same time treats such 'toy' emotions with irony.

LATE
NINETEENTH
-EARLY
TWENTIETH
CENTURIES

K. A. SOMOV

FIFTY
RUSSIAN
ARTISTS
201

4

In the picture *Echo of Past Time* (1903, TG) we see an elegant lady in a dress like a foaming wave and a gossamer head-dress. She sits in a rather artificial pose and resembles a doll with large motionless eyes and finely outlined eyebrows and lips. Her pallid cheeks, puffy eyelids and dry parchment skin betray old age. Outside the balcony door it is sunny and scorching, but in the depths of the shady room there is cold, dampness and decay. *Echo of Past Time* is not irony, but bitterness and sadness.

Anguish and morbidity are even more prominent features in his 'Harlequinade' series (*Firework, Pierrot and Columbine, Harlequin and*

FIFTY
RUSSIAN
ARTISTS
202

K. A. SOMOV

LATE
NINETEENTH
-EARLY
TWENTIETH
CENTURIES

Lady). The critic S. Ernst wrote of Somov: 'His art gives off a sharp odour of falling roses and decay.'

When Somov turned to portraiture he was demonstrably the pupil of Repin and a worthy contemporary of Serov. From Repin he inherited the ability to show the highly individual, unique characteristics of a man through gesture, pose and expression, but in his interest in the workings of the mind he was closer to Valentin Serov. In the words of Alexander Benois, 'Somov's series of portraits will tell as fully and truthfully about our age as do the drawings of Holbein and the pastels of La Tour about theirs'.

Many of Somov's portraits are well-known, for example those of his father the art-critic Andrei Somov (1897, RM), the graphic-artist Anna Ostroumova-Lebedeva (1901, RM), the poet Alexander Blok (1907, TG), A. Kuzmin (1909, TG), the scene-painter and graphic-artist Mstislav Dobuzhinsky (1910, TG), the artist Yevgeny Lanseré (1907, TG), Viktor Ivanov (1909, TG) and V. Nuvel (1914, RM).

In the famous picture-portrait *Lady in Blue* (1900, TG)—of the artist Ye. Martynova, who died at an early age—Somov achieved great psychological depth. The young woman stands, deep in thought, with a book in her hand, against a decorative landscape. Her gentle, delicately featured face, fragile shoulders and graceful hands are painted with careful, smooth brush-strokes. Ye. Martynova's appearance has the charm of youth and intellect; her captivating womanliness is intermingled with oversensitivity and inner tiredness.

Somov's portraits are a striking page in the development of twentieth-century realist art. And not only his portraits, but his landscapes too. Whether it is his blazing *Camp-Fire* or his suite of the seasons (*Autumn, Spring, Summer, Rainbow in Summer*)—all are lyrical and romantic: the combination of decorativeness and a filigree graphic quality adds to the generalised, sometimes symbolic imagery. Benois and Os-

troumova-Lebedeva remarked upon Somov's intricate technique and ornamental skill, and other of his contemporaries were delighted by his decorative sense of colour.

Somov's work displayed features that were very typical of the age—an age which Sergei Diaghilev, one of the organisers of the 'World of Art', understood and assessed with great precision: 'We live in a terrible time of change; we are condemned to die in order that the new culture, which shall take from us what remains of our weary wisdom, should live. History says so, and aesthetics confirms it. We are witnessing the greatest historical moment of stock-taking and ending, for the sake of a new, unknown culture.'

Somov's art reflected the complexity and sharp contrasts of the age. Apart from works which manifested his oversensitivity and tendency to hide from the surrounding world, he produced brilliantly painted portraits and landscapes; they will always remain landmarks in Russian realist art of the turn of the century.

Konstantin Somov died in Paris in 1939.

LATE
NINETEENTH
-EARLY
TWENTIETH
CENTURIES

FIFTY
RUSSIAN
ARTISTS
203

Mstislav Valerianovich
DOBUZHINSKY

(1875-1957)

1

Mstislav Dobuzhinsky belonged to the magnificent cluster of artists which formed around the 'World of Art' society at the turn of the century. As a graphic artist and theatrical designer, Dobuzhinsky was one of the most important members of the group.

He was born in Novgorod. His father was an artillery officer, later a general, and his mother —a graduate of the St. Petersburg Conservatoire —was an opera singer in provincial theatres.

The artist spent his childhood in St. Petersburg. The family library was extensive, and Mstislav's father, who himself was fairly competent at drawing, taught his son to illustrate the books he read. The boy was particularly keen on history books. Gradually drawing changed from a childhood pastime into a veritable passion, and even before he went to grammar-school Mstislav went to drawing lessons at the Society for the Furtherance of the Arts for two winters running.

His father's work entailed frequent changes of abode, and the family lived by turns in Kishinyov, Vilno, Tambov province, on the Volga and in the outskirts of St. Petersburg. The young Mstislav drew a great deal and his powers of observation developed. In 1895 he began studying in the Law Faculty of St. Petersburg University, and at the same time tried to get into the Academy of Arts. Although his drawings were singled out by Repin, however, he was not accepted for the Academy. While at university he studied history of art on his own and attended classes at the private studio of Dmitriev-Kavkazsky. Dobuzhinsky's drawings appeared in student magazines. It was also while still a student that he decided to see something of the world and travelled to Germany and Switzerland. He made up his mind to study abroad, and after graduating from university in 1899 he set off for Munich, which was then—together with Paris—the leading artistic centre in Europe. Dobuzhinsky studied at the famous A. Ažbè school and then transferred to S. Hollósy's studio. Many other Russian artists—Grabar, Kardovsky, Krav-

1. Self-Portrait
2. A Man in Spectacles
3. St. Petersburg
4. Illustration for F. M. Dostoyevsky's
   short novel *White Nights*

FIFTY
RUSSIAN
ARTISTS
204

M. V. DOBUZHINSKY

LATE
NINETEENTH
-EARLY
TWENTIETH
CENTURIES

2

chenko, Favorsky, Braz and Narbut, to name but a few—also perfected their professional skills in the Munich studios, some earlier, some later.

Dobuzhinsky's early leanings towards graphic art were quickly spotted, and when he returned to Russia he was advised by Igor Grabar to study etching under Professor V. Mate at the Academy. But these classes were presently curtailed, and Dobuzhinsky did not take up engraving again until 1918.

In 1901 Dobuzhinsky joined the 'World of Art', which by then had got over its period of organisational difficulties. He was its youngest and least experienced member, but he quickly became a celebrity. Typical of Dobuzhinsky's art of this period are his town landscapes: views of Vilno, Tambov, Novgorod, Rostov-on-Don and, of course, St. Petersburg. For open letters put out by the St. Eugene Community, he pro-

duced a series of drawings depicting the architecture of St. Petersburg from the eighteenth and early nineteenth centuries. In other landscapes Dobuzhinsky emphasised another aspect of the city's life: behind the eye-catching façades hide gloomy courtyards with faceless symmetrical windows; instead of picturesque colonnades and porticos we see thick fire-proof walls. Dobuzhinsky became known as the 'artist of the city'.

A Man in Spectacles (1906, TG) is one of the artist's most frank utterances about his contemporaries. The man stands before a window through which a city landscape is visible. His face is impenetrable and his stance immobile, but his inner concentration can be felt and a sense of reticence and loneliness arises.

The public-spiritedness of Dobuzhinsky's art clearly found expression during the events of the 1905-07 revolution, when he published a se-

LATE
NINETEENTH
-EARLY
TWENTIETH
CENTURIES

M. V. DOBUZHINSKY

FIFTY
RUSSIAN
ARTISTS

205

ries of biting political cartoons in the journals *Bugbear* and *Infernal Post.* One of the most expressive drawings was *Appeasement,* which showed Moscow drowned in a sea of blood. At this period Dobuzhinsky and other members of the 'World of Art' set up satirical periodicals, in which he called upon artists to work for the people.

After 1910 the artist travelled a lot—in the Scandinavian countries, Germany, Holland and Italy. As before, he drew many urban landscapes. In Amsterdam he did a study—*Peter the Great in Holland* (1910)—which echoed Serov's picture *Peter the Great.*

Dobuzhinsky's *Province of the 1830s* (1907-09) is similar in mood to Gogol's novel *Dead Souls:* the provincial backwater depicted here was symbolic, in the artist's eyes, of officialdom in Russia under Nicholas I.

From 1907, Dobuzhinsky attached consider-

able importance to working in the theatre. His collaboration with the Moscow Art Theatre, for which he designed twelve productions, was very fruitful. One of his best sets was for Stanislavsky's production of Turgenev's *A Month in the Country* in 1909. With excellent stage-sense and knowledge of life, he recreated the unhurried rhythm of life on a country estate. In his scenery for a stage version of Dostoyevsky's *The Possessed* Dobuzhinsky underlined the dramatic qualities and intensity of the author's fictional characters.

Dobuzhinsky left pencil portraits of Stanislavsky and the actors at the Art Theatre, which are exceptionally apt in their psychological characterisation. The artist benefited greatly by the many years he worked with Stanislavsky; and as for the producer's opinion of Dobuzhinsky: 'One could hardly wish for a better painter,' he said.

Another sphere in which Dobuzhinsky excelled was book-illustration. His pen illustrations for S. Ausländer's story *The Night Prince* (1909) subtly convey the unsteady, semi-fantastic nature of the plot. Gradually his illustrations made fuller use of contrasts and shaded patches. In his drawings for Pushkin's *Lady into Lassie (1919) he employed the silhouette technique which was so popular in Pushkin's days. The book was conceived by Dobuzhinsky as an organic combination of all graphic elements, subordinated to a single idea and a single emotional framework. The same features were seen in one of the artist's best works—his illustrations for the Hans Christian Andersen tale The Swine-Herd* (1917). Dobuzhinsky also designed head-pieces, illuminated letters, types, publishers' marks and book-plates—all executed with great virtuosity and skill.

At the time of the October Revolution Dobuzhinsky was already a mature master, well-known both at home and abroad. He took an active part in designing the early revolutionary festivals, worked in the theatre and taught. His album of lithographs *Petrograd in 1921* shows

FIFTY
RUSSIAN
ARTISTS
206

M. V. DOBUZHINSKY

LATE
NINETEENTH
-EARLY
TWENTIETH
CENTURIES

the austerity and coldness of the city during this difficult period.

Dobuzhinsky's illustrations for Dostoyevsky's short novel *White Nights* (1923) are fine examples of Russian graphic art. The Petersburg landscapes are particularly expressive, conveying both the mood of the novel and its heroes' solitude and pure emotions. With a minimum of pen-work the artist manages to get across the ghostly luminescence of the sky and its reflection on the cobbled streets; he achieves a classical harmony of black and white, of subtle calculation and sincere emotion.

In 1924 Dobuzhinsky went to live in the homeland of his forebears, Lithuania. From now on most of his successes were linked with the theatre. He designed sets for more than seventy productions, the best of them Russian and world classics: Tchaikovsky's *The Queen of Spades* and *Eugene Onegin*, Mussorgsky's *Boris Godunov,* Mozart's *Don Giovanni,* Shakespeare's *Hamlet* and *King Lear*. In 1927 he made studies of scenery for Gogol's *The Government Inspector*; here he returned to a familiar theme —provincial Russia of the 1830s—but this time a gentle smile gave way to satire and the grotesque.

The new Soviet literature appealed to Dobuzhinsky as a book-illustrator, and in 1929 he illustrated Yury Olesha's *Three Fat Men*.

Starting in 1939, Dobuzhinsky worked in the Mikhail Chekhov Theatre in America. His scenery for Mussorgsky's and Prokofiev's operas at this time showed great originality and skill. In 1941 he collaborated with the outstanding Russian choreographer M. Fokine on a ballet entitled *The Russian Soldier*, which was dedicated 'To the Russian Soldiers of the Second World War'. Fokine, with whom the artist worked for many years in Diaghilev's theatre, based the libretto of the ballet on Yury Tynyanov's story *Second Lieutenant Kizhe,* and used music by Prokofiev.

A year later Dobuzhinsky wrote a ballet libretto to the music of Shostakovich's Seventh (Leningrad) Symphony, designed scenery for the ballet, and also produced illustrations to Shostakovich's music.

Towards the end of his life Dobuzhinsky returned to the theme of the city which had inspired his art for so long.

He died in 1957.

LATE
NINETEENTH
-EARLY
TWENTIETH
CENTURIES

FIFTY
RUSSIAN
ARTISTS
207

Zinaida Yevgenyevna SEREBRYAKOVA

(1884-1967)

1. At the Dressing-Table. Self-Portrait

Zinaida Serebryakova was born on the estate of Neskuchnoye near Kharkov. Her father, Yevgeny Lanseré, was a well-known sculptor, and her mother, who was related to Alexander Benois, was good at drawing. One of Zinaida's brothers, Nikolai, was a talented architect, and her other brother, Yevgeny Lanseré, has an important place in Russian and Soviet art as a master of monumental painting and graphic art.

Zinaida's childhood and youth were spent in St. Petersburg, where her grandfather the architect N. L. Benois lived, and at Neskuchnoye. The family was so artistic that no one was surprised by the girl's talent and desire to become an artist.

Her years of study did not last long. In 1901 she studied at the art school headed by Ilya Repin, and later she was taught by Osip Braz.

Zinaida's early works, which appeared at an exhibition in 1909, already showed her own style and field of interests. While studying classical art in the Hermitage and in the museums of France and Italy, she was drawn to the works of Tintoretto, Poussin, Jordaens and Rubens by their powerful plastic forms and national character. But most of all she was captivated by the purity and chastity of Venetsianov's images. She could feel the importance of the simplicity and inner harmony inherent in Venetsianov's peasants and saw the inseparable link between these traits and Russian nature. 'I cannot see enough of this wonderful artist,' she wrote afterwards.

Another influence on the artist's work was her life at Neskuchnoye: she was delighted by the pure colours of the local countryside, by the leisureliness of country life and by the freedom and plasticity of the movements of the peasants at work.

Ever since her youth Zinaida Serebryakova strove to express her love of the world and to show its beauty. Her earliest works—*Country Girl* (1906, RM) and *Orchard in Bloom* (1908, private collection)—speak eloquently of this search, and of her acute awareness of the beauty

FIFTY
RUSSIAN
ARTISTS
208

Z. YE. SEREBRYAKOVA

LATE
NINETEENTH
-EARLY
TWENTIETH
CENTURIES

2

of the Russian land and its people. These works are études done from nature, and though she was young at the time her extraordinary talent, confidence and boldness were apparent.

Broad public recognition came with Serebryakova's self-portrait *At the Dressing-Table* (1909, TG), first shown at a large exhibition mounted by the Union of Russian Artists in 1910.

Alexander Benois wrote about the portrait: 'A young woman lives in a remote country area . . . and has no other pleasure, no other aesthetic enjoyment on winter days that seclude

her from the whole world, than to see her gay young face in the mirror and to watch the play of her bare arms and hands with a comb . . . Her face and everything else in the picture is young and fresh. There is not a trace of modernistic refinement. But the simple, real-life atmosphere, illuminated by youth, is joyous and lovely.'

The self-portrait was followed by *Girl Bathing* (1911, RM), a portrait of Ye. K. Lanseré (1911, private collection) and a portrait of the artist's mother Yekaterina Lanseré (1912, RM)—mature works, strict in composition.

LATE
NINETEENTH
-EARLY
TWENTIETH
CENTURIES

Z. YE. SEREBRYAKOVA

FIFTY
RUSSIAN
ARTISTS
209

2. At Dinner
3. Self-Portrait
4. The Peasants
5. Landscape

4

In 1914-17 Zinaida Serebryakova was in her prime. During these years she produced a series of pictures on the theme of Russian rural life, the work of the peasants and the Russian countryside which was so dear to her heart: *Peasants* (1914-15, RM), *Sleeping Peasant Woman* (private collection).

The most important of these works was *Bleaching Cloth* (1917, TG) which revealed Zinaida Serebryakova's striking talent as a monumental artist. The figures of the peasant women, portrayed against the background of the sky, gain majesty and power by virtue of the low horizon. The colour composition, built around a combi-

nation of large areas of red, green and brown, lends the smallish picture the character of a monumental-decorative canvas, or part of a large frieze. This magnificent work is like a hymn to peasant labour.

Serebryakova joined the 'World of Art' society, but stood out from the other members of the group because of her preference for popular themes and because of the harmony, plasticity and generalised nature of her paintings.

When in 1916 Alexander Benois was commissioned to decorate the Kazan Station in Moscow, he invited Yevgeny Lanseré, Boris Kustodiev, Mstislav Dobuzhinsky and Zinaida

FIFTY
RUSSIAN
ARTISTS
210

Z. YE. SEREBRYAKOVA

LATE
NINETEENTH
-EARLY
TWENTIETH
CENTURIES

Serebryakova to help him. Serebryakova took on the theme of the Orient: India, Japan, Turkey and Siam are represented allegorically in the form of beautiful women. At the same time she began compositions on subjects from classical mythology, but these remained unfinished.

The deeply personal, feminine element in Zinaida Serebryakova's work continued to develop, and this came to the fore particularly in her self-portraits: in them the naive coquetry of a girl alternated now with an expression of maternal joy, now with tender, lyrical sadness.

Many of the artist's plans were not to be realised. Her husband (Boris Serebryakov, a railway engineer) died suddenly of typhus, and Zinaida was left with her mother and four children on her hands. In 1920 the family moved to Petrograd. The elder daughter went in for ballet, and from then on the theme of the theatre ran through Serebryakova's work. The range of her work narrowed: most often she depicted

5

ballerinas before a performance, and for all the merits and beauty of these pictures they canno have statisfied her.

In the autumn of 1924 Serebryakova went to Paris, having received a commission for a large decorative mural. On finishing this work she intended to return to Russia, where her mother and two children remained. But life turned out differently and she stayed in France.

Serebryakova's long years away from Russia were full of nostalgia and brought her neither joy nor creative satisfaction. The works she produced after 1924 indicate that even in a strange land she still stuck to her favourite theme of popular life, remaining faithful to the art of realism.

Zinaida Serebryakova travelled a great deal And everywhere, be it in Brittany, Algeria or Morocco, it was the common folk that appealed to her artist's mind. Among the best works she produced as a result of these travels are her portraits of peasants and fishermen in Brittany.

The salient feature of her later landscapes and portraits is the artist's own personality—her love of beauty, whether in nature or in man And yet, the most important thing was missing—the connection with what was near and dear to her.

In 1966 a large exhibition of Zinaida Serebryakova's works was mounted in Moscow, Leningrad and Kiev. The public response and the Soviet state's recognition of this great master's services brought her enormous joy. Many of Serebryakova's works were acquired by Soviet museums after the exhibition.

On 19 September 1967, at the age of eighty-two, Zinaida Serebryakova died in Paris.

LATE
NINETEENTH
-EARLY
TWENTIETH
CENTURIES

FIFTY
RUSSIAN
ARTISTS
211

Pavel Petrovich TRUBETSKOI

(1866-1938)

The turn of the century brought to Russian art a highly original master who created deeply psychological images in all the various forms of sculpture—from small-scale pieces to monumental works. Pavel Trubetskoi gained renown as a sculptor who showed a striking and poetic affinity with nature.

He was born on his parents' estate near the Italian town of Intra, near Lake Maggiore. His father, Pyotr Trubetskoi, was a Russian prince, his mother was American. From the age of eight Pavel became interested in sculpture, and under the influence of his brother Pietro, a scene-painter, he made his first sculptures for a puppet theatre; two years later he attended classes with the artist Danielo Ranzoni. Serious lessons in sculpture began in 1884 in Milan, first at Donato Barcaglia's studio, and then with Ernesto Bazzaro. Trubetskoi never, in fact, received a systematic artistic training, but his rare talent and willpower assured his success.

It was in 1886 that the young sculptor first displayed one of his works—a statue of a horse—at an exhibition in the Italian town of Brera; thereafter his works appeared at exhibitions in France and America. He sculptured portraits and small animal figures, and experimented in monumental art. In 1891 he took part in competitions to design monuments to Garibaldi and Dante.

In 1897 Trubetskoi came to Russia, the homeland of his father. Inspired by new impressions, he began to work very intensively, and soon started teaching at the Moscow School of Art, Sculpture and Architecture.

The bronze sculpture *A Moscow Cab Driver* (1898, RM) was the first work he completed in Russia. It is a genre composition with an apparently traditional subject. Similar genre scenes were quite common in the work of the Russian sculptors Ye. A. Lanseré and L. V. Posen. For Trubetskoi this work was an embodiment of his first Russian impressions, devoid of any 'ethnographic' speculation, touchingly sincere, and with great plastic expressiveness in its gentle, flowing forms.

1. V. A. Serov. Portrait of P. P. Trubetskoi
2. A Moscow Cab Driver
3. Dunya

FIFTY
RUSSIAN
ARTISTS
212

P. P. TRUBETSKOI

LATE
NINETEENTH
-EARLY
TWENTIETH
CENTURIES

2

Trubetskoi's exhibition works were sharply criticised in the conservative circles of the St. Petersburg Academy, where his innovatory method was considered a violation of 'classical' canons; but they attracted the attention of leading representatives of Russian society and of the artistic intelligentsia. He got to know such people as Ilya Repin, Isaak Levitan, Valentin Serov and Fyodor Chaliapin, and got on very well with Lev Tolstoy. In the words of V. A. Bulgakov, Tolstoy's secretary, 'The sculptor Paolo Trubetskoi was one of Tolstoy's favourites ... He loved him for his simple, open heart, his uprightness, his hatred of high-society conventions, his love of animals and his vegetarianism.' Tolstoy willingly sat for Trubetskoi, and they had long conversations both in the sculptor's studio and at the writer's estate, Yasnaya Polyana.

His bust of Lev Tolstoy (1899, RM) and the statuette *Lev Tolstoy on a Horse* (1900, RM)

are famous throughout the world. In them, the sculptor reveals the salient qualities in the character of the great Russian writer: calmness and wisdom; intolerance of hypocrisy; simplicity and generosity.

In 1900 Trubetskoi's works were displayed in the Russian pavilion at the World Exhibition in Paris. For his portraits of Tolstoy and L. Golitsyn and his *Moscow Cab Driver* Trubetskoi received joint first prize—the 'Grand Prix'—together with Auguste Rodin.

After this Trubetskoi produced a series of excellent portrait figurines, each unique in its characterisation: e.g. an elegant and emotional likeness of Levitan (1899, RM), an inspired Chaliapin (1899-1900, RM) and a cheerful, good-natured Doctor Botkin (1906, RM). Trubetskoi's sculptures employ vivid artistic devices, displaying mobility and clarity of plastic forms, and a desire to avoid smooth, even,

LATE
NINETEENTH
-EARLY
TWENTIETH
CENTURIES

P. P. TRUBETSKOI

FIFTY
RUSSIAN
ARTISTS
213

and therefore inert, surfaces. It is in this mobility of form that the innermost, spiritual aspects of the model are revealed.

Trubetskoi's female portraits are distinguished by keen perceptiveness, softness of modelling and lyricism. All are unique works of art, from the striking portrait of M. K. Tenisheva in her ball gown (1899, RM) and the aristocratic Golitsyna (1911, State Art Museum of Byelorussia, Minsk) to *Mother with Child* (1898, RM, TG), *Mother with Son* (1901, RM) and the charming *Dunya* (1900, RM).

His portraits of children are especially poetic: cf. *Children—Nikolai and Vladimir Trubetskoi* (1900, RM) and *Girl with Dog (Friends)* (1901, RM). His animals portraits are also remarkably profound psychologically: *Dog* (1899, TG), *Horse and Foal* (1899, Smolensk Regional Museum of Local History), *Siberian Husky* (1903, RM) and *A Saddled Horse* (1898, RM).

Between 1899 and 1909 Trubetskoi worked on a large-scale monument to Alexander III. For this purpose he was given a special studio-pavilion of glass and steel on Old Nevsky Prospekt, near the Alexander Nevsky Monastery. In the preparatory stages of this work, Trubetskoi made eight small-scale models, four life-size ones and two on the scale of the proposed monument.

Emerging in 1900 as winner of a competition for the right to create a monument to Alexander III, Trubetskoi paid little attention to the jury's remarks about the structure of his monument. S. Witte in his *Memoirs* complained about the sculpture's 'unaccommodating character'. Trubetskoi disregarded both this comment and that of the Grand Prince Vladimir Alexandrovich, who saw the monument as a caricature of his brother. The Tsar's widow, however, who liked the portrait's verisimilitude, allowed Trubetskoi to complete the work.

The monument is essentially different from most other monuments to Russian tsars in that the sculptor sought neither idealisation nor outward splendour. Ilya Repin very succinctly summed up the idea behind the work: 'Russia, oppressed by the burden of one of the most reactionary of tsars, has dug in its heels and refuses to go on.'

In the monument Trubetskoi embodied his creative credo: 'A portrait should not be a copy. In clay or on a canvas I convey the idea of the person portrayed, that which I see as characteristic of him.' Whether the words 'I'm not interested in politics; I merely depicted one animal on top of another' were really spoken by Trubetskoi or not, the monument conveys the impression of a dull, crushing force. Alexander Benois remarked that this was a result 'not merely of the master's good fortune, but of his profound penetration of the task at hand.'

Even before the monument was unveiled, Trubetskoi could sense the hostility of many members of the tsar's family and of high-ranking civil servants. Nicholas II wanted it removed to Irkutsk, 'to send it into exile in Siberia, as far as possible from my offended filial eyes', and to have another monument erected in the capital. S. Witte recalled that the sculptor did not even receive his invitation to the unveiling ceremony in time, and arrived too late in St. Petersburg.

Having fallen into disfavour with the authorities and having been deprived of the possibility of starting work on a new commission, Trubetskoi went abroad.

Between 1906 and 1914, in Paris, he made, sculptural portraits of Auguste Rodin, Anatole France, Giacomo Puccini and S. A. Muromtsev, and in London, one of George Bernard Shaw. However he continued to participate in competitions and art exhibitions held in Russia. Personal exhibitions of his work were mounted in 1912 in Chicago and Rome.

In 1914 Trubetskoi went to America, where he constructed monuments to Dante (San-Francisco) and General Otis (Los Angeles).

In 1921 he returned to Paris, and the last years of his life were spent in Italy. He carved a marble statue of the famous Caruso for the La

FIFTY
RUSSIAN
ARTISTS
214

P. P. TRUBETSKOI

LATE
NINETEENTH
-EARLY
TWENTIETH
CENTURIES

3

Scala Opera House in Milan, designed a war memorial for the town of Brera, did a sculptured portrait of Gabriele D'Annunzio, a self-portrait for the Uffizi Gallery in Florence, and a portrait of one of the most famous Italian artists, Giovanni Segantini.

He travelled to Egypt (1934) and Spain (1935) with exhibitions of his own work.

Pavel Trubetskoi died in Italy on 12 February 1938.

Although he spent a comparatively short time in Russia, Trubetskoi made an invaluable contribution to Russian art. His profundity, spirited forms and distinctive styles have had an enormous influence on the development of Soviet sculpture.

LATE
NINETEENTH
-EARLY
TWENTIETH
CENTURIES

FIFTY
RUSSIAN
ARTISTS
215

Abram Yefimovich ARKHIPOV

(1862-1930)

1. Photograph of A. Ye. Arkhipov

Abram Yefimovich Arkhipov made his name in the history of Russian art of the turn of the century as a sensitive, poetic artist who devoted all his talent to themes from peasant life. He was born into a poor peasant family in a remote village in Ryazan Gubernia. As a boy he first showed an interest in drawing at his local school. His parents gave him every possible encouragement, and in 1876, having painstakingly gathered together the necessary means, they sent him to study at the School of Art, Sculpture and Architecture in Moscow. At that time people such as Ryabushkin, Kasatkin and Nesterov were among his fellow-students. The heart of the School, and the best-loved teacher was Vasily Perov, and other teachers included Makovsky, Polenov and Savrasov.

Arkhipov studied eagerly and with great application. His works received prizes at exhibitions. In his third year he completed the painting *A Game of 'Svaika'*, and in the early 1880s painted *The Second-Hand Shop* (1882, TG), *The Drunkard* (1883, TG) and *The Tavern* (1883, TG). Perov's lessons, which urged the artist to be truthful and not to shy from the darker sides of life, clearly did not fall on stony ground. Arkhipov started out as a genre-artist, in the footsteps of his teacher.

In 1883, after seven years at the School, Arkhipov decided to continue his education at the Academy of Arts. The academic system of teaching disappointed him, however. Despite the fact that his study *Man Falling from the Saddle* and various other drawings were hailed as masterpieces and donated to the Academy's permanent collection, Arkhipov left the Academy and returned to the Moscow School. After Perov's death he studied under Polenov, whose art, permeated with light and a joyful perception of life, also exerted an influence on his work.

One of the most important works drawing together the threads of Arkhipov's student period was *Friends* or *Visiting the Sick Woman* (1885, TG), which depicts the artist's mother. Her head sadly inclined, her eyes fixed on one point, a sick

FIFTY
RUSSIAN
ARTISTS
216

A. YE. ARKHIPOV

LATE
NINETEENTH
-EARLY
TWENTIETH
CENTURIES

LATE
NINETEENTH
-EARLY
TWENTIETH
CENTURIES

A. YE. ARKHIPOV

FIFTY
RUSSIAN
ARTISTS
217

woman is sitting on a straw-filled bed in a miserable, dark hut. Beside her, with the same dimmed, sorrowful look in her eyes, is her neighbour, come to pay the sick woman a visit. The postures of the two women, their tired, unhappy faces—everything tells of their humility, hopelessness and sadness. Only the sunlight, bursting in through the open door, is a reminder that happiness and beauty do exist somewhere. The painting contains both quiet melancholy and a feeling of deep compassion for human sorrow.

In 1888 Arkhipov set off on a trip along the Volga with his friends from the School. They stayed in villages, drawing a lot and painting many études. This was where he conceived the idea for the small painting *On the Volga* (1889, RM), in which for the first time he tried to achieve a successful fusion of genre scene and lyrical landscape.

Two years later Arkhipov was accepted as an active member of the *Peredvizhniki* Society. That same year, he completed one of his best known works, *Along the River Oka* (TG), which shows a barge floating along the river with tired peasants, deep in thought. Its meaning extends beyond the bare subject-matter, however. It is a story about people who are capable of enduring a great deal without losing their strength and steadfastness. It is an affirmation of the beauty of Russian nature, with its blue horizons, the spring flooding of its rivers, and its streams of sunlight. The muted colour-scheme is in harmony with the general mood of the painting. Arkhipov's artistic style has changed. Compared to the careful detail of his early works, his style has become freer, more expansive and passionate.

'The whole picture is painted in sunlight,' wrote Stasov about this painting, 'and this can be felt in every patch of light and shade, and in the overall wonderful impression; among the people on the barge, the four women—idle, tired, despondent, sitting in silence on their bundles—are portrayed with magnificent realism.'

In the 1890s Arkhipov painted mostly in the open air, portraying his heroes not in their small, stuffy studios and rooms but in the wide-open spaces of the Volga, in broad, sunlit squares, green meadows and roads. The painting *The Ice Is Gone* (1895, Ryazan Regional Art Gallery) breathes the cheerfulness of spring. The river is freeing itself of ice, throwing off the fetters of winter. The inhabitants of the surrounding villages—old men, women and children—have come to observe the ceremonious awakening of Spring. Everything is bathed in the first rays of the sun. In Arkhipov's works, people are closely bound up with nature. Their thoughts and feelings are refracted through the prism of the landscape, which—like Russian folk tales and songs—has an epic breadth and sweep and is full of lyricism and gentle poetry.

Later, Arkhipov also painted highly dramatic works. The first of them—*The Convoy* (1893, TG)—deals with a new theme for the artist: that of the tragic fate of the peasants, ruined and impoverished, worn down by poverty and landlessness. Silent and submissive, they patiently bear their cross.

In his painting *Women Labourers at the Iron Foundry* (1896, TG), Arkhipov dealt with one of the nineteenth century's most poignant themes: the bitter fate of Russian women. The painting depicts the women resting from their exhausting labour, but the artist draws more attention to their milieu. The drifting black smoke, the sun-scorched earth and the low, wooden buildings help us to imagine the dreadful conditions that these women worked in from dawn to dusk.

Arkhipov's paintings seldom depict acute situations or actions. The basic meaning is revealed through the milieu or surroundings in which the events take place. This was a characteristic device for artists at the end of the nineteenth century. One of Arkhipov's best and most interesting works is the painting *The Washer-Women*, of which there are two versions: (1899, RM; and 1901, TG). While working on it, the artist searched tirelessly for a mod-

FIFTY
RUSSIAN
ARTISTS
218

A. YE. ARKHIPOV

LATE
NINETEENTH
-EARLY
TWENTIETH
CENTURIES

3

el. He visited wash-houses, and spent hours watching the movements of the women at work. When the painting was almost finished, he noticed an old washer-woman sitting in a wash-house at the Smolensk market in Moscow. Her hunched back, her lowered head and her limply hanging arm—everything spoke of utter exhaustion, deep spiritual apathy and hopelessness. Profoundly moved by all this, Arkhipov decided to start a new canvas, and in this way the second version came about. The artist ignored many unnecessary details, enlarging the figures by moving them closer to the spectator. He raised the picture to a universal level, epitomising the hopelessness and doom of these women's existence.

The Washer-Women is an example of the artist's new searchings in the realm of colour. In contrast to his other works, the painting is also,

to a certain extent, accusatory, a trait which brings it in line with the best traditions of critical realism of the second half of the nineteenth century.

The early 1900s saw the creation of Arkhipov's Northern landscapes. They represent nature in all its splendour, with muted colours, distinctive wooden buildings, rickety cottages huddled together along river-banks, deserted wooded islands, and huge boulders by the seaside. He worked enthusiastically on *A Northern Village* (1902, TG), *A Jetty in the North* (1903, TG), and *In the North* (1912, TG), the greyish colour-range of which is amazingly rich in subtle shades and half-tones.

At this time, too, Arkhipov painted an unusual series of portraits of peasant women and girls from the Ryazan and Nizhny Novgorod regions. They are all dressed in bright national costume,

LATE
NINETEENTH
-EARLY
TWENTIETH
¯CENTURIES

A. YE. ARKHIPOV

FIFTY
RUSSIAN
ARTISTS
219

with embroidered scarves and beads. Painted with broad, lively strokes, the paintings are marked by their decorativeness and buoyant colours, with rich reds and pinks predominating.

Arkhipov also expended much time and energy on his activities as a teacher. He started teaching in 1894 in the Moscow School of Art, Sculpture and Architecture, and carried on there after the Revolution. In 1924 he joined the Association of Artists of Revolutionary Russia, and in 1927—to mark his fortieth year as an artist—he was among the first who were awarded the title of People's Artist of the Russian Republic.

Abram Arkhipov died in 1930.

2. The Washer-Women
3. The Guests

Sergei Vasilievich IVANOV

(1864-1910)

1

2

Sergei Vasilievich Ivanov was born in the town of Ruza in Moscow Gubernia into the family of an exciseman. The boy's artistic leanings became apparent at an early age, but his father considered that he would never make an artist, or that at the most he might become 'a sign-painter'. Discerning no difference between painting and drawing, he decided that his son should become an engineer, and sent him in 1875 to the Konstantinovsky Institute of Land Surveying. The Institute oppressed him, and on the advice of P. P. Sinebatov, a colleague of his father's and an 'eternal student' at the Academy of Arts, in the autumn of 1878 he started studying at the Moscow School of Art as an external student. The following year he left the Institute and began full-time at the School of Art. In 1882 he entered the St. Petersburg Academy of Arts, and in 1883 completed his first painting *Blind Folk* (Sverdlovsk Art Gallery), which was the fruit of a journey to the Volga area. His interest in the way of life of peasant resettlers also undoubtedly dates from this time.

Ivanov's studies at the Academy were successful, but both his dissatisfaction with academic practises and his own financial difficulties forced him—by this time in his final year—to leave the Academy and return to Moscow, where he re-entered the School of Art. The works painted during the last stage of his studies include *The Sick Woman* (1884, whereabouts unknown), *At the Tavern* (1885, whereabouts unknown), *A Request to the Lady of the Manor* (1885, whereabouts unknown), *At the Jail* (1884-85, TG) and *The Agitator in a Train Carriage* (1885, Museum of the Revolution).

The direction of the young artist's work is quite clear. He is interested in the life of the peasants, and in the last of the above-mentioned paintings his subject is a revolutionary. His artistic style is also taking shape; the most successful of these paintings from the point of view of expression and colour harmony is *At the Jail*.

The theme of 'resettlers' was attracting the artist more and more; on obtaining permission

LATE
NINETEENTH
-EARLY
TWENTIETH
CENTURIES

S. V. IVANOV

FIFTY
RUSSIAN
ARTISTS
221

3

from the Moscow Art Society to visit the districts between Moscow and Orenburg, he left the School without even a certificate qualifying him to teach drawing. From that time on Ivanov became a kind of chronicler of the tragedy that befell many Russian peasants after the reform of 1861, about which Lenin wrote: 'The ruined, impoverished, hungry masses of ... centre—the "heart" of Russia—rushed for resettlement.'

The well-known art critic Sergei Glagol says the following about this period in Ivanov's life and work: '. . . Scores of miles he covered with the resettlers in the dust of the Russian roads, in rain and in the scorching sun of the steppe; many nights he spent with them, filling his album with drawings and sketches; many tragic scenes passed before his eyes, and a series of pictures took shape in his head—an epic telling of the resettlement of the Russian peasantry.'

Ivanov's pictures and drawings present horrifying scenes from the life of the resettlers. Hope and despair, illness and death were the constant companions of those people wandering in the vast expanses of Russia. One of the most impressive is the painting *Resettlers Returning* (1888, Syktyvkar, The Komi ASSR Art Museum), in which one is made acutely aware of the tragedy of the peasants' position. The fate of one of these unfortunate people—in the painting *On the Road. The Death of a Resettler* (1889, TG)—is presented as the logical outcome of an inconsolable situation.

The next chapter of Ivanov's social epic was the 'prisoners series', work on which coincided to some extent with the 'resettlers cycle'; it was at this time that the artist painted his *Uprising in the Country* (1889, Museum of the Revolution). Consequently, various aspects of the lives of the Russian people at that time became connected

FIFTY
RUSSIAN
ARTISTS
222

S. V. IVANOV

LATE
NINETEENTH
-EARLY
TWENTIETH
CENTURIES

in the mind of the artist as links in the same chain: poverty and lack of rights 'on the land', all the burdens of resettlement, jails, exile, and finally the peasant uprising. It is clear that the artist did not consider the fugitives, convicts and prisoners a 'band of robbers', for he understood the social reasons which were the ultimate cause of people being sent to prison or into exile. Ivanov had no opportunity to meet the political prisoners who swamped the tsarist prisons, but he managed to discern the human soul even among criminals. When he got to know them a bit better, and spoke to many of 'these dishonoured outcasts, with their shaven heads', it became clear to him 'that most of them, despite years of wandering from one prison to another, and from Russia to Siberia and back again, were neither vicious nor were they the dregs and parasites of society.'

With great expressiveness the artist conveys the state of mind of a fugitive peasant who has found his way to his own home, from which he will again have to flee to hide from his pursuers (*The Fugitive*, sketch, 1886, TG). Ivanov does not disguise his sympathy for the handsome, black-bearded peasant, one of the Mironov brothers, 'who were on their way to Siberia for beating a village policeman and a witness'. The characters in the painting *The Tramp* (1890, whereabouts unknown) are portrayed with great psychological accuracy, the indifference of the policeman being contrasted with the guardedness of the arrested man. The painting *The Dispatch of the Prisoners* (1889, Museum of the Revolution) produces a feeling of oppression. This is largely due to its colour composition: the large, dismal, dark-green expanse of the prisoners' carriage, the dirty grey shades of the station arches, the dark-red wall, the muddy snow and the brownish crowd of people seeing the prisoners off. The painting *The Halting Place* (1891, the painting itself has not survived, facsimile in the Radishchev Art Gallery in Saratov) seems to sum up the 'prisoners series'. Prostrate bodies, shackled in irons, are shown in a sharp

foreshortening perspective, and singled out among these sleeping figures is the face of a shorn prisoner. The painting acquires great expressiveness from the compositional device of magnifying the subject, which makes one feel that one is actually beside that tangle of bodies, in which, in the artist's own words, 'you see a pile of arms, legs and backs, and cannot distinguish individual bodies, and then suddenly you catch sight of a pair of eyes which are fixed on you'. This compositional technique increases the poignancy of the painting's protest against the social reality of the time.

A new period in Ivanov's creative life began in the mid-1890s, when he turned to historical themes. His historical paintings contain features that liken him to Surikov and Ryabushkin. He understood the state of the masses at crucial moments (cf. *Discord* 1897, I. I. Brodsky Flat-Museum, Leningrad, *Judgment of the People's Council*, 1896, private collection), he was attracted by the strength of the Russian national character, and, like Ryabushkin, found beauty in the everyday life of the people and asserted their understanding of this beauty. He was acutely aware of the artistic searchings of his time; and his works during these years are distinguished by their rich colour combinations.

Ivanov also worked with great enthusiasm on paintings of the leaders of popular uprisings —Stepan Razin and Yemelian Pugachov.

Ivanov exhibited one of his works—*The Arrival of Foreigners in Seventeenth-Century Moscow* (TG)—at a *Peredvizhniki* Exhibition in 1901 (he was admitted to the Society in 1899). The painting depicts the various attitudes of the Muscovites to the newcomers: mistrust, surprise and naive curiosity; the characters, the details and the magnificent winter landscape all have a peculiar historical flavour.

In 1902 Ivanov exhibited his painting *The Tsar. Sixteenth Century* (TG) at an exhibition of 'The Union of 36'—the nucleus of the future Union of Russian Artists, one of whose founders and organisers he was. This painting, like

LATE
NINETEENTH
-EARLY
TWENTIETH
CENTURIES

S. V. IVANOV

FIFTY
RUSSIAN
ARTISTS
223

4

The Arrival of Foreigners, depicts a winter's day. Only here there are no curious onlookers: everyone is kissing the ground. Along this unusual 'corridor', past rows of people with their heads buried in the snow, the tsar's guards in red caftans solemnly proceed. The tsar himself is seated on a richly decorated horse; he is fat and clumsy, and holds high his foolish, pompous face.

The painting got a mixed reception in the press. Some saw in the prostrated bodies and in the tsar's shining garments 'an awareness of the greatness of the moment', others were puzzled: 'the tsar's face can scarcely be called regal; he is more like a well-fed merchant in tsar's clothing'. The *Moskovskiye vedomosti* spotted that 'Ivanov's disgusting lampoon' was a caricature of the Russian tsar.

In 1903 at the First Exhibition of the Union of Russian Artists Ivanov displayed his paintings *Strike* and *The March of the Muscovites. Sixteenth Century* (TG). The latter again depicts an icy winter's day, brought to life by the noisy, energetic troops surging along the road.

In 1910 Ivanov completed a painting entitled *The Family* (TG), on which he had been working for many years. If it can be said that *The March of the Muscovites* and many other of Ivanov's paintings are similar to those of Surikov, then *The Family* can be likened to paintings by Ryabushkin depicting the Russian patriarchal way of life. Ivanov's interest in history can also be seen in his illustrations for Gogol's *Taras Bulba*, and in various picture-plates on historical themes which he made for the Knebel Publishing House.

The public-spiritedness of Ivanov's work came to the fore during the 1905-07 revolution. As early as 1903 his painting *Strike* (The Uzbekistan Museum of Fine Arts, Tashkent) was

FIFTY
RUSSIAN
ARTISTS
224

S. V. IVANOV

LATE
NINETEENTH
-EARLY
TWENTIETH
CENTURIES

shown at an exhibition of the Union of Russian Artists; this was the first depiction of the proletariat in rebellion in the history of Russian art. In 1905 he painted one of his most impressive historical-revolutionary works, *Execution* (Museum of the Revolution). Here, the ideas adumbrated in *At the Jail* and *Uprising in the Country* were expressed with even greater acuteness.

An empty grey square, hung over by huge buildings, separates the soldiers from the demonstrators. A volley is fired, and the first victims fall to the ground. In the rays of the setting sun the colour contrasts of violet, yellow, crimson and brown on the buildings seem sinister. The splashes of blue and dark-red in the dead men's clothes on the evenly lit square strike a tragic note. The meaning of the events is clear: the courage of the bearers of the red flag marching to their death, and the cruelty of their punishers.

Ivanov made a magnificent etching (Pushkin Fine Arts Museum, Moscow) from the painting *Execution;* he also etched another historical-revolutionary work entitled *Beside the Wall. An Episode from 1905.*

The Victors (1905, Museum of the Revolution) was the sarcastic title Ivanov gave to his water-colour depicting the results of 'victorious' actions of the tsarist henchmen: a snow-covered square, corpses, and a woman fleeing with a little girl, seized by terror. Ivanov exposed the meaning of the tsarist manifesto about 'freedoms' in the drawings *The Suppressors* and *The Search.*

On 20 October, the day of the revolutionary N. Bauman's funeral, Ivanov was among those guarding the university from the police. That night in the university—which the students turned into a temporary hospital—has been immortalised in sketches and drawings by Ivanov. An album of rough drafts for the painting *The Funeral of Bauman* has also been preserved.

Teaching occupied an important position in Ivanov's life. He taught for eleven years in the Moscow School of Art and in the Stroganov College, and many Soviet artists owe a great deal to him for the development of their talent.

Ivanov was a modest, self-effacing man, but he possessed a vivid, unique talent. In his works he revealed the story of Russia, past and present, and the 'movement of life' towards the future.

Sergei Ivanov died at the age of forty-six on 3 August 1910.

1. O. E. Braz. Portrait of S. V. Ivanov
2. Execution
3. The Family
4. The Arrival of Foreigners in 17th-Century Moscow

LATE
NINETEENTH
-EARLY
TWENTIETH
CENTURIES

FIFTY
RUSSIAN
ARTISTS
225

Andrei Petrovich
RYABUSHKIN

(1861-1904)

Ryabushkin made a name for himself in the history of Russian art as a talented master of historical genre-painting and a sensitive portrayer of the peasant way of life. He was born in the village of Stanichnaya Sloboda in Tambov Gubernia. His father and elder brother were icon-painters, and the young Ryabushkin helped them in their work. The boy was orphaned at the age of fourteen, and remained with his elder brother who had by then taken up his father's profession. Chance had a hand in Ryabushkin's becoming an artist: while staying at Stanichnaya Sloboda, A. Preobrazhensky, a student at the Moscow School of Art, Sculpture and Architecture, noticed Ryabushkin's talent. He took the boy with him to Moscow, enrolled him at the School of Art, and thereafter played a very active part in his life.

The first works which Ryabushkin completed at the School of Art—*The Pirates' Attack, The Carnival Procession, A Summer Evening in the Country* (1881, RM) and others—revealed his interest in subjects connected with life in the Russian countryside. His most independent work of this period was his *Peasant Wedding in Tambov Gubernia* (1880, TG). This painting already shows signs of the artist's individual traits: his sensitive power of observation, his restraint and tenderness in conveying feelings, and his good-natured, indulgent irony.

Ryabushkin did not complete his course at the Moscow School of Art. He went to St. Petersburg after the death of his teacher Vasily Perov and entered the Academy of Arts in 1882. He was greatly aided in his professional training by his teacher there, Pavel Chistyakov. Ryabushkin's picturesque study *The Model* (1887, Academy of Arts Research Museum) was given to the Academy as one of the best examples of pupils' work. During these years Ryabushkin worked on subjects from the Bible, classical mythology and Roman history, in accordance with the Academy's programme.

The teachers at the Academy observed the young artist's boldness and innovatoriness, his

. Self-Portrait

FIFTY
RUSSIAN
ARTISTS
226

A. P. RYABUSHKIN

LATE
NINETEENTH
-EARLY
TWENTIETH
CENTURIES

2

ability to achieve realism, the persuasiveness of his compositions and the naturalness of his characters. At this time, Ryabushkin also amused himself by doing illustrations for the popular magazines *World Illustration* and *Niva*.

Ryabushkin chose a religious theme—*The Removal from the Cross* (1890, TG)—for his diploma work at the Academy. During his work on it, however, he cooled towards the original sketch which had been approved by the Council of the Academy, and, unafraid of the consequences, painted a completely new composition in the month before the work was due to be submitted. This breaking of the rules led to his being denied the first-class gold medal.

On leaving the Academy in 1890 Ryabushkin was at last able to realise a dream of his, and set off on a tour of ancient Russian towns. He was attracted by the architecture and decoration of the old Russian buildings. In the museums he studied traditional fabrics and costumes, household equipment and utensils, and weapons. He also had a passionate interest in historical literature, chronicles and folk legends. Presently he went to stay on the estate of his friend I. Tyumenev not far from the village of Lyuban, near St. Petersburg, and in 1901 moved to the estate of

Didvino, which belonged to his close friend V. Belyaev. Here he had a studio and small house built to his own design, where he lived quietly and almost uninterruptedly, engrossed in music and painting. His closest advisers and friends, and the severest critics of his work were the peasants, to whose weddings, christenings and family celebrations he was always being invited. Ryabushkin owed his best works to the countryside, whose inexhaustible wealth of material constantly nourished his art.

In 1891 he exhibited one of his works—*Awaiting the Newly-weds in Novgorod Gubernia* (1891, RM)—for the first time at a *Peredvizhniki* Exhibition. According to the reminiscences of friends, this painting was inspired by Ryabushkin's impressions after attending a peasant wedding. It depicts the poignant moment when the wedding guests, friends, relations and match-makers are sitting in silence, awaiting the return of the newly-weds. Ryabushkin conveys various shades of human feelings with great simplicity and restraint. He takes pleasure in his characters, whose moral integrity and dignity are close to his heart. The directness of style and the vitality of the characters make this a typical product of the 1890s.

LATE
NINETEENTH
-EARLY
TWENTIETH
CENTURIES

A. P. RYABUSHKIN

FIFTY
RUSSIAN
ARTISTS
227

3

FIFTY
RUSSIAN
ARTISTS
228

A. P. RYABUSHKIN

LATE
NINETEENT
-EARLY
TWENTIETH
CENTURIES

Ryabushkin's travellings throughout Russia, and his fascination with Russian history and the folk epic, aroused his interest in the historical genre. In 1892 he painted *The Game Regiment of Peter I in a Pot-House* (TG), treating one of the important events of the Petrine era, the conflict between the streltsi—the members of the old army—and Peter's new, young Game soldiers. But in Ryabushkin's treatment the inner conflict takes on a peaceful, commonplace character; the artist was never drawn to dramatic or tense situations. His friends were aware of this unique, original approach to a historical theme. Repin wrote that the painting 'transports' one into the distant past . . . 'Everything is so unexpected, so natural and authentic—an excellent work!' Stasov remarked that Ryabushkin had 'an originality all his own, a fresh, distinctive approach . . .'

In 1893 Ryabushkin painted the work *Tsar Mikhail Fyodorovich in Session with Boyars* (TG). In it he conveys with delicate but biting irony the air of boredom and formal self-importance which prevailed at such 'sessions'. It is as though dummies in boyar clothing are discussing affairs of state, their faces indifferent and apathetic. Here, for the first time, the artist uses a completely new, unusual colour-scheme. Whereas before his main concern was to achieve an exact likeness of his model, in this painting he set himself another, no less important task—to reveal 'the spirit of history' through the overall colour-structure of the painting.

During the 1890s Ryabushkin completed a good many drawings and water-colours commissioned for various albums and publications, and also made studies for the proposed redecoration of St. Sophia's Cathedral in Novgorod. His finest historical canvas of this decade was the painting *Moscow Street in the Seventeenth Century* (1896, RM).

Choosing an everyday scene from life in Moscow of the seventeenth century, Ryabushkin recreated here a page from Russia's distant past, bringing to life a typical corner of old Moscow, with its low stone and wooden buildings and it impassable mud. People lift high the hems c their clothing; a young woman in red, with white scarf, carefully picks her way along timbered footway; a boyar sits astride a blac horse; a pauper seated in front of an icon i begging for alms . . . The artist had witnesse many such scenes in provincial Russian town and was therefore able to achieve remarkabl vividness and naturalness in his portrayal.

The landscape plays an important role in thi work. The cold autumnal day, the dark cloud and the thinning foliage on the trees all lend melancholy note to the atmosphere. The artist' attitude to his subject is sensitive, good-nature and slightly ironic. Yet at the same time he ad mires the primitiveness, the naive simplicity, th attractiveness and colourfulness of this way c life. For the painting's decorative effect Rya bushkin drew on the traditions of Russian icon and frescoes. He is not striving for an illusor portrayal of objects. His style of painting is dis tinguished by its density, vivid decorativenes and localised patches of colour. This style wa his own creative discovery, the result of his ow interpretation of the problems of historical genre art.

Ryabushkin's interest in the seventeenth cen tury led him to plan a series of historical por traits depicting representatives of the variou social strata of that period. Only one portrait however, was realised—*The Merchant's Fami ly* (1897, RM). It is remarkable for the sta tic quality of its composition and the im mobility of the characters, who are neithe caricatured nor idealised.

Dissatisfied with his first attempt, and striv ing to achieve more unity in the artistic inter pretation of the piece, Ryabushkin reworke it, strengthening its humanistic basis and mak ing the images of the girls more attractiv and lively.

In 1899 Ryabushkin completed one of his fa vourite paintings, *Seventeenth-Century Russia Women in Church* (TG). Displaying a rare sens

LATE
NINETEENTH
-EARLY
TWENTIETH
CENTURIES

A. P. RYABUSHKIN

FIFTY
RUSSIAN
ARTISTS
229

of decorativeness, Ryabushkin created an integrated colour ensemble from the gaily-coloured clothes and the brightly painted interior of the church. With its flowing, sing-song rhythm, rich colours and lucid harmony, the painting is reminiscent of an old, melodic song. Its refined elegance recalls the ancient Yaroslavl frescoes, or old enamel-work and miniatures. Both this painting and *The Merchant's Family* were awarded honorary diplomas at the International Exhibition in Paris.

In 1901 Ryabushkin painted one of his best works, *A Wedding Procession in Moscow* (TG), which again evokes Moscow in the far-off seventeenth century. The noisy, brightly-coloured procession is moving swiftly along a street. Against the background of a dark-grey shed, we see the well-dressed figure of an unhappy young girl who is trying to remove herself as far as possible from the splendid, gay festivities. The artist has left much unsaid, leaving it to the spectator to interpret the painting in his own way. The landscape is portrayed with particular subtlety —it is still and pensive, brushed by the last rays of the setting spring sun. In places the canvas has scarcely been touched by the artist's brush, certain details have not been elaborated, and Ryabushkin himself considered the painting incomplete; yet for all this, it is an integrated work, full of emotional expressiveness.

In the last years of his life Ryabushkin illustrated many Russian epic tales, and also painted pictures on village themes, such as *Going to*

the Well (1898), *In a Village* (1902, private collection), *Young Man Joins a Round Dance* (1902, TG), *In a Village. Going to Liturgy* (1903, TG). His attitude to contemporary village life was reflected in one of his later works, *Tea Drinking* (1903, Moscow, private collection), in which his former poetisation of life in the Russian countryside was no longer in evidence. In its psychological depth, the work may be likened only to Korovin's *Village Meeting*.

In the last years of his life Ryabushkin was seriously ill with tuberculosis. In 1903 he went to Switzerland on the advice of his doctors, but sadly his health did not improve. He returned to Russia and died on 10 May 1904 in his studio at Didvino, surrounded by his friends. Russian art lost a great, original and truly national artist.

4

Nikolai Konstantinovich ROERICH

(1874–1947)

1. B. M. Kustodiev. Portrait of N. K. Roerich

Nikolai Konstantinovich Roerich, an out
standing artist, scholar and public figure, wa
born in St. Petersburg. His ancestors, of Danish
and Norwegian stock, had settled in Russia in
the first half of the eighteenth century. His
father, who owned a notary office, was a highly
cultured man with a wide range of interests, and
many leading scholars of the day were attracted
to the Roerich household.

From childhood the future artist loved read
ing historical books and listening to ancient leg
ends, and dreamt of travelling. He developed a
rich imagination and a keen interest in ancient
Rus. During his years at the gymnasium he took
part in archeological excavations, and it was also
at this time that his talent for drawing became
apparent.

On leaving the gymnasium in 1893, Roerich
became a student both at the Academy of Arts
and in the Law Faculty of the University. His
interest in the mysteries of the past, however
continued to grow, and he also attended lectures
in the Department of History. As a member of
the Russian Archeological Society, he spent the
summer months on excavations.

In 1895, after meeting Vladimir Stasov, who
was at that time in charge of the art section of
the Public Library, Roerich began a serious
study of ancient books, manuscripts and deeds.

Roerich's teacher, Kuinji, played an important role in shaping the young artist's talent. In
Kuinji's studio Roerich began to paint landscapes from nature, and also completed his first
historical works. In 1897 he and Kuinji's other
pupils left the Academy as a sign of protest at
the dismissal of their beloved teacher. He continued working on a series of paintings based on
the life of the ancient Slavs, which he entitled
The Beginning of Rus; the Slavs.

The conception of this series was quite original. Roerich was not trying to recreate particular historical events, and although he resurrects
the past on the basis of scientific archeological
findings, the essence of his work is not
reconstruction of a past age, but its poetic em-

LATE
NINETEENTH
-EARLY
TWENTIETH
CENTURIES

N. K. ROERICH

FIFTY
RUSSIAN
ARTISTS
231

bodiment. Characteristic of Roerich's painting are his rich fantasy, his emotional perception of ancient times, and his ability to convey the special flavour of those times.

Of the early works in this series—*The Herald; Clan Rises Against Clan* (1897, TG), *The Meeting of the Elders* (1899, RM), *The Campaign* (1899, whereabouts unknown)—the first is the most successful. Here, by means of the twilight colours and the shimmering of the moon, the artist expresses a mood of impending danger, a foreboding of bad news. Roerich painted two other works—*Idols* (1901, RM) and *Merchants From Overseas* (1901, TG; 1902 version in RM)—in Paris, where he spent some time working in the studio of the historical artist Fernand Cormon.

Idols depicts a pagan temple: behind a fence decorated with the skulls of sacrificed animals, in the midst of elaborate stone idols, an old sorcerer is wandering, deep in thought; the world of Slavonic superstitions comes to life before us, and one can sense the atmosphere of ancient mysteries. The artistic idiom of this work is significantly different from Roerich's earlier works, the novelty lying in its generalisation of form, precise outlines, and a complete, integrated composition.

The search for new imagery was particularly clear in the painting *Merchants From Overseas,* in which the artist's talent as a colourist came into its own. The exultant colours of this picturesque work bring back to life the age of discovery of new lands. The Vikings' long boats sail across a blue sea amidst green islands; a high wind fills the brightly-coloured sails, and white seagulls swoop down to meet them with a loud cry. Here, Roerich reworked certain folk art techniques to produce a highly decorative, colourfully harmonious and joyful work.

The artist returned to Russia in 1901 and continued to work on Slavonic themes: *Small Town* (1902, RM), *Alexander Nevsky Strikes Birger-Jarl* (1904, RM), *A Town Is Built* (1902, TG),

The Dnieper Slavs (1905, RM) and others. Completed in 1901, the painting *Omens* (RM) is of particular interest. It portrays a derelict shore, with dark silhouettes of ravens perched on huge boulders, under a cold sky, evoking evil presentiments.

In the summers of 1903 and 1904 Roerich and his wife made a tour of ancient Russian towns, studying their architecture, painting, applied arts, folklore and traditional dances. This led to a series of ninety picturesque canvases portraying monuments of old Russian architecture. In these artistically subtle works one can feel the artist's deep understanding of the style of ancient buildings and his enthusiasm for the inspired creations of ancient Russian masters. At this time, too, Roerich published several articles popularising old Russian art and appealing for the preservation of Russia's ancient national heritage.

In 1906 Roerich began work on an unusual series of paintings about human prehistory: *The Stone Age* (1910, whereabouts unknown), *Coastal Dwellers. Morning* (1906, Gorlovka Picture Gallery), *The Forefathers of Man* (1911, whereabouts unknown; later copy in RM). This latter painting is typical of the series. It depicts a young Slav playing on a pipe, and bears, enchanted by the magical sounds, are peacefully settled on the green hills around him. In this series Roerich gave symbolic expression to his philosophical outlook, which was linked to the ideas of the Enlightenment. He contrasts contemporary society with a past idyll, where people were motivated by goodness and love, and lived in harmony with nature. Roerich believed that the key to the transformation of reality lay in man's moral perfection, and that radiant, purifying art could serve this goal.

Also at this time, Roerich painted a number of unusual historical landscapes which reflected his pantheistic conceptions of the ancient Slavs, who spiritualised nature and believed in mystical powers which influenced man's life. These paintings included *The Herald* (1914, RM),

FIFTY
RUSSIAN
ARTISTS
232

N. K. ROERICH

LATE
NINETEENTH
-EARLY
TWENTIETH
CENTURIES

2

Astral Runes (1912, whereabouts unknown), *Heavenly Battle* (1909, England; copy 1912, RM). They are noteworthy for their emotional and poetic qualities, and for their interesting associations with fairy-tale images.

In the pre-war years, works appeared with complex symbolic imagery, fantastic subject-matter, intense expressiveness and generalised artistic language. Such, for example, were *The Serpent's Cry* (1913, Pskov Museum) and *A Doomed City* (1914, whereabouts unknown), in which there was a foreboding of the tragic events to come. The latter depicts a white city in the clutch of a giant fiery boa.

Of enormous interest are the sets which

Roerich designed for the theatre, especially those for Meaterlinck's play *Sister Beatrice* (1914), Ibsen's *Peer Gynt* (1912), Rimsky-Korsakov's opera *The Woman of Pskov* (1909) and Borodin's opera *Prince Igor* (1914). Roerich brilliantly conveyed the national colouring and emotional atmosphere of each of these works. Particularly original and poetic was his design for Stravinsky's ballet *The Rite of Spring* (1913), for which he also wrote the libretto, based on the life of the ancient Slavs.

Roerich also worked in the genre of monumental art, making sketches for the decoration of secular buildings and churches. His murals

LATE
NINETEENTH
-EARLY
TWENTIETH
CENTURIES

N. K. ROERICH

FIFTY
RUSSIAN
ARTISTS
233

for the Church of the Holy Ghost in Talashkino (1911) are among his best.

He was sympathetic towards the revolution and joined the Arts Commission set up in March 1917 on the initiative and under the chairmanship of Maxim Gorky. In May 1917, owing to a serious lung disease, Roerich went to the Karelian Isthmus, and in the spring of the following year, when the interventionists attacked Russia, he found himself abroad.

In 1918 Roerich travelled in Finland, Norway, Denmark and England with an exhibition of his works, and in 1920 he went to America, where his work was particularly well received. In America he made an effort to popularise Russian art, organised an Art University, an Artists' Union, and 'The Crown of the World' International Art Centre, the aim of which was to foster cultural collaboration between the peoples of different countries. In 1923 a Roerich Museum was opened by a group of his admirers.

In that same year the artist left America and went to France via Italy and Switzerland. From France he sailed East, having made up his mind to realise a long-cherished dream—to make a tour of India and Central Asia. This unusual expedition lasted for five years. Roerich's group crossed the Himalayas and carried on into some of the most inaccessible areas of Central Asia; in May 1926 the travellers crossed into the Soviet Union and made their way to Moscow. Here, Roerich met the Minister of Culture Lunacharsky and presented the Soviet government with some of his works. The following summer the travellers went to the Altai mountains, then through Siberia into Mongolia and further across the Gobi Desert, Tsaidam, Tibet, and back across the Himalayas to their starting point, the town of Darjeeling. They encountered many dangers and obstacles, and during a forced winter stop in the Tibetan mountains they nearly died of hunger and cold. But throughout the expedition Roerich continued to work, even in the most extreme conditions; the fruits of this trip amounted to some five hundred paintings and sketches. His scientific findings were also substantial: Roerich made a thorough study of the art, ancient manuscripts, rites, traditions and religions of all the areas he visited. In 1928, for the purpose of sorting out the collected material, he set up the Himalayan Institute for Scientific Research in the Kulu Valley (Western Himalayas). In 1930, after a short visit to America, Roerich and his family settled permanently in the Kulu Valley, where he was visited by famous Indian artists and politicians.

The works which Roerich painted in India are extremely diverse in character. During the 1920s he worked on a cycle of paintings directly linked to his study of ancient oriental philosophy and the problems of ethics. He painted portraits of those whom he considered to be preachers of the eternal norms of morality—Mohammed, Buddha, Christ, Confucius, Lao Tzu and others. Linked to this cycle are the religious paintings *Compassion* and *Madonna of Work*. The canvas *The Advent of Time* occupies a special place in his work. It depicts, on an enormous scale, a wise man's head with features similar to those of Lenin. The artist thus connected his ideas about the liberation of the peoples of the East to the name of the leader of the Russian Revolution.

Roerich's principal works during the last twenty years of his life, however, were landscapes, which were as a rule suffused with a deep philosophical content. In them Roerich glorified the majesty and eternal, ennobling beauty of nature.

He painted over six hundred pictures of the Eastern Himalayas, which together constitute a beautiful epic poem on canvas. They include paintings such as *Remember!* (1945, RM), *The Himalayas; Glaciers* (1937, RM), and *The Himalayas, Nanda-Devi* (1941, RM).

These works are executed in tempera, a technique which allowed the artist greatest expression for his artistic searchings.

FIFTY
RUSSIAN
ARTISTS
234

N. K. ROERICH

LATE
NINETEENTH
-EARLY
TWENTIETH
CENTURIES

3

In the cycle *The Strongholds of Tibet* Roerich harmoniously combined the landscape and the ancient architectural monuments of the East: cf. *Lhasa* (1942, RM), *Stupa Ladak* (1941, RM), *Tibetan Monastery* (1942, RM) and *Royal Monastery; Tibet* (1932, TG). Often the artistic monuments depicted by Roerich are connected with ancient superstitions, and have a symbolic meaning. An example of this is the series devoted to Maitreya, the Buddha of the future, who is destined to bring happiness to Earth. Typical of this series is the painting *Maitreya the Conqueror* (1925, Gorky Art Museum), in which, besides the depiction of the deity hewn out of a rock, there is also a symbolic image—the sil-houette of a horseman in the clouds. Roerich depicts the Indian gods Buddha and Krishna in a number of works.

Popular rites and ceremonies also interested Roerich. In one of his most poetic works, *Lights on the Ganges* (1945, RM), he depicts an ancient method of fortune-telling. In the dark-blue light of dusk a woman sets fires floating on the water to tell her fate by their movements. In such works Roerich sensitively portrayed the local colour and way of life of a country that became very dear to him.

Roerich's activities also extended into public life: he was a member of forty international cultural organisations. One of his most significant

LATE
NINETEENTH
-EARLY
TWENTIETH
CENTURIES

N. K. ROERICH

FIFTY
RUSSIAN
ARTISTS
235

achievements was the famous 'Roerich Pact', the aim of which was to safeguard valuable monuments in the event of war. This led to the signing in the Hague in 1954 of the final act of the international convention on protection of cultural values in case of armed conflicts which was ratified by thirty-nine countries.

The artist died in India, and a monument was erected at the spot where he was cremated in the Kulu Valley with the inscription 'Here, on 13 December 1947, was cremated the body of Nikolai Roerich, the great Russian friend of India'. Ten years later, his son Yuri came to the Soviet Union with a large collection of his father's works, which the artist had bequeathed to his native land.

2. Sketch of scenery for Henrik Ibsen's play *Peer Gynt*
3. Merchants from Overseas
4. Remember!

4

Boris Mikhailovich KUSTODIEV

(1878-1927)

1

Boris Kustodiev has a place of honour among those artists of the early twentieth century who worked to create a new socialist culture. A talented genre-painter, master of psychological portraiture, book illustrator and stage-set artist, Kustodiev produced masterpieces in almost all the imitative arts. But his talent is most apparent in his poetic paintings on themes from the life of the people, in which he conveyed the inexhaustible strength and beauty of the Russian soul. He wrote, 'I do not know if I have been successful in expressing what I wanted to in my works: love of life, happiness and cheerfulness, love of things Russian—this was the only "subject" of my paintings . . .'

The artist's life and work are inseparably linked with the Volga and the wide open countryside of the area, where Kustodiev spent his childhood and youth. His deep love for this area never left him all his life.

Boris Kustodiev was born in Astrakhan. His father, a schoolteacher, died young, and all financial and material burdens lay on his mother's shoulders. The Kustodiev family rented a small wing in a rich merchant's house. It was here that the boy's first impressions were formed of the way of life of the provincial merchant class. The artist later wrote, 'The whole tenor of the rich and plentiful merchant way of life was there right under my nose . . . It was like something out of an Ostrovsky play.' The artist retained these childhood observations for years, recreating them later in oils and water-colours.

The boy's interest in drawing manifested itself at an early age. An exhibition of *peredvizhniki* which he visited in 1887, and where he saw for the first time paintings by 'real' artists, made a tremendous impression on him, and he firmly resolved to become one himself. Despite financial difficulties his mother sent him to have lessons with a local artist and teacher A. Vlasov, of whom Kustodiev always retained warm memories. Graduating from a theological seminary in 1896, Kustodiev went to St. Petersburg and entered the Academy of Arts. He studied in

1. Self-Portrait. Hunting
2. The Fair
3. The Merchant's Wife
4. The Bolshevik

LATE
NINETEENTH
-EARLY
TWENTIETH
CENTURIES

B. M. KUSTODIEV

FIFTY
RUSSIAN
ARTISTS
237

Repin's studio, where he did a lot of work from nature, trying to perfect his skill in conveying the colourful diversity of the world. 'I pin great hopes on Kustodiev,' wrote Repin. 'He is a talented artist and a thoughtful and serious man with a deep love of art; he is making a careful study of nature . . .'

When Repin was commissioned to paint a large-scale canvas to commemorate the hundredth anniversary of the State Council, he invited Kustodiev to be his assistant. The work was extremely complex and involved a great deal of hard work. Together with his teacher, the young artist made portrait studies for the painting, and then executed the right-hand side of the final work. At this time too, Kustodiev made a series of portraits of contemporaries whom he felt to be his spiritual comrades. These included the artist Bilibin (1901, RM), Moldovtsev (1901, Krasnodar Regional Art Museum) and the engraver Mate (1902, RM). Working on these portraits considerably helped the artist, forcing him to make a close study of his model and to penetrate the complex world of the human soul.

In the summer of 1903 Kustodiev undertook a long trip down the Volga from Rybinsk to Astrakhan, in search of material for a programme painting set by the Academy. The colourful scenes at bazaars along the Volga, the quiet provincial side-streets and the noisy quays made a lasting impression on the artist, and he drew on these impressions for his diploma work, *Village Bazaar* (not preserved). Upon graduating, he obtained the right to travel abroad to further his education, and left in 1903 for France and Spain.

Kustodiev studied the treasures of Western European art with great enthusiasm and interest, visiting the museums of Paris and Madrid. During his trip he painted one of his most lyrical paintings, *Morning* (1904, RM), which is suffused with light and air, and may be seen as a hymn to motherhood, to simple human joys. However, no matter where Kustodiev happened

to be—in sunny Seville or in the park at Versailles—he felt the irresistible pull of his motherland. After five months he returned to Russia. Joyfully he wrote to his friend Mate that he was back once more 'in our blessed Russian land'.

The revolutionary events of 1905, which shook the foundations of society, evoked a vivid response in the artist's soul. He did work for the satirical journals *Bugbear* and *Infernal Post*, drawing vicious caricatures of prominent tsarist officials such as Ignatiev, Pobedonostsev and Dubasov. He also made drawings directly related to the revolutionary events *(The Agitator* and *Meeting)* which for the first time showed a revolutionary leader together with a mass of working people. In paintings such as *Meeting at Putilovsky Factory, Strike, Demonstration* and *The May-Day Demonstration at Putilovsky Factory* (1906, Museum of the Revolution, Moscow), he depicted workers risen in the struggle against autocracy.

Kustodiev was deeply distressed by the defeat of the revolution. His drawing *Moscow. Entry* (1905, TG) is an allegory on the cruel suppression of the December uprising. Houses are being destroyed, people are dying. Soldiers fire on the demonstrators, and Death reigns over all. Scenes of bloody violence against demonstrating workers are also portrayed in the drawing *February; After the Dispersal of a Demonstration* (1906).

In 1905 Kustodiev first turned to book illustrating, a genre in which he worked throughout his entire life. He illustrated many works of classical Russian literature, including Gogol's *Dead Souls, The Carriage* and *The Overcoat,* Lermontov's *The Lay of Tsar Ivan Vassilyevich, His Young Oprichnik and the Stouthearted Merchant Kalashnikov* and Lev Tolstoy's *How the Devil Stole the Peasant's Hunk of Bread* and *The Candle.*

Kustodiev also continued to work in portraiture. His *Portrait of a Priest and a Deacon* (1907, Gorky Art Museum) and *The Nun* (1908, RM) are complex and vivid in their char-

FIFTY
RUSSIAN
ARTISTS
238

B. M. KUSTODIEV

LATE
NINETEENTH
-EARLY
TWENTIETH
CENTURIES

acterisation. His sculptured portraits are also varied in form and characterisation. That of I. Yershov (1908, Kirov Opera and Ballet Theatre) shows us the noble, imposing figure of the singer, while in the sculpture of Mstislav Dobuzhinsky we see the artist's troubled, searching nature. It was at this time that the circle of images and themes formed which would serve as the basis of the bulk of Kustodiev's work. He was very fond of folk art—painted toys from Vyatka and popular prints—and studied folk tales, legends and superstitions. He believed that in the minds of ordinary people art was always connected with celebration and rejoicing.

In 1906 he painted *The Fair* (TG), in which a colourful crowd is seen milling about outside the merchants' stalls. Although the scene portrayed is commonplace and seemingly haphazard, much thought and care was put into the composition of the piece. The bold combinations of bright colours lend it a decorativeness not unlike that of popular prints of the time.

Kustodiev was also attracted by the theme of gay village festivals and merrymaking, with their brightness, spontaneity and coarse folk humour: cf. *Village Festival* (1907, TG), *Merrymaking on the Volga* (1909, Kostroma Museum of Local History). These paintings were very popular at exhibitions both in Russia and abroad.

LATE
NINETEENTH
-EARLY
TWENTIETH
CENTURIES

B. M. KUSTODIEV

FIFTY
RUSSIAN
ARTISTS
239

In 1909 Kustodiev was awarded the title of Academician of Art. He continued to work intensively, but a grave illness—tuberculosis of the spine—required urgent attention. On the advice of his doctors he went to Switzerland, where he spent a year undergoing treatment in a private clinic. He pined for his distant home-land, and Russian themes continued to provide the basic material for the works he painted during that year. In 1912 he painted *Merchant Women* (Kiev Museum of Russian Art), in which fact and fantasy, genuine beauty and imitation, are intermingled. Well-dressed, stately, healthy-looking merchant women are having an un-hurried conversation in the market-place. Their silk dresses shimmer with all the colours of the rainbow, and their painted shawls are ablaze with rich colours. Roundabout, the brightly-coloured signs above the stalls seem to echo all this. In the distance a red church with golden cupolas and a snow-white bell-tower are clearly visible. The artist's perception of the world is festive, cheerful and unclouded.

Although his illness became progressively worse, Kustodiev's work remained radiant and optimistic.

... The Moscow cab drivers seated round their glasses of tea in the painting *Moscow Inn* (1916, TG) are acting out the tea-drinking ritual with great solemnity and seriousness. A gramophone is straining, a cat is purring and a waiter is dozing in a chair. The picture is full of witty, pointed details.

The inhabitants and life of provincial towns were the main subjects of Kustodiev's genre-painting at this time. His talent is especially apparent in three paintings in which he sought to create generalised, collective images of feminine beauty: *The Merchant's Wife* (1915, RM), *Girl on the Volga* (1915, Japan) and *The Beauty* (1915, TG).

In the *Merchant's Wife* we have a captivating picture of a dignified Russian beauty, full-busted and glowing with health. The radiant yellows, pinks and blues of the background land-

scape set off the reddish-brown tone of her dress and her flowery shawl, and everything mingles together in her bright, colourful bouquet.

Another of Kustodiev's characters, in *The Beauty*, cannot fail to attract the viewer. There is great charm and grace in the portrayal of the plump, fair-haired woman seated on a chest. Her funny, awkward position reflects her naivety and chaste purity, and her face is a picture of softness and kindness. Maxim Gorky was very

FIFTY
RUSSIAN
ARTISTS
240

B. M. KUSTODIEV

LATE
NINETEENTH
-EARLY
TWENTIETH
CENTURIES

4

fond of this painting, and the artist presented him with one of the variants he made of it.

The genre works which Kustodiev painted at this time describe the world of small provincial towns: cf. *The Small Town* (1915, private collection, Moscow) and *Easter Congratulations* (1916, Kustodiev Art Gallery, Astrakhan). This series was completed by one of his finest paintings, *Shrovetide* (1916, RM), which continued the theme of popular festivals.

Despite his serious illness, Kustodiev continued to work. He underwent a complex operation, but to no avail. Now his legs were completely paralysed. He wrote, 'Now my whole world is my room.'

Kustodiev was one of the first artists to welcome the Revolution. In his painting *27 February 1917*

(1917, private collection, Leningrad) he depicted the view from his studio window on that portentous day when the fate of tsarism was decided.

In 1918 Kustodiev painted several large panels to decorate the squares of Petrograd during the celebrations for the first anniversary of the Revolution. His large-scale monumental work *Stepan Razin* (1918, RM) was painted for this purpose. In the first years after the Revolution the artist worked with great inspiration in various fields. Contemporary themes became the basis for his work, being embodied in drawings for calendars and book covers, and in illustrations and sketches of street decorations. His covers for the journals *The Red Cornfield* and *Red Panorama* attracted attention because of their vividness and the sharpness of their subject-

LATE
NINETEENTH
-EARLY
TWENTIETH
CENTURIES

B. M. KUSTODIEV

FIFTY
RUSSIAN
ARTISTS
241

matter. Kustodiev also worked in lithography illustrating works by Nikolai Nekrasov. His illustrations for Leskov's stories *The Darner* and *Lady Macbeth of Mtsensk District* were landmarks in the history of Russian book-designing, so well did they correspond to the literary images. Kustodiev worked on the illustrations for *Lenin and Children, Lenin and Young Leninists* and *A Day With Lenin* with a great sense of the responsibility and seriousness of the task. His drawings portray Lenin with great warmth and truthfulness.

The artist was also interested in designing stage scenery. He first started work in the theatre in 1911, when he designed the sets for Ostrovsky's *An Ardent Heart*. Such was his success that further orders came pouring in; in 1913 he designed the sets and costumes for *The Death of Pazukhin* at the Moscow Art Theatre. His talent in this sphere was especially apparent in his work for Ostrovsky's plays: *It's a Family Affair, A Stroke of Luck, Wolves and Sheep* and *The Storm*. The milieu of Ostrovsky's plays—provincial life and the world of the merchant class —was close to Kustodiev's own genre paintings, and he worked easily and quickly on the stage sets.

In his post-Revolutionary works, Kustodiev sought to create generalised images which might convey the greatness and importance of the changes which had taken place in the country. He invented a new type of national hero. In *The Bolshevik* (1919-20, TG) we see the giant figure of a Bolshevik bearing a red banner and striding through a town. The image is indomitable, energetic, full of strength and will. Despite its naivety and artificiality, the painting moves one by its bold style and composition, and by the sincerity of the artist's response to the events of the time.

In 1920-21 Kustodiev was commissioned by the Petrograd Soviet to paint two large colourful canvases on the theme of national celebrations: *Festivities on Uritsky Square in Honour of the Second Congress of the Comintern* (RM) and *Night-time Celebrations on the Neva* (Museum of the Revolution, Moscow). Kustodiev worked enthusiastically on the image of the great leader of the Revolution: he painted several portraits of Lenin intended for mass reproduction.

Kustodiev's sudden death on 26 May 1927 was a great loss to Soviet art, but his bright, optimistic works live on, a source of great pleasure for millions.

A LIST OF ILLUSTRATIONS

A. YE. ARKHIPOV

Photograph of A. Ye. Arkhipov
The Washer-Women
The Guests

S. V. IVANOV

O. E. Braz. Portrait of S. V. Ivanov
Execution
The Family
The Arrival of Foreigners
   in the 17th-Century
Moscow

A. P. RYABUSHKIN

Self-Portrait
A Wedding Procession in Moscow
   (17th Century)
A Moscow Girl, Seventeenth Century
Novgorod Church

N. K. ROERICH

B. M. Kustodiev. Portrait
   of N. R. Roerich
Sketch of scenery for Henrik Ibsen's
   play "Peer Gynt"
Merchants from Overseas
Remember!

B. M. KUSTODIEV

Self-Portrait. Hunting
The Fair
The Merchant's Wife
The Bolshevik

Request to Readers

Raduga Publishers would be glad to have your opinion of this book, its translation and design and any suggestions you may have for future publications.

Please send all your comments to 17, Zubovsky Boulevard, Moscow, USSR.